Always Keep Your Bags Packed

SANDEEP CHAVAN

Published by SANDEEP CHAVAN, 2024.

While every precaution has been taken in the preparation of this book, the publisher assumes no responsibility for errors or omissions, or for damages resulting from the use of the information contained herein.

ALWAYS KEEP YOUR BAGS PACKED

First edition. November 8, 2024.

Copyright © 2024 SANDEEP CHAVAN.

ISBN: 979-8227168399

Written by SANDEEP CHAVAN.

Table of Contents

Preface 1
Chapter 1: The Struggle to Get In 3
Good Morning Mumbai!!! 7
Chapter 2: The Struggle, Frustration, and the Moment of Clarity 10
Chapter 3: The Road Less Traveled – The Struggle and Reinvention ... 14
Chapter 4: The Journey of Keeping Bags Packed 18
Chapter 5: The Ongoing Adventure 21
Chapter 6: The Art of Adaptability 24
Chapter 7: Readiness for Change 50
Chapter 8: Non-Attachment to Outcomes 64
Chapter 9: Embracing Uncertainty 78
Chapter 10: Lifelong Learning and Growth 95
Chapter 11: Purpose Beyond Material Success 114
Chapter 12: The Importance of Being Present 131
Chapter 13: Building Resilience through Adversity 150
Chapter 14: The Wisdom of Letting Go 168
Chapter 15: Living with the Bags Packed 192
Conclusion: The Journey Continues 211
Acknowledgments 216

To my peers, my students, and everyone who has been part of my journey—

This book is for you, the ones who stood beside me, encouraged me, and believed in the power of transformation. You have been my teachers, my supporters, and my inspiration.

Thank you for being part of this journey and for helping me discover the courage to embrace each new chapter.

—Sandeep Chavan

When Life Surprises You,

Make the Most of It

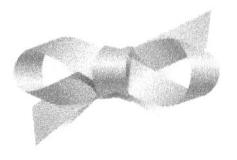

Preface

In our fast-paced world, change is the only constant. Yet, despite this inevitability, many of us cling to the familiar—the comfort of what we know, the safety of routines, and the predictability of our lives. But what if, instead of resisting change, we embraced it? What if we lived every day with the readiness to step into the unknown, with a heart open to new experiences and a mind willing to adapt?

This is the essence of the philosophy I present in this book: "Always Keep Your Bags Packed: Embrace Life's Transitions."

The metaphor of keeping your bags packed is not about physical luggage, but about mental, emotional, and spiritual preparedness. It's a way of living that encourages us to remain open, agile, and ready for whatever life throws our way. It means acknowledging that while we cannot predict the future, we can certainly prepare ourselves to face it with confidence, courage, and clarity.

In my own life, I've experienced countless transitions—moving from a technical career in industrial engineering to becoming a mentor and educator, stepping away from old business ventures, and constantly redefining my path. Through all of these shifts, the one constant has been my commitment to keeping my metaphorical bags packed. It's been my guiding principle, one that has allowed me to embrace new opportunities, shed outdated beliefs, and remain open to personal and professional reinvention.

This book is a culmination of my journey and the lessons I've learned along the way. It's a reflection on how we can all live with more freedom, purpose, and growth by staying ready for change and by letting go of the attachments that hold us back. It's about releasing what no longer serves us, embracing the unknown with grace, and focusing on the present moment, knowing that the future will unfold in ways we can't yet imagine.

In the pages that follow, you'll find actionable steps, reflections, and stories—both mine and others—designed to help you live a life with your bags packed. Whether you're facing a career transition, navigating personal challenges, or simply looking to cultivate a more open and flexible mindset, this book will guide you in embracing change with ease.

Life is not about reaching a destination; it's about being ready for the journey ahead, no matter where it takes us. By always keeping your bags packed, you'll find that you're not just prepared for the unexpected—you're ready to thrive in it.

I invite you to walk this path with me. Together, let's embrace the adventure of life with open arms and a packed bag, ready for the next step.

Sandeep Chavan

Chapter 1: The Struggle to Get In

Welcome, friends. Before we delve deeper into the essence of this book, let's meet our central character—Hemant. His journey is more than just a personal story; it reflects the struggles, dreams, and hopes of countless young professionals in India. Hemant, like many others, aspired to a life of success, stability, and fulfillment. Yet, what seemed like a straight path to success soon turned into an unpredictable, challenging journey.

At first glance, Hemant's story might seem like just another tale of an ambitious engineer chasing his dreams. But as we unfold his experiences, it becomes clear that there is something deeper at play—something that transcends ambition and success. It's a philosophy, one that teaches the power of resilience, the necessity of adaptability, and most importantly, the wisdom of being ready for change, even when it feels uncertain or uncomfortable. This book is about that—how to stay prepared for the unexpected, how to recognize when it's time to walk away from something, and why it's crucial to always be ready for a fresh start. We will see how the title of this book, "Always Keep Your Bags Packed: Embrace Life's Transitions," reflects not just a way of life but a philosophy that can shape the path to fulfillment in today's unpredictable world.

Let's take a journey into Hemant's life—his struggle to get in, to make a mark, to find his place in the world.

Hemant grew up with dreams that many young boys share. From a small town in rural India, his mind often wandered to distant places—cities with towering buildings, cutting-edge technology, and the bright future of an engineer at the helm of progress. He dreamed of designing complex systems, working on groundbreaking projects, and contributing to a world that was always advancing. But reality, as it often does, had other plans.

The journey to becoming an engineer wasn't a smooth one. Hemant faced many challenges from the very start. The Indian education system, particularly for students in technical fields, is known for its intensity and competition. Hemant, coming from a rural background, found himself up against a formidable wall: limited seats in prestigious engineering institutes, and the harsh realities of a reservation system that seemed to favor others. Despite his relentless hard work and high academic performance, the doors to the top institutes remained closed. In a world that often felt unfair, he wondered if the dream he held onto so dearly was slipping through his fingers.

But Hemant wasn't one to give up easily. With determination fueling him, he enrolled in a smaller, lesser-known engineering college. While many students from more renowned institutions would go on to secure high-paying jobs, Hemant's path was uncertain. The college lacked the resources and infrastructure that would have made his education easier. But Hemant, ever the resourceful one, took matters into his own hands. He sought practical knowledge beyond textbooks, took on independent projects, and relentlessly pushed himself to learn in ways that many of his peers didn't. While others were content with theoretical knowledge, Hemant immersed himself in the real-world application of what he was learning.

Graduation arrived, and with it came a cruel awakening. Hemant's dreams of walking straight into a high-paying job were dashed. Without a shiny campus placement or an offer from top companies, he was left to face the harsh reality of the job market. His friends from more prestigious institutions were already receiving job offers from multinational companies, while Hemant was left scrambling.

For months, Hemant pounded the pavement, sending out resumes, attending interviews, hoping that somewhere, someone would recognize his potential. But the competition was fierce, and opportunities were few. In a country of over a billion people, where the demand for jobs far outstrips supply, only a few would be fortunate enough to secure positions at top companies—and Hemant wasn't one of them.

It was in the midst of this struggle that the first of many setbacks came. Hemant finally managed to land a position as a trainee engineer at a small, local firm. It wasn't the dream job he had envisioned, but it was something—a foot in the door. He worked tirelessly, learning on the job, applying his engineering knowledge, and growing with each passing day. But after a year, the company restructured, and Hemant found himself without a job once again. The disappointment was crushing, and he questioned everything. Was all this struggle for nothing?

But giving up wasn't an option. The survival instinct kicked in, and Hemant took up temporary marketing jobs just to make ends meet. His mornings were spent job hunting, sending resumes, while his evenings were filled with calls to recruitment agencies, praying for a chance to prove himself. His life was a blur of uncertainty, self-doubt, and exhaustion. Yet, through it all, Hemant kept pushing, unwilling to let go of the dream he had nurtured for so long.

Still, Hemant understood that he needed to do something different. With the hope of improving his prospects, he enrolled in an MBA program, hoping that a business degree would open new doors. But even as he attended classes, deep down, he knew that his heart still belonged to engineering. He was not ready to leave that world behind, but he needed to find something more.

Then, one day, a phone call came—a call that would change his life forever. A well-known Mumbai-based company, renowned for its technical expertise and global reputation, offered him a job. This was it. This was the break he had been waiting for. Without hesitation, Hemant left his MBA program and packed his bags. With a mixture of excitement and apprehension, he boarded a train to Mumbai, stepping into a new chapter of his life.

What Hemant didn't know was that this was just the beginning of an even greater journey. It would be a journey filled with challenges, realizations, and—most importantly—lessons that would shape his entire perspective on life and career.

As we move forward in Hemant's story, we'll begin to uncover the philosophy that guided him through his struggles and triumphs. "Always Keep Your Bags Packed: Embrace Life's Transitions" isn't just about physical preparedness—it's about the mental and emotional readiness to embrace change, to adapt, and to take bold steps when necessary. It's about recognizing that while we cannot control everything, we can always control how we respond to the unexpected.

Hemant's journey is one of self-discovery, of mistakes made, of lessons learned, and of a man who, despite all odds, learned how to keep his bags packed—not just for the next big opportunity, but for whatever life had in store for him.

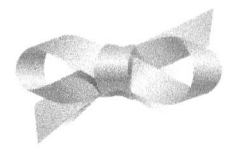

Good Morning Mumbai!!!

Hemant finally made it to an MNC in Mumbai—the city of dreams, joy, and struggle. Mumbai is where the hustle is real, where the skyline is as tall as the ambitions of its people, and where dreams are built and shattered with equal intensity. For Hemant, Mumbai was a promise—a gateway to endless possibilities. He had fought tooth and nail to get here, overcoming challenges, pushing through self-doubt, and finally landing in one of the most prestigious companies in the industry. His excitement was palpable as he stepped into this new chapter of his life, eager to prove his worth.

In the beginning, everything was perfect. The work seemed manageable, the tasks were routine, and there was no pressure—yet. The company, a 30-year-old manufacturing facility with a German parent company, was undergoing a transition phase, and Hemant was eager to be a part of the changes. The smooth start was comforting; the paycheck was better than he expected. As an industrial engineer, Hemant had the opportunity to interact with various aspects of the company, including its management strategies.

But, as the months went by, things started to shift. Special orders began to come in, and suddenly Hemant found himself handling more significant responsibilities. The work became intense, and deadlines loomed large. He threw himself into the grind, believing that he was contributing to something big. Every day was a rush of deadlines, and for a while, it felt fulfilling. It felt like he was on the verge of something extraordinary.

However, the initial excitement soon faded. Hemant began noticing that the company, despite receiving these lucrative orders, was stuck in a rut. The same old methods were being followed; there was no room for innovation. The management was too set in its ways, content with playing it safe and maintaining a routine. Hemant, being the enthusiastic engineer that he was, began speaking up. He wanted to push boundaries, to drive change, but his suggestions fell on deaf ears. The company's culture was too rigid, and any attempt at introducing change was swiftly shut down.

It was then that Hemant realized a painful truth: the decisions that were shaping the company's future were not being made in Mumbai or even India, but halfway across the world—in Germany. Hemant wasn't the first to face this reality. Many engineers and managers in MNCs across India often find themselves in the same position—working in a system where the corporate direction is dictated by foreign offices. The head office, far removed from the ground realities in India, takes decisions based on profit margins, ignoring local challenges, culture, and market dynamics. And so, despite the hard work of engineers, managers, and employees, the company's growth is always tethered to the whims of a faraway boardroom.

Hemant's frustration grew as the company's management stuck to its limited vision, unwilling to adapt to changing times. His efforts to bring new ideas were dismissed as unnecessary, and he soon realized that no matter how hard he worked, the company was only interested in profits. The focus was on cutting costs and maximizing returns for shareholders, with no consideration for innovation, employee growth, or the broader impact on society.

It was the same story when Hemant left Mumbai and joined another MNC in Pune. He had hoped for a fresh start, but within a year, he found himself facing the same challenges. The decisions were still being made in foreign countries, and the local offices were simply expected to execute them. The work culture was toxic, with little scope for creativity or growth. Hemant started noticing that the only thing that truly mattered to the higher-ups was the bottom line. He was disheartened by the fact that his contributions—despite being significant—seemed to be secondary to the company's profit-driven agenda.

It wasn't long before Hemant realized that the MNC life wasn't for him. But his next step didn't bring the relief he hoped for. He joined an Indian giant, hoping to find a more locally driven, innovation-friendly environment. Instead, he was confronted with another kind of challenge—union issues. The management was embroiled in constant negotiations with unions, and the work environment became a battlefield of egos and demands, with little focus on progress. The environment was deeply politicized, and Hemant, once again, found himself at a crossroads.

As an industrial engineer, Hemant had always prided himself on understanding the broader business dynamics. He could see the underlying issues in every organization he worked with—how profit, not people, was always at the center of decision-making. He saw how employees were often treated as cogs in the machine, their creative potential overlooked in favor of maximizing profits. The higher you rose in the corporate ladder, the more you realized the game wasn't about innovation or personal growth—it was about hitting targets and keeping shareholders happy.

And that's when Hemant had an epiphany. He realized that no matter where he went—whether to an MNC or an Indian giant—the core issue remained the same. Companies, more often than not, were driven by one goal: profits. There was no room for meaningful growth, no space for innovation. It was all about the bottom line. For the first time in years, Hemant asked himself, "What am I really working for?"

Frustrated, Hemant took a break. He walked away from it all, deciding to reset. He spent a year reflecting on his journey—looking at the bigger picture, seeing what his life had become. He realized that, despite the corporate world's hollow promises, he had grown. He had gained invaluable experience, honed his skills, and learned the art of navigating corporate politics.

But now, he needed something different. Hemant had come to understand a harsh truth—the corporate world was driven by profits and not by people. He needed to find a place where he could grow, where his contributions mattered, and where innovation wasn't just a buzzword, but a way of life.

So, with renewed clarity, Hemant decided to venture into something entirely new. It wasn't going to be easy. It would require him to step out of his comfort zone and embrace uncertainty. But Hemant knew one thing for sure: Life wasn't about settling. It was about growth, adaptation, and finding meaning in everything you do.

As he took that leap into the unknown, Hemant was ready for the next chapter of his life—where success wasn't just defined by profit margins, but by the ability to make a difference, to innovate, and to be true to himself.

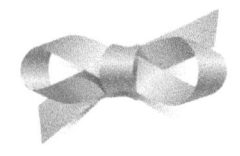

Chapter 2: The Struggle, Frustration, and the Moment of Clarity

Hemant's journey had reached a point where the grind had become unbearable. After leaving his first MNC in Mumbai, he joined another organization, hoping for a fresh start, yet the situation remained unchanged. The same sense of monotony, the same routines—punch and lunch duties, as Hemant liked to call them. He was still locked in a cycle that offered little fulfillment.

The frustration was mounting. Hemant had dreams, ambitions, and a desire to make a difference, but the reality was vastly different. He spent his days working on projects that felt insignificant, surrounded by colleagues who seemed content with just following instructions. No one was questioning the status quo, no one was innovating. The company's focus was narrow, and growth seemed to be an afterthought. Hemant knew that this kind of work wouldn't lead him anywhere. He had learned that he wasn't just working for a paycheck; he wanted more—he wanted to contribute, to grow, and to feel the sense of fulfillment that came with a purpose-driven job.

But the deeper truth was that, as an industrial engineer, Hemant began to understand the stark reality of how corporations operate. He was quickly realizing that many engineers and managers were stuck in similar situations. The decisions that shaped the future of the company weren't being made in India, but in boardrooms far away—often in foreign countries, thousands of miles away. His current MNC, like most others, followed directives that originated from their global headquarters. The people in those boardrooms, far removed from the realities of local markets, were often driven by one thing: profits. The decisions, no matter how they impacted the people or the local culture, were aimed at meeting financial goals, often at the cost of employee well-being and innovation. The personal growth he longed for, and the deep sense of purpose he desired, were constantly undermined by the corporate machine focused purely on maximizing profits for shareholders.

Hemant saw it clearly now. The systems he was working within weren't designed for creativity or innovation—they were designed for efficiency, and efficiency alone. Engineers and managers weren't expected to think outside the box; they were just cogs in the wheel, following instructions, implementing decisions made far above their pay grade. The system was set up in a way that the real power lay in foreign boardrooms, where corporate strategies and policies were formulated with no regard for local cultures, challenges, or growth opportunities.

As he observed his colleagues, Hemant realized that many were simply going through the motions—content with staying in their roles without ever questioning whether the company, or even the industry, was really a fit for their personal aspirations. They had become comfortable, like gears in a machine. But Hemant was different. He had entered the field with a vision, a dream of contributing meaningfully, of using his engineering expertise to solve problems that would make a difference. Yet, in the corporate world, his dream seemed increasingly irrelevant.

He began to wonder if he had made a mistake by staying in this field. The frustration mounted. The more he worked, the more he saw his colleagues, and even his superiors, simply going through the motions, playing the corporate game without ever questioning its meaning. There was no room for change, no space for new ideas. His attempts to bring fresh perspectives were met with indifference. The company culture, rigid and profit-driven, had no place for innovation or risk. And as the months dragged on, Hemant realized that no matter how hard he worked, the company had no intention of changing. The focus would always be on bottom-line profits—no matter the personal cost.

But beyond work, things weren't any better in Hemant's personal life either. His relationships were strained, his health had started to deteriorate, and his sense of isolation grew stronger each day. Despite working harder, he felt increasingly disconnected—not just from the people around him, but from his own sense of self. The work that once gave him purpose now seemed hollow, and the sense of fulfillment he had hoped for had vanished, replaced by a growing emptiness and frustration.

His social life, which once provided comfort, now seemed like a distant memory. The joy of spending time with friends had become rare. Hemant couldn't help but feel like he was living someone else's life. The man he had hoped to become, the engineer who would bring about change, seemed to have disappeared somewhere along the way. He had invested so much time, energy, and hope into this job and career, but it felt like he had nothing to show for it. The dream had faded into the background, and all that remained was the grind.

It was in this moment of frustration that Hemant realized he was stuck. Stuck in a job that no longer aligned with his values. Stuck in a system that wasn't designed for growth or innovation. He realized that, like many engineers and managers, he had become another cog in the corporate wheel, his efforts absorbed into a larger system that didn't care about him as an individual. The more he worked, the more he felt like he was losing touch with who he really was, and what he truly wanted from life.

This sense of stagnation made him restless. He began to wonder if he was making a mistake by staying in this field. Why was he still doing this? What was he really gaining? For the first time in his life, he started questioning everything—the choices he had made, the path he was on, and the future that seemed so uncertain. Hemant had spent so many years pushing himself, following the rules, trying to climb the corporate ladder. But he was finally starting to see the truth: The climb was an illusion. He was climbing a ladder that wasn't leading anywhere he wanted to go.

Then came the pivotal moment—a meeting with Stephen, an old friend from his college days. Stephen had always been one of those people who seemed to have it all figured out. He had a calm, collected demeanor that Hemant envied. Over the years, they had lost touch, but now their paths had crossed again. Hemant invited Stephen over for a cup of tea, hoping to get some advice or simply to vent about the frustration that had built up inside him.

As they sat down together, Hemant shared his struggles, the frustration with his job, his lack of fulfillment, and the emotional toll it was taking on him. Stephen listened quietly, nodding occasionally. When Hemant had finished venting, Stephen took a deep breath and said something that Hemant would never forget:

"If you can't change it, leave it."

At first, Hemant didn't understand. He had put so much time and effort into his career. Could he really just walk away? Wasn't that a failure? But Stephen's words echoed in his mind, over and over again. "If you can't change it, leave it."

Stephen went on to explain that sometimes, staying in a situation that was draining you emotionally, physically, and mentally was more detrimental than leaving it. No job, no career, and no situation was worth sacrificing your happiness or your well-being. Hemant realized that he had been holding on to a dream that wasn't his anymore. The company, the job, and the career path he was on weren't aligned with the person he had become. He had been so focused on the idea of success, the idea of staying in the game, that he hadn't stopped to ask if it was really the right fit for him anymore.

Stephen told him that the real courage came from knowing when to leave, when to move on, when to admit that something wasn't working and to step away from it. There was no shame in leaving if it meant preserving one's mental health and happiness. Hemant realized that this was the clarity he needed. It wasn't about success or failure—it was about being true to himself.

That night, Hemant went home and thought long and hard about everything Stephen had said. The more he reflected, the more he realized that it was time to leave. He had to trust his instincts. The job wasn't going to change, and neither was the company. Hemant wasn't the same person who had walked into that first job in Mumbai years ago. He had grown, learned, and evolved. But the environment around him hadn't. He needed to leave to preserve his own sense of identity and find something that would truly fulfill him.

It was a difficult decision, but Hemant knew it was the right one. The next day, he handed in his resignation letter. For the first time in a long while, he felt a sense of relief. It wasn't the end, but it was the beginning of something new. He didn't know exactly what that new path would look like, but he was ready to find it.

Chapter 3: The Road Less Traveled – The Struggle and Reinvention

After Hemant resigned from the corporate world, he had hoped for peace and time to reflect, but the reality was far more complicated than he had anticipated. Returning to his hometown, he faced the disapproval of his family and friends, who questioned his decision at every turn. The weight of their judgment bore down on him, suffocating his thoughts and making it harder to find clarity.

"Why would you leave such a secure life, Hemant? A job with a high salary in a city like Mumbai, only to come back here?" His family asked, and his brothers, particularly, couldn't understand why he had chosen to walk away from the comforts of city life. "Isn't the dream to settle down with a good job? Why throw it all away?"

These questions haunted him daily, and no matter how much Hemant tried to explain, it felt like he was justifying a decision that no one, not even himself, could fully explain at the time. The tension at home was palpable. Every glance felt like an accusation, every comment a reminder that he was stepping away from a conventional path.

Even his parents, who had been his pillars of support through past struggles, expressed concern. "Are you sure about this, Hemant? Leaving everything behind?" His father's voice was filled with doubt, a reflection of the traditional values that had been instilled in him since childhood. And for the first time, Hemant found himself unsure of how to answer. He only knew that something had to change. But what? And how?

Hemant's home, once a place of comfort, now felt like a cage. The familiar surroundings, the once-comforting voices, now only added to his growing anxiety. The quiet of the house became suffocating. He needed to escape, not just physically, but mentally. He needed space to breathe and think clearly, away from the ever-present expectations of his family. So, he made a decision. He would leave and move to a nearby town, away from the prying eyes and the judgments. Though it wasn't a drastic change, it was enough to give him some breathing room.

Yet, even in the new town, the weight of uncertainty followed him. Hemant's struggle to find his next step felt like a constant tug-of-war between the dreams he had abandoned and the pressure to find something new. His path ahead was unclear, and every step seemed burdened by doubt.

It was during this period of self-reflection and quiet frustration that fate intervened. Hemant reconnected with an old college friend, Prakash, who had been working as a teacher at a nearby engineering college. Prakash mentioned there was a teaching position available. Initially, Hemant dismissed the idea; teaching had never been on his radar. He was trained as an engineer, after all. But something in Prakash's tone made him stop and listen. The job wasn't glamorous, nor was it lucrative, but it felt right—an opportunity to do something different, something with a sense of purpose beyond the constraints of a corporate office.

With a mixture of hesitation and resolve, Hemant agreed to take the job. It wasn't about salary or perks anymore. It was about finding a way forward, stepping out of the suffocating cycle he had been trapped in for so long. Taking the teaching job was not a dream come true, but it was a chance to reset, to redefine what success meant to him.

When Hemant first stepped into the classroom, it felt foreign, almost surreal. He had spent years as a student, but now, as the teacher, the responsibility weighed heavily on him. The classroom was his stage, but there was no script. The students, just like him in his younger years, came with dreams and aspirations. Yet, he realized, just as he had felt in the corporate world, they were stuck. They were learning theories, formulas, and concepts, but there was little connection to the skills they would need to face the rapidly changing world outside the classroom.

The education system, which he had once thought of as the key to success, was failing these young minds. They were being prepared for jobs that no longer existed, for a world that was evolving too fast for the system to keep up. Hemant saw the same confusion and helplessness in their eyes that he had once felt in his own. The realization hit him hard: the education system wasn't just flawed—it was broken.

But instead of despairing, Hemant found himself energized by the challenge. He realized he couldn't be a passive observer of this system. He had to make a change. He couldn't simply teach the same outdated material and expect things to improve. The students needed more than knowledge—they needed guidance, they needed to develop the skills that would help them thrive in the real world.

The more Hemant thought about it, the clearer his vision became: he would start his own coaching institute. He wanted to create a space where students could learn not just the academic theories, but the practical skills that would prepare them for the ever-evolving job market. He wanted to bridge the gap between education and industry, to help students navigate the complexities of the modern world and equip them with the tools to succeed. This was the next step in his reinvention.

At the same time, Hemant took a break from his busy schedule and spent time with the tribal communities living in the nearby forests. Their simple, yet profound, way of life gave him a new perspective on what truly mattered. He embarked on a 300-kilometer journey, walking through villages, staying with the people, learning their ways, and observing their connection to the earth. They had so little, yet they seemed so content. It was humbling and eye-opening. It made Hemant realize that fulfillment wasn't found in wealth or status but in living with purpose, in making a positive impact, no matter how small.

The experiences in the classroom and with the tribal communities became the foundation of Hemant's new career. Teaching, for him, was no longer just about imparting knowledge—it was about shaping individuals who could think critically, act responsibly, and make a difference. It became his mission. And slowly, he began to see the impact of his work. Students who once felt lost and uncertain were starting to find their direction. They were beginning to understand that the world needed more than just degrees—it needed people who could think for themselves, solve problems, and innovate.

Hemant realized that his journey wasn't one of fame or fortune, and it was far from the glossy success stories in business magazines. He wasn't a celebrity, nor was he a billionaire. He was an ordinary man who had made extraordinary decisions to reinvent his life. His story was one that millions of others could relate to—people caught in a system that didn't always serve them, who struggled to find their place in a rapidly changing world.

Hemant knew that not everyone would find their purpose in the same way he did. Some would continue to chase the corporate dream, others would find fulfillment in different paths. But his story was a testament to the power of reinvention. It was proof that even when everything seemed uncertain, it was possible to carve your own path. Sometimes, the road less traveled was the one that led to the most meaningful destinations.

In the end, Hemant understood that success wasn't defined by titles or wealth—it was defined by the impact you had on others, the authenticity of your choices, and the fulfillment that came from knowing you were living your purpose. His journey had taught him that the road to reinvention is never easy, but it is always worth it.

Chapter 4: The Journey of Keeping Bags Packed

As Hemant reflected on his journey, he stood in a place of profound contentment. His family, once doubtful of his path, was now proud of him. His students, who had once been strangers with vague dreams, now saw him as a mentor who had guided them toward clarity and purpose. In the educational circles of his town and beyond, his name had become synonymous with dedication and transformation. The coaching institute he had founded was thriving, not only because of its curriculum but because it was built on the values he held dear: adaptability, perseverance, and self-discovery.

But for Hemant, true fulfillment wasn't solely about these achievements. It was about the path he had walked, the lessons he had learned, and the continuous journey of self-improvement. He had come to realize that the journey never truly ends. With each success, he saw not a stopping point but a new threshold—an invitation to keep moving forward, learning, and evolving. For Hemant, "Keeping Bags Packed" had become more than just a phrase; it was a personal mantra, a commitment to growth and resilience that kept him in a state of readiness for whatever life might bring.

Over the years, Hemant learned that true growth lay in embracing change rather than resisting it. This idea of "keeping bags packed" was not about physical travel or switching jobs; it was a mindset—a state of mental readiness, a commitment to stay adaptable and flexible no matter where life's path took him. Life had shown him time and again that it could throw unexpected challenges and opportunities his way. He realized that growth didn't happen in comfort zones. The most transformative moments of his life had often come during periods of discomfort, periods that required him to leave behind what was familiar and step into the unknown.

For Hemant, "keeping bags packed" was also about not letting complacency settle in. He saw how easily people could get caught in routines, even when they reached success. Too often, he had seen individuals achieve their goals, only to let themselves fall into a stagnant pattern, reluctant to pursue new ambitions or take further risks. Hemant was determined not to let this happen to him or his students. He wanted his life to be a testament to the idea that success wasn't a final destination but a continuous journey. Each milestone he achieved became a reminder that he could—and should—continue to aspire, learn, and evolve.

As an educator, Hemant knew he had a responsibility to model this mindset for his students. He wanted them to see that change and uncertainty were not obstacles to be feared but essential parts of personal growth. Hemant often shared this idea in his classes: "Success isn't about reaching a final destination; it's about staying ready for the next part of your journey. Keep your bags packed, keep your minds open, and stay curious. No matter where life takes you, never stop evolving."

He had come to view the idea of "keeping bags packed" as essential in today's fast-paced world. With industries transforming at rapid speeds, new skills and adaptability were more critical than ever. The world was no longer a place where people could settle into one job or one skill set for life. Hemant knew that this was the reality his students would face, and he felt a deep responsibility to prepare them for it. The goal wasn't just to impart knowledge or skills but to instill in them the courage to face change head-on, to remain resilient in the face of setbacks, and to keep seeking opportunities even when they seemed elusive.

One day, while teaching a class on life skills, Hemant decided to share his own journey with his students. He recounted the many times he had been forced to adapt, to change course, and to leave behind comfortable situations in pursuit of something better—even when he wasn't sure what that "better" was. He spoke about the challenges he faced, the doubts and insecurities he had overcome, and the risks he had taken that had led him to where he was now. "Success," he told them, "isn't just about hard work or talent. It's about staying ready for opportunities, even when they seem out of reach. It's about maintaining a mindset that is open to change and always believing that the next chapter of your life is waiting to be written."

For Hemant, the concept of "keeping bags packed" extended beyond his professional life. It was also about staying adaptable in his personal life, ready to embrace whatever changes might come. His relationships with his family and friends had grown stronger over time, but he had come to understand that even personal connections required flexibility and willingness to evolve. Hemant's children, now young adults themselves, looked up to him, not just as a father but as an example of what it meant to lead a life of integrity and purpose.

In the quiet moments of his life, Hemant often found himself reflecting on the path that had brought him here. He had made mistakes, taken risks, and sometimes walked paths that led to dead ends. But he held no regrets. Each decision, no matter how daunting, had taught him something invaluable and had contributed to the person he had become. He felt grateful for those experiences, understanding that each one had been a step in his journey toward self-discovery and fulfillment.

Hemant had come to realize that his story wasn't about extraordinary achievements or fame. It was about resilience, humility, and the courage to follow an unconventional path. His journey was not the type that would be celebrated in headlines, but it was a story shared by countless others—ordinary people navigating a complex world, striving to find their place, and refusing to settle for anything less than a life of purpose and meaning. Hemant's story was one of growth, reinvention, and the belief that no matter where life's journey took him, his bags would always be packed, ready for the next adventure.

Chapter 5: The Ongoing Adventure

Hemant had come to embrace a profound truth: life was an unending journey, an ongoing adventure that required a commitment to evolve, adapt, and grow continuously. Although he had reached a place of stability with his coaching institute, he knew that this was not the end of the road. In fact, Hemant had come to understand that true success meant never becoming stagnant. To him, life was about seizing every opportunity, meeting each challenge head-on, and always being ready for the unexpected.

The coaching institute that he had built was flourishing, a source of pride and fulfillment. Yet, Hemant realized that there was potential for even more growth, not just within himself but in the way he impacted others. The world around him was changing rapidly: technology was advancing at lightning speed, online education was reshaping the landscape, and the demand for lifelong learning was growing. Hemant knew he couldn't afford to stand still; he had to keep pace with these changes.

One evening, after a particularly enlightening session with his students, Hemant sat at his desk, reflecting on his journey so far. He had often spoken to his students about "Keeping Bags Packed"—a phrase that had come to mean so much more than just readiness for a career move or life transition. Now, it resonated with him on a deeper level. It symbolized a way of living with purpose, a commitment to constant self-improvement, and a drive to make an impact that extended beyond his immediate environment.

With the rise of digital learning, Hemant saw an opportunity to reach beyond the four walls of his coaching institute. For years, he had dreamed of connecting with students from all corners of the country, especially those in remote areas who longed for knowledge, guidance, and mentorship. The traditional classroom setting, while effective, had its limitations. The world was increasingly shifting to a digital platform, and Hemant felt that he, too, should explore this frontier.

He wondered, "What if I could bring the same sense of connection and mentorship to a virtual space? What if I could offer quality education to students in the smallest villages, and even beyond our country's borders?" The idea excited him. "Why not?" he thought. After all, "Keeping Bags Packed" was about being open to new opportunities, taking risks, and adapting to whatever life presented.

Without wasting any time, Hemant began the groundwork for his new venture—a digital learning platform that would complement his existing coaching institute. He knew that entering the world of online education wouldn't be without its challenges. There were technology barriers to overcome, competition to face, and a new teaching approach to adopt. But, over the years, Hemant had learned that challenges were not obstacles; they were opportunities to grow.

As he began planning his online courses, Hemant's vision expanded. It wasn't just about teaching academic subjects anymore. The modern world demanded a more comprehensive approach to education—students needed skills that went beyond textbooks. Critical thinking, emotional intelligence, problem-solving, resilience—these were the skills that would prepare his students for life. His platform would focus not only on academic excellence but on equipping students to face the complexities of the world.

To ensure the best experience for his students, Hemant immersed himself in the world of digital learning. He studied new tools, platforms, and methodologies that would help him create an engaging online experience. Despite the technological shift, Hemant believed that maintaining a human touch was crucial. His online courses would be structured to offer the same level of personalization and care he provided in person. This approach, he believed, was key to creating a connection, even in a virtual environment.

The transformation was astonishing. As Hemant expanded his digital presence, he saw a spark in his students' eyes. Now, students from places he had never even visited could access his guidance. For many, this was the first time they felt truly connected to a teacher who understood their challenges, dreams, and aspirations. Hemant's work was reaching beyond his small town, touching the lives of thousands of students who, like he once had, dreamed of a better future.

While his physical coaching center remained a cornerstone of his life, the online platform was quickly becoming a powerful new chapter in his story. Hemant was once again at a turning point. But this time, it wasn't about abandoning one role for another. It was about broadening his impact, about taking everything he had learned and using it to make a difference on a much larger scale.

Through all of this, Hemant held firmly to his principle of "Keeping Bags Packed." It had become a philosophy that transcended his career—it was a way of life. He recognized that no matter how successful or comfortable he became, there would always be another challenge to face, another opportunity to pursue, and another lesson to learn. Hemant was ready to expand his influence, tackle the nuances of online education, and guide a new generation toward success.

As he reflected on his journey, Hemant had a powerful realization: his story was no longer just about him. It was about every student, every dreamer, and every individual who had ever felt lost or uncertain about their path. He was no longer just a teacher or a coach; he was a mentor, a guide, a symbol of what it meant to keep moving forward. His journey was an example of resilience, growth, and the willingness to embrace the unknown.

Hemant understood that "Keeping Bags Packed" was not about reaching a destination; it was about the willingness to adapt, to remain curious, and to keep moving forward. Life would continue to change, and with it, so would he. The future held endless possibilities, and Hemant was ready to face each one with an open mind and an unyielding spirit. His adventure was far from over—it was only beginning.

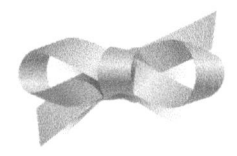

Chapter 6: The Art of Adaptability

In a world where the pace of change is accelerating faster than ever before, adaptability is not just an asset; it's an essential skill for survival and success. As we explore the philosophy of "Keeping Bags Packed," we discover that adaptability isn't simply about adjusting to circumstances—it's about preparing yourself to face the unknown, to embrace change, and to thrive in environments where predictability is a luxury.

Hemant's journey is a testament to the power of adaptability. His career is a mosaic of transitions: from a small-town engineering graduate struggling to find his footing in a large and competitive job market, to his eventual move into the world of education, teaching, and entrepreneurship. Each phase of his life required him to adapt not just to external conditions, but to his own evolving understanding of who he was, what he wanted, and how he could contribute meaningfully to the world.

The Essence of Adaptability in Hemant's Journey

From the moment Hemant left behind his stable job in Mumbai, a world of towering skylines, bustling streets, and endless energy, he knew he was stepping into the unknown. He returned home to his small town, where life moved at a slower, quieter pace, worlds apart from the life he'd built in one of India's most dynamic cities. To many, this return was baffling, even reckless. Why would anyone walk away from a well-paid, prestigious position in Mumbai? For those who had watched him work his way up, Hemant's choice seemed like a retreat, an abandonment of comfort and ambition. But Hemant saw it differently. To him, this was an opportunity, a necessary turning point that would allow him to redefine his life's purpose. It was not a step back but a step inward, a moment to ask himself what truly mattered.

Initially, Hemant faced confusion and disapproval, even from his family. They struggled to understand why he had left a secure future to return to a small town with fewer opportunities. To them, Mumbai represented stability, while his hometown seemed like a step into obscurity. Yet, Hemant felt a stirring within him, a call to rediscover his roots and reconnect with a side of himself that had gone dormant amid the city's relentless pace. This decision wasn't just about leaving a job; it was a conscious step toward a new way of life. Hemant knew that if he stayed in a place that no longer fulfilled him, he would only be conforming to expectations instead of following his own path.

Adapting to his new reality wasn't easy, but it was a challenge he embraced with a sense of calm resilience. Instead of mourning what he had left behind, Hemant focused on what lay ahead. He began to see his small-town surroundings with fresh eyes, recognizing the strength and simplicity of his community. The warmth, the familiar faces, the unhurried conversations—they reminded him of a life that had more to offer than material success. With time, he shifted his mindset from what he had "lost" to what he could gain by exploring this new path.

His journey of adaptation took on even deeper meaning when he decided to enter the field of education. Teaching wasn't just a career change; it was a leap of faith into a world that held both challenges and potential. Hemant took up a position in a local school, stepping into classrooms with more passion than he'd ever felt behind a desk in Mumbai. He quickly realized that his students were full of curiosity and ambition, but they were often limited by a system that failed to connect their education to the real-world skills they needed to thrive. Hemant saw how, despite their potential, many students were held back by an outdated education system that wasn't in tune with the demands of the modern job market.

This gap between theory and practice struck a chord in him. He couldn't shake the thought that these students deserved more—they deserved an education that would empower them to stand confidently in the world, to secure their futures, and to turn their dreams into reality. This was more than an observation; it was a calling. Hemant knew he had the knowledge and the experience to bridge this gap, and he decided to take matters into his own hands.

Determined to make a difference, Hemant launched his own coaching institute. It was a bold move, but he was ready for the challenge. He poured his heart into crafting a curriculum that combined academic knowledge with practical skills, teaching students not just to memorize but to understand, analyze, and apply their learning. In his institute, students weren't just preparing for exams—they were preparing for life. Hemant guided them to think critically, to problem-solve, and to become self-sufficient, capable individuals. For Hemant, this wasn't just a job; it was a mission. He had found his purpose, and every day, he watched it come alive through his students.

Hemant's adaptability had not only transformed his career but had also deepened his sense of fulfillment. Each student's progress was a testament to his journey—a journey defined by courage, resilience, and the willingness to change. The risk he had taken, the comfort he had sacrificed, had brought him to a place of true impact and meaning. And as he watched his students step confidently into their futures, Hemant knew that the path he had chosen, though unconventional, had been the right one all along.

Why Adaptability is Key in Today's World

In today's rapidly evolving world, adaptability has become an essential skill for thriving in every area of life—whether in careers, relationships, or mental well-being. With each passing year, the world becomes more interconnected and technologically advanced, but also more unpredictable. The modern era is defined by volatility, uncertainty, complexity, and ambiguity (often summarized as VUCA), and the COVID-19 pandemic has been one of the most striking reminders of this reality. Within weeks, countless people had to shift from familiar routines to new ways of working and living, adapting to remote work, unfamiliar technologies, and entirely different social dynamics. Those who were resilient and flexible found ways to cope, and even thrive, amid these changes.

Hemant's story is a perfect example of why adaptability is not only important but inevitable in a world where change is the only constant. His decision to leave a stable, high-paying job in Mumbai to return to his hometown was a bold move, one that many would see as risky. It wasn't the obvious path, nor was it easy. But Hemant saw it as an opportunity to realign his career with his values and personal growth goals. Rather than letting the weight of societal expectations hold him back, he embraced change, opening doors to new experiences that ultimately brought him a sense of purpose and fulfillment he hadn't found before. By taking calculated risks and approaching each new situation with an open mind, Hemant built a path that was both rewarding and meaningful.

Adaptability goes beyond simply adjusting to new circumstances; it requires mental flexibility—the capacity to view situations from multiple perspectives and to understand that life doesn't always unfold in a predictable, linear fashion. Hemant's path is a testament to this. His journey zigzagged through different industries, roles, and skill sets, from corporate life in Mumbai to teaching and launching his own coaching institute in a small town. With each turn, Hemant adapted, embracing the changes rather than resisting them. His willingness to pivot, to learn from his experiences, and to grow from each challenge contributed not only to his professional success but to his growth as an individual.

Adaptability also means accepting that the future may look different from the past. In the digital age, where advancements in technology are reshaping industries, and global challenges like climate change are influencing every aspect of life, adaptability is about staying ready to shift perspectives, to learn, and to relearn as circumstances evolve. Hemant's journey exemplifies this mindset. By stepping away from a traditional career path and into the unknown, he demonstrated a remarkable openness to the future. His journey reminds us that while change can be uncomfortable, it is also a source of growth, resilience, and personal evolution.

Ultimately, adaptability is not about abandoning stability; it's about building resilience to navigate the inevitable ups and downs of life. Like Hemant, those who are adaptable find a way to use each experience as a stepping stone, to align their lives with their true passions and values. In a world that is constantly changing, adaptability is not just a skill—it is a way of life, a mindset that allows us to embrace uncertainty with courage and grace, and to see each twist and turn as a part of a greater journey.

Core Philosophy of Adaptability

At its heart, adaptability is more than just adjusting to new situations; it is a way of thinking, a mindset that views change as a powerful force for growth and discovery. It requires the courage to let go of rigidity and embrace life's natural ebb and flow. Adopting this mindset involves nurturing a few core principles that can help guide you through life's transitions and challenges.

Embrace Change, Don't Fear It

Change is one of the few constants in life. However, most of us tend to resist it, clinging to the familiar as a source of comfort. Yet, resisting change often leads to frustration and a sense of stagnation, blocking us from our true potential. Embracing change, on the other hand, is a mindset that allows us to move fluidly with life's rhythms, opening ourselves to growth, resilience, and unexpected opportunities.

Rather than viewing change as something to endure, we can start to see it as a catalyst for growth—a way to expand beyond what we thought was possible. Hemant's journey is a prime illustration of this principle in action. Each significant shift in his life, whether stepping away from the stability of the corporate world or choosing a new, uncharted path as an educator, represented more than just a change in occupation. It was a conscious decision to allow himself to evolve. By seeing change as an invitation to explore, Hemant wasn't just navigating life's transitions; he was actively shaping his own destiny.

This approach to change—viewing it as an opportunity rather than a threat—allows us to redefine our lives with each transition. Embracing change means letting go of rigid expectations and stepping into the unknown with a spirit of curiosity. It's about trusting that each transition, no matter how daunting, brings with it the potential for something greater. For Hemant, each career shift became a stepping stone to deeper fulfillment, offering fresh insights into his life's purpose.

To truly embrace change, we need to cultivate flexibility within ourselves. This involves building an open-minded attitude, a willingness to take risks, and the courage to redefine ourselves as circumstances shift. Change, by its very nature, pushes us to step beyond the boundaries we've set for ourselves. Hemant found that, with each new chapter, his sense of self expanded. As he moved from one role to another, he was able to see that his true value didn't lie in any single job or title but in his adaptability, his willingness to learn, and his openness to growth.

In this sense, change is an invitation to shed the old and create space for the new. Each experience and each shift serves as a learning moment, a chance to let go of what no longer serves us. Instead of fearing change, we can choose to meet it with a sense of possibility. Each transition, whether a shift in career, a change in relationship, or an unexpected life event, becomes a doorway to a new version of ourselves. Embracing change is not just a survival skill; it's a way to thrive, to evolve, and to live with purpose.

Stay Curious and Open-Minded

Adaptable individuals are often driven by an innate curiosity—a genuine desire to understand the world around them and their place within it. This curiosity becomes a fuel, constantly pushing them toward new experiences, perspectives, and skills. For adaptable people, learning is not confined to formal education or restricted to particular phases of life; it's an ongoing journey. This relentless pursuit of knowledge equips them with the mental agility needed to navigate an ever-changing landscape, transforming challenges into opportunities for growth and discovery.

Hemant's journey provides a powerful example of this principle in action. When he shifted from a stable corporate career to an entirely new field, he didn't just change jobs—he chose to immerse himself fully in the process of lifelong learning. For Hemant, each step forward was an opportunity to gain deeper insight and understanding. His curiosity led him to explore not only the technicalities of a new career path but also the broader, interconnected nature of knowledge itself. He discovered that every skill and insight gained, regardless of its origin, contributed to a fuller, more versatile understanding of his own capabilities and goals.

By embracing an open-minded attitude, Hemant cultivated a mindset of growth and resilience, enabling him to welcome change with a spirit of enthusiasm rather than resistance. He actively sought out new knowledge and perspectives, making a conscious effort to learn from diverse sources. This approach allowed him to stay ahead of shifts in his career and life, ensuring that he was not only prepared to adapt to new circumstances but also able to find ways to flourish within them. His journey exemplifies how curiosity and open-mindedness transform challenges into avenues for enrichment, as they invite us to question assumptions, challenge our own limitations, and broaden our understanding of what we can achieve.

Curiosity doesn't only drive personal growth; it enriches how we interact with others and our surroundings. Hemant's openness to new ideas allowed him to build meaningful connections across different fields and with people from diverse backgrounds. He learned from others' experiences, taking inspiration from their successes and insights. This openness made him a more versatile individual, able to approach problems from multiple angles and contribute unique solutions. By fostering curiosity and open-mindedness, Hemant wasn't just learning for himself; he was enhancing his ability to make a positive impact on those around him.

In a world that is constantly evolving, curiosity and open-mindedness serve as essential tools. They help us break free from the limitations of familiarity and prepare us to face the unknown with confidence. Instead of being bound by rigid expectations or past experiences, adaptable individuals stay open to the possibilities around them. They view each moment as an opportunity to learn, to evolve, and to contribute in new, meaningful ways.

For those seeking to embrace this philosophy, the key lies in cultivating a sense of curiosity in everyday life. Stay open to new ideas, perspectives, and possibilities. Challenge yourself to learn something new, no matter how small, every day. Be open to different ways of thinking and different ways of approaching problems. As Hemant's story shows, this commitment to growth is what enables us not only to adapt but to thrive, finding fulfillment and purpose in the journey itself.

Focus on the Journey, Not the Destination

In a world that often glorifies achievement and reaching the finish line, adaptability requires a shift in perspective—one that emphasizes the journey over the destination. Adaptable people understand that life is not a series of fixed goals to be conquered but rather an unfolding experience that offers endless opportunities to learn and grow. This approach shifts the focus from a narrow fixation on outcomes to a broader appreciation for the process itself, enabling us to stay engaged, flexible, and ready to make the most of each moment.

Hemant's journey exemplifies this principle beautifully. Rather than being locked into a rigid vision of what his life "should" look like, Hemant learned to find value in each step of his path. From his corporate career to his transition into teaching, he understood that each experience was shaping him, imparting unique lessons and skills that would prepare him for future challenges. By not limiting himself to a specific end goal, he was able to stay open to unexpected opportunities—ones that he might have overlooked had he been solely focused on reaching a particular endpoint.

This emphasis on the journey allowed Hemant to stay resilient, even during uncertain periods where the path forward wasn't clear. He discovered that, by valuing each stage of his journey for what it offered, he could find meaning and purpose even in moments of struggle or ambiguity. In a way, his adaptability was strengthened by this outlook, as it allowed him to view setbacks and obstacles as integral parts of his personal growth rather than as barriers to success. By embracing the journey in its entirety, he was able to maintain a positive and resilient attitude, finding motivation and fulfillment in the present rather than postponing satisfaction for a distant future.

Focusing on the journey rather than the destination also keeps us grounded in the present, which is essential for true adaptability. When we're fully engaged in the here and now, we're better able to respond to changes as they arise. We become more attuned to our surroundings and more receptive to new ideas and opportunities. Hemant's experience illustrates this beautifully; by not being overly concerned with "where" he was going, he was free to explore different avenues, try new approaches, and embrace change as it came. This presence of mind allowed him to pivot gracefully, making decisions that aligned with his evolving goals and values rather than being bound to a fixed outcome.

This mindset shift also encourages us to redefine success. Success becomes less about a single, fixed result and more about continual learning, growth, and the ability to adapt. Hemant's adaptable journey highlights that true success lies in our ability to evolve, to remain open to life's lessons, and to transform along the way. In his case, the "destination" became less about a specific role or achievement and more about developing a life filled with meaning, purpose, and positive impact. By focusing on the journey, he found that each step, each challenge, and each small victory contributed to a larger sense of fulfillment and satisfaction.

For those looking to cultivate this principle in their own lives, it can be helpful to practice mindfulness and gratitude for the present. Instead of constantly looking forward to the next milestone or achievement, take time to appreciate the growth you're experiencing right now. Celebrate the small wins and recognize the ways in which each experience, even the difficult ones, is shaping you. This approach not only makes the journey more enjoyable but also builds the resilience and adaptability needed to handle whatever lies ahead.

In the end, focusing on the journey over the destination isn't about dismissing our goals or ambitions—it's about approaching life with a sense of openness and curiosity. By immersing ourselves in the process, we remain adaptable, receptive to change, and better equipped to handle whatever comes our way. As Hemant's story illustrates, when we embrace the journey fully, we discover that each step, each twist, and each turn adds richness to our lives, bringing us closer to a more fulfilling and adaptable way of being.

Be Willing to Let Go of the Old to Make Room for the New

Adaptability often requires us to step away from what is familiar, leaving behind old habits, roles, and even identities to create space for something new. This process of letting go isn't about discarding the past but recognizing when it's time to move beyond it. It takes courage to release the comfort of what we know in favor of what is unknown, and it's a leap that many are hesitant to take. However, letting go is often the first step toward growth and transformation, allowing us to embrace new experiences, perspectives, and opportunities that enrich our lives.

Hemant's journey illustrates this principle powerfully. He had invested years building a successful career in the corporate world—a role that came with a stable income, respect, and a sense of accomplishment. But as his values and goals evolved, he began to feel the pull toward something different. Transitioning from the corporate world to a career in teaching was not an easy decision; it meant stepping away from a secure, well-paying job and moving toward something with less certainty. However, he knew that staying in his old role would limit his growth and keep him from pursuing a life more aligned with his passions and values.

By choosing to let go of his corporate job, Hemant opened up a path toward a more meaningful career that allowed him to make a lasting impact on others as a teacher and mentor. This move required him to release the societal expectations and self-imposed ideas of what "success" should look like, freeing himself to follow a new path. Hemant's decision to let go wasn't just about changing careers—it was a symbolic act of creating room in his life for personal transformation. He recognized that clinging to the old would only restrict his ability to grow into the person he aspired to be.

Letting go is often one of the most challenging aspects of adaptability because it demands that we confront our fears and insecurities. The comfort of the familiar can be a strong pull, and stepping away from it can feel like a loss. However, growth and progress require a willingness to clear away the outdated or unfulfilling aspects of our lives. This doesn't mean that what came before was without value. Hemant's corporate career, for instance, provided him with valuable skills, insights, and experiences. But he understood that in order to grow in a direction that truly resonated with him, he had to make room for new possibilities.

In making this choice, Hemant was also practicing one of the core principles of adaptability: flexibility. He was willing to redefine his concept of success, shifting it from an externally validated status to a personally meaningful one. This shift allowed him to create a life that reflected his evolving values, and ultimately, it led him to a place where he could make a greater impact. By letting go, he freed himself from a fixed identity, allowing him to adapt and find fulfillment in a role that resonated with his goals.

For those looking to embrace this principle, it's helpful to start by examining areas of life that may feel stagnant or misaligned with current values. Ask yourself: Is there something that I'm holding onto out of habit, fear, or security? Recognize that letting go doesn't mean abandoning everything you've gained. Instead, it's about clearing space for new growth, allowing room for the next chapter of your journey. Whether it's a career, a relationship, a lifestyle, or even a mindset, releasing the old frees up the energy to invest in something that truly aligns with your present self.

Ultimately, letting go is an act of faith in the process of change. By willingly creating space, we invite new experiences and opportunities that help us evolve and adapt in ways we may not have initially imagined.

Hemant's story is a testament to the power of letting go, as it allowed him to transition into a life that felt more meaningful and aligned with his goals. When we are willing to release the old, we set ourselves up for transformation and prepare ourselves to embrace whatever the future may bring. Through this act of adaptability, we allow ourselves to grow into new possibilities, making room for a life that is both purposeful and fulfilling.

Develop Emotional Resilience

Adaptability is not just about intellectual flexibility or openness to new ideas; it requires a robust inner strength that empowers us to handle challenges and setbacks with grace. Emotional resilience is this strength—a foundation that allows us to withstand life's storms and maintain our sense of purpose, even in difficult times. While many view adaptability as simply the ability to shift direction or pivot when needed, true adaptability goes deeper. It relies on emotional resilience as a core element, enabling us to bounce back from hardships, process our emotions constructively, and keep moving forward.

Hemant's journey is filled with moments that tested his resilience, from career changes to personal challenges. Each setback had the potential to derail his path, yet he used these moments as opportunities for self-growth. When he encountered obstacles, he didn't let disappointment consume him. Instead, he leaned into the lessons each experience offered, understanding that resilience meant more than just enduring hardship; it meant actively finding ways to grow from it. This mindset transformed setbacks into stepping stones and disappointments into valuable lessons, contributing to a stronger, more adaptable outlook on life.

Developing emotional resilience requires embracing both the highs and lows of our experiences. Rather than suppressing difficult emotions or pretending that challenges don't affect us, resilience asks us to confront our feelings head-on, process them, and then move forward. This might mean allowing ourselves to feel disappointed, frustrated, or even scared when things don't go as planned, but it also means refusing to let these emotions dictate our actions. Hemant's resilience enabled him to face disappointments without losing sight of his goals or his sense of self-worth. He recognized that emotional resilience wasn't about ignoring setbacks but about learning to handle them in a way that preserved his forward momentum.

Resilience is a vital skill in today's fast-paced world, where change and uncertainty are constants. Without emotional resilience, even minor setbacks can feel overwhelming, and significant challenges can become immobilizing. When we build resilience, we cultivate the strength to keep the larger picture in focus, even when life feels chaotic. This ability to "zoom out" and remember the broader journey helps us to avoid becoming overly focused on immediate disappointments, allowing us to approach challenges with a sense of perspective. Hemant's resilience kept him grounded and allowed him to view each experience as part of a larger, unfolding story.

Emotional resilience also involves a level of self-compassion. Being adaptable doesn't mean being unaffected by hardship, nor does it mean pushing ourselves past healthy limits. When Hemant encountered setbacks, he didn't berate himself for struggling; instead, he accepted that challenges are a natural part of life. This acceptance allowed him to build resilience without exhausting himself in the process. He gave himself permission to feel and process his emotions, understanding that resilience doesn't demand perfection but progress. By cultivating self-compassion, he maintained his emotional well-being and prevented burnout, which in turn sustained his adaptability.

For anyone looking to develop emotional resilience, it helps to start with small steps. Begin by recognizing that setbacks and challenges are opportunities to build strength, not signs of failure. When faced with difficulties, take time to reflect on what you can learn from the experience. Practice mindfulness or journaling to process your emotions, allowing yourself to feel them fully before moving forward. Over time, these practices build a foundation of resilience that makes it easier to handle future challenges with greater calm and clarity.

Building emotional resilience is a journey, not a destination. Hemant's story shows us that resilience is cultivated through each experience, each hardship, and each moment of self-reflection. With each challenge, his resilience grew stronger, and this strength gave him the courage to face new, even more demanding, changes. By prioritizing resilience, he developed a mindset that didn't just help him survive change but enabled him to thrive within it.

Ultimately, emotional resilience is the anchor that keeps us steady in a constantly shifting world. It allows us to remain adaptable and flexible without losing sight of our values or our goals. In developing resilience, we prepare ourselves to face life's uncertainties with courage, and we equip ourselves to find stability within, even when everything around us feels unstable. As Hemant's journey reveals, this inner strength is an essential aspect of adaptability—one that allows us to move through life's challenges not just intact, but stronger, wiser, and more prepared for whatever lies ahead.

Trust Yourself

Adaptability is rooted in one's ability to trust themselves—an inner assurance that allows us to face the unknown with courage and conviction. At the core of this self-trust is the belief that, regardless of external circumstances, we have the inner resources to navigate whatever challenges come our way. It's the quiet confidence that whispers, "I may not know exactly where this road leads, but I am capable of handling whatever I find along the way." This trust forms the foundation of adaptability, making it possible to move forward even when the path is uncertain.

Hemant's journey offers a powerful example of self-trust in action. Each pivotal decision, from leaving the corporate world to embarking on a new career as an educator, required a leap of faith—not in the certainty of the outcomes, but in his own ability to handle those outcomes, no matter what they might be. He didn't wait for a guarantee that his new path would be a success or that he would have all the answers immediately. Instead, he relied on his inner compass, trusting that he could learn, adapt, and grow with each step.

Self-trust is especially important when faced with decisions that challenge the comfort and security of the familiar. When Hemant decided to shift careers, he was stepping away from a stable and predictable environment. For many, such a transition would evoke hesitation or fear of failure. But his self-trust allowed him to move forward without getting paralyzed by "what-ifs." He knew that even if he encountered obstacles or setbacks, his resilience and adaptability would guide him. This inner trust became a wellspring of strength, allowing him to thrive in uncertainty.

Building self-trust is essential for anyone seeking to become more adaptable. It's a process of gradually strengthening your belief in your abilities, your values, and your instincts. Often, we are taught to rely on external validations—grades, job titles, or social approval—to affirm our worth and capabilities. But true self-trust is an internal, unshakable belief that you can depend on yourself to make sound choices and manage the consequences of those choices. This confidence isn't about arrogance; it's about developing a realistic, grounded understanding of your strengths and using them as a source of stability.

Trusting yourself also means embracing the fact that mistakes are part of the journey. Hemant's self-trust didn't mean he expected perfection from himself. Instead, it allowed him to accept that he might stumble or face unforeseen challenges, but he trusted himself to learn from those experiences. He saw each mistake not as a failure, but as an opportunity for growth and refinement. This mindset helped him approach change with openness and curiosity, rather than fear or self-doubt. In this way, self-trust becomes a protective buffer against the inevitable uncertainties of life, allowing us to see challenges as opportunities rather than threats.

To cultivate self-trust, start with small acts of courage. Give yourself permission to make decisions without second-guessing every detail. Recognize that, while input from others can be helpful, your intuition is a valuable guide as well. Begin by setting small, achievable goals, and follow through on them consistently. Each success, no matter how minor, reinforces your belief in your own abilities. Over time, these small acts of self-reliance compound, creating a strong foundation of self-trust that supports you when facing more significant challenges.

Self-trust also grows when we are honest with ourselves about our strengths and limitations. Hemant's ability to trust himself wasn't based on a belief that he could do anything without effort, but rather on a realistic assessment of his skills and an understanding of where he needed to grow. By embracing both his strengths and areas for improvement, he developed a balanced sense of confidence. This honesty created a flexible and resilient foundation that allowed him to remain adaptable, even in moments of doubt.

In the end, self-trust is what allows us to face the unknown with courage. It's the inner confidence that supports us through each twist and turn of life's journey, grounding us in the belief that we are equipped to handle whatever comes. Hemant's journey exemplifies this quality, showing how, when we trust ourselves, we become more open to life's possibilities. Instead of shying away from new challenges, we find ourselves willing to embrace them, confident that no matter where the journey leads, we have what it takes to navigate it with grace and resilience.

In a world where change is constant, self-trust is a vital anchor. It's the belief that, no matter how turbulent the journey, we can rely on ourselves to find our way. As Hemant's story demonstrates, this trust doesn't just help us survive change—it allows us to thrive within it, transforming each new chapter into a meaningful and fulfilling experience.

In a world that is constantly shifting and evolving, adaptability is a skill that enables us to remain steady in the face of uncertainty. It requires curiosity, resilience, self-trust, and, above all, a willingness to let go of what no longer serves us in order to make room for growth. Hemant's journey serves as a powerful reminder that while the path may be unpredictable, a mindset rooted in adaptability can transform each twist and turn into an opportunity for learning and self-discovery. As life continues to change, this mindset becomes more than just a strategy; it becomes a way of life, empowering us to face the future with courage, grace, and optimism.

Actionable Insights for Staying Adaptable

As we reach the end of this chapter, let's shift from concepts to practical, tangible strategies for fostering adaptability in your daily life. Embracing adaptability is about developing habits that allow you to remain open, flexible, and resilient—qualities that prepare you for whatever life may bring.

Cultivate a Growth Mindset

Adaptability begins with the belief that we're capable of learning, evolving, and expanding beyond our current state. This belief is at the core of what's known as a *growth mindset*—the understanding that intelligence, skills, and personal potential are not static traits but are capable of continuous improvement through effort, dedication, and resilience.

Embracing a growth mindset allows us to see challenges not as insurmountable barriers but as opportunities to stretch our abilities and deepen our understanding.

People with a growth mindset view setbacks as integral parts of the learning journey, rather than final judgments on their worth or capability. They recognize that each misstep or challenge offers valuable insights, helping them refine their approach and ultimately progress. Instead of fearing failure, they welcome it as an instructor, knowing that every setback has something to teach. By adopting this perspective, adaptable individuals become more resilient, open to feedback, and ready to pivot when circumstances demand it.

Hemant's journey is a powerful example of the growth mindset in action. At various stages in his life, he encountered unexpected challenges that could have led to frustration or self-doubt. Yet, each time, he saw these obstacles as stepping stones, a chance to pause, reassess, and grow. Rather than viewing difficulties as setbacks, he considered them as pivotal points that pushed him toward new insights and directions. This mindset enabled him to remain optimistic, patient, and proactive, even in the face of uncertainty.

To cultivate a growth mindset in your own life, start by challenging any internal narratives that suggest your abilities or intelligence are fixed. Reframe limiting beliefs by reminding yourself that you have the power to improve and adapt. For instance, if you encounter a new task that seems daunting, view it as an opportunity to build a new skill, not as a measure of your limitations. By actively choosing to believe in your capacity for growth, you create a foundation of adaptability that encourages you to pursue new experiences, even when they may feel outside your comfort zone.

Another aspect of the growth mindset is the willingness to embrace lifelong learning. In today's fast-evolving world, adaptability depends on our ability to keep expanding our knowledge and skills. For Hemant, learning didn't stop when he changed careers; instead, he actively sought new knowledge and tools that allowed him to succeed in each new role. This commitment to continuous learning not only fueled his growth but also made him more versatile and capable of navigating change with confidence.

Developing a growth mindset also involves reframing how we see effort. In a fixed mindset, hard work is often perceived as a sign of inadequacy, as though the need to put in effort suggests a lack of natural talent. However, with a growth mindset, effort becomes a tool for improvement. The more we practice, the better we become, regardless of where we started. Seeing effort as a path to mastery encourages us to persevere, even when the journey is tough. It reminds us that improvement is always within reach as long as we're willing to put in the work.

Building this mindset can also involve setting small, achievable goals that encourage progress and growth. Each time you meet a goal, no matter how minor, you reinforce the idea that growth is possible. For instance, if you're learning a new skill or adapting to a new environment, start with small steps that make the process feel manageable. Celebrating these incremental successes creates positive reinforcement, motivating you to continue growing and expanding your adaptability.

One practical way to maintain a growth mindset in challenging times is to adopt a reflective practice, such as journaling or regular self-assessment. This can help you track your progress, recognize patterns in your thinking, and pinpoint areas where your mindset may be limiting your adaptability. Reflecting on past experiences, both successes and setbacks, reminds you of your resilience and growth over time, reinforcing your belief in your ability to handle whatever comes next.

In summary, a growth mindset is the foundation for adaptability. It's the belief that change isn't just something to be tolerated but an opportunity for personal evolution. By staying open to growth, embracing effort, and remaining curious about what we can achieve, we prepare ourselves to handle the unexpected with resilience and creativity. With each challenge we face, we build the skills and confidence needed to not only adapt to change but to thrive within it. Just as Hemant did, we can turn every obstacle into a stepping stone, viewing each moment as an invitation to grow and to continue moving forward.

Expand Your Comfort Zone

While our comfort zones offer a sense of security and familiarity, they can also limit our growth and prevent us from realizing our full potential. Adaptability requires us to challenge the boundaries of this comfort, venturing into new and sometimes uncomfortable territory to experience life more fully and develop resilience. Each step beyond what's familiar helps us become more open to change, more flexible in our thinking, and ultimately, more capable of navigating life's uncertainties.

Expanding your comfort zone can begin with small but intentional steps, such as trying a new activity, engaging in different types of conversations, or setting goals that push you just beyond your current limits. Taking these small steps on a regular basis builds your confidence in facing unfamiliar situations. When you regularly step into the unknown, you learn to manage discomfort and anxiety, making you more prepared to handle significant changes when they arise. For example, if you're used to working independently, you might start by collaborating with a colleague on a project or volunteering for a task that requires public speaking. These experiences may feel challenging at first, but they're valuable opportunities to expand your skills and adapt to new demands.

One of the most effective ways to expand your comfort zone is through learning new skills. Each new skill requires practice, patience, and a willingness to be vulnerable, especially if the process includes moments of struggle or failure. As you acquire these new skills, you develop adaptability, resourcefulness, and a readiness to tackle a broader range of challenges. Whether it's learning a new language, mastering a new technology, or pursuing a creative hobby, each new skill adds to your toolkit, empowering you to face unexpected situations with a wider range of abilities.

In Hemant's journey, his decision to leave a secure corporate role and step into the realm of education exemplifies the power of expanding one's comfort zone. Teaching was uncharted territory for him, and it required a complete shift in perspective and approach. By stepping into this new role, Hemant was able to uncover strengths he hadn't known he possessed, like the ability to connect with students, to communicate complex ideas simply, and to inspire others through mentorship. This leap not only broadened his professional skills but also deepened his personal growth, opening up a path that allowed him to make a meaningful impact on others' lives.

Expanding your comfort zone also involves engaging with people who hold different perspectives or come from different backgrounds. These interactions encourage you to see the world from diverse viewpoints, fostering empathy, tolerance, and flexibility. Conversations with people from different fields, cultures, or ideologies challenge your assumptions and expand your understanding, helping you to become more adaptable in both personal and professional contexts. By exposing yourself to a range of ideas and perspectives, you learn to approach problems from multiple angles, increasing your resilience and creativity when faced with complex situations.

As you step outside your comfort zone, it's natural to experience discomfort or even self-doubt. However, these feelings are often signs of growth. Each time you push through discomfort, you build a new layer of emotional strength and adaptability, making it easier to confront future challenges. Embracing discomfort as a part of growth teaches you to welcome uncertainty rather than avoid it, ultimately making you more adaptable and open to life's unexpected twists and turns.

Expanding your comfort zone doesn't mean abandoning everything familiar or taking reckless risks. It's about gradually challenging yourself to try new things, to experiment, and to embrace a little more uncertainty with each step. This approach helps you build confidence and adaptability incrementally, in a way that feels manageable. Over time, the unfamiliar becomes less intimidating, and you develop a sense of competence and courage that serves you well in any area of life.

Another essential benefit of expanding your comfort zone is the personal fulfillment that comes from discovering new aspects of yourself. By stepping into new experiences, you may uncover talents, interests, or strengths you didn't realize you had. Hemant's journey is an example of this self-discovery; by moving into teaching, he discovered a deep sense of purpose and a passion for helping others. Expanding beyond your comfort zone opens up possibilities for growth and self-discovery that can lead to a more fulfilling and meaningful life.

In conclusion, expanding your comfort zone is a powerful strategy for cultivating adaptability. Each step outside the familiar builds resilience, enriches your perspective, and strengthens your ability to handle change. Just like Hemant, you may find that stepping into the unknown not only reveals new strengths but also deepens your sense of purpose and connection with others. By regularly challenging yourself to explore beyond the comfort zone, you prepare yourself to face whatever comes next with confidence, curiosity, and an open mind.

Practice Mindfulness

Mindfulness, at its core, is the practice of being fully present in the moment, without distraction or judgment. It is the art of focusing your attention on what's happening right now, rather than getting lost in the past or worrying about the future. This practice helps to reduce stress, anxiety, and the overwhelming sense of uncertainty that often accompanies change, making it a powerful tool for adaptability. Mindfulness isn't just about quieting the mind; it's about training yourself to become more aware of your thoughts, emotions, and the world around you. By cultivating this awareness, you can navigate transitions with more ease and grace, allowing you to approach new situations with clarity and a calm mind.

In times of change or upheaval, the unknown can often feel daunting, and our natural instinct is to resist it. We may find ourselves worrying about potential outcomes, regretting past decisions, or imagining worst-case scenarios. This kind of mental clutter can make it even harder to adapt, keeping us trapped in a cycle of uncertainty and fear. Mindfulness, however, acts as a counterbalance to this mental chaos. It teaches us to stay focused on the present moment, helping us to quiet the inner dialogue that fuels anxiety and stress. Instead of dwelling on what might happen in the future or getting stuck in past mistakes, mindfulness encourages us to take a deep breath and focus on the here and now. This approach allows us to deal with change in a grounded, balanced way, making it easier to navigate life's inevitable shifts.

The power of mindfulness lies in its ability to shift our mindset. When we practice mindfulness, we train ourselves to respond to change with openness, rather than resistance. Instead of automatically feeling threatened by a new challenge or fearing what lies ahead, we learn to approach it with curiosity and acceptance. This mindset shift is particularly important for adaptability, as it allows us to embrace the unknown instead of feeling overwhelmed by it. When you are fully present and engaged, you can see challenges as opportunities rather than obstacles, making it easier to adjust to the evolving circumstances around you.

For Hemant, mindfulness was a key strategy in his journey of adaptation. Each time he faced a new transition—whether it was leaving a well-established career in the corporate world or stepping into the role of a teacher—he practiced mindful reflection. He took time to reconnect with his core values and goals, asking himself questions like, "What matters most to me right now?" and "How can I align this change with my vision for the future?" By taking the time to pause, reflect, and center himself in the present moment, Hemant was able to make decisions that were grounded in clarity and purpose, rather than being clouded by fear or uncertainty. This mindfulness practice provided him with the mental space he needed to make thoughtful, deliberate choices, rather than reacting impulsively or out of stress.

Moreover, mindfulness helps to process emotions in a healthier way. In the face of significant change, it's natural to feel a mix of emotions—fear, excitement, confusion, or even sadness. However, mindfulness enables us to sit with these emotions without judgment, allowing us to understand and process them in a constructive manner. Rather than suppressing emotions or allowing them to control us, mindfulness teaches us to acknowledge them and then let them pass. This emotional resilience is crucial for adaptability, as it enables us to maintain a sense of inner peace and stability during times of upheaval.

Mindfulness also enhances our ability to focus and make better decisions. In the midst of change, it can be easy to become distracted or overwhelmed by external noise, making it difficult to prioritize and stay on track. However, mindfulness sharpens our concentration, helping us to stay focused on what truly matters. When we are present in the moment, we are better able to assess situations with a clear mind, weighing options thoughtfully before taking action. This focused attention allows us to make decisions that are aligned with our long-term goals, even when faced with uncertainty.

Practicing mindfulness can be as simple as setting aside a few minutes each day for deep breathing, meditation, or simply paying attention to your surroundings without distraction. It doesn't require a lot of time, but the benefits are profound. By incorporating mindfulness into your daily routine, you train your mind to remain calm, open, and receptive to whatever challenges or changes arise. Over time, mindfulness becomes an ingrained habit, a natural part of your approach to life, enabling you to face new experiences with a greater sense of ease and confidence.

Another key benefit of mindfulness is that it fosters self-awareness, allowing us to better understand our reactions to change. By observing our thoughts and feelings without judgment, we become more attuned to the automatic patterns that shape our behavior. For example, you might notice that you tend to resist change because it makes you feel insecure or fearful. Through mindfulness, you can recognize these emotional triggers and choose to respond differently. Instead of reacting impulsively or withdrawing, you can respond to change with intentionality, choosing the mindset that serves you best.

Ultimately, mindfulness isn't just about coping with change; it's about thriving within it. By practicing mindfulness, you create a mental and emotional foundation that supports your adaptability. Instead of being swept away by the tides of change, you become the steady presence in your own life, able to ride those waves with grace and resilience. Mindfulness empowers you to remain fully engaged in the present moment, ensuring that you don't miss the opportunities that lie in each transition. It's about living with intention, embracing life's ups and downs, and always staying connected to what matters most—regardless of what the future may hold.

In conclusion, mindfulness is a transformative practice that helps you adapt more effectively to life's changes. By staying present, reducing anxiety, and approaching transitions with a calm and open mind, you can cultivate the emotional and mental strength needed to thrive during times of uncertainty. Hemant's use of mindfulness to navigate his journey is a testament to the power of this practice, and by incorporating it into your own life, you can build the resilience needed to face whatever challenges come your way.

Surround Yourself with Adaptable People

The individuals you choose to surround yourself with play a significant role in shaping your mindset and approach to life's challenges. The importance of having adaptable people in your circle cannot be overstated. When you are surrounded by individuals who embrace change, who see setbacks as opportunities for growth, and who are unafraid to challenge the status quo, their energy and perspective can help you navigate your own journey with greater resilience and confidence. In times of uncertainty, the influence of adaptable people can be the difference between stagnation and progress.

Adaptability is not a solitary trait; it's often cultivated through collaboration and interaction with others. When you are part of a group or network that values flexibility, growth, and learning, you are more likely to adopt these qualities yourself. The energy of adaptable people is contagious. They inspire you to think differently, to approach problems from new angles, and to stay open to alternative solutions. When you find yourself in a difficult or uncertain situation, having someone who can offer a fresh perspective or lend a word of encouragement can make all the difference in helping you stay adaptable. These individuals remind you that change doesn't have to be feared; it can be an exciting opportunity for personal and professional development.

A key benefit of surrounding yourself with adaptable people is that it exposes you to different ways of thinking and problem-solving. No two individuals approach challenges in exactly the same way, and when you are exposed to a variety of perspectives, you gain a broader understanding of how to adapt to new situations. For instance, a mentor or colleague who has faced similar challenges may offer strategies and insights that you hadn't considered, providing you with a roadmap to navigate your own obstacles. Likewise, engaging with people from different backgrounds or industries can open your mind to innovative ideas and approaches that you might not have encountered otherwise. The diversity of thought and experience within an adaptable circle can help you build a more flexible mindset and equip you with the tools needed to adapt effectively.

For Hemant, the people in his life played a pivotal role in his journey of transformation. He didn't navigate his career shifts or personal growth alone. Throughout his transitions, he actively sought out mentors who had walked similar paths and who could offer guidance and wisdom. These mentors weren't just advisors—they were role models who embodied the qualities of adaptability that Hemant sought to cultivate in himself. By observing their resilience, their ability to embrace change, and their willingness to explore new opportunities, Hemant learned that adaptability is not just a personal trait, but a collective journey. The support and encouragement he received from these individuals allowed him to take calculated risks, reassess his goals, and adapt to the shifting circumstances of his career and life.

In addition to mentors, Hemant also surrounded himself with peers who shared his passion for growth and learning. Having a network of like-minded individuals helped him to stay motivated and inspired, even during challenging times. These peers, who also embraced change and viewed setbacks as growth opportunities, became a source of strength for Hemant. Together, they created an environment where adaptability wasn't just encouraged—it was celebrated. This camaraderie and mutual support created a culture of continuous improvement, where everyone was motivated to stretch beyond their comfort zones and explore new possibilities.

Moreover, adaptable people often challenge you in ways that push you to become a better version of yourself. They don't simply offer comfort or validation; they encourage you to think critically, question assumptions, and take ownership of your own growth. In Hemant's case, his peers didn't just support him through the tough transitions; they held him accountable for staying true to his values and purpose. They reminded him to remain focused on his broader vision and not to get bogged down by short-term setbacks or challenges. This accountability and encouragement were vital in helping him remain resilient and adaptable in the face of uncertainty.

Another aspect of having adaptable people around you is that they can provide constructive feedback when needed. They help you identify areas where you may be holding yourself back or where your mindset may be limiting your growth. Rather than offering empty praise, adaptable individuals offer feedback that challenges you to reflect and improve. They help you see your strengths and weaknesses from a balanced perspective, empowering you to take action and continue evolving. Hemant's network of supportive peers and mentors provided him with honest, constructive feedback that helped him make more informed decisions and stay on track during his journey.

The collective nature of adaptability also means that when you face difficult times, you don't have to shoulder the burden alone. The people around you can offer emotional support, share their own experiences, and provide a sense of reassurance that you are not isolated in your struggles. This sense of community can be incredibly reassuring when you are navigating periods of uncertainty or change. Knowing that others have faced similar challenges and come out stronger on the other side can give you the confidence to keep moving forward, even when the path ahead seems unclear.

In today's world, adaptability is becoming an increasingly important trait, and having a supportive, adaptable circle can significantly enhance your ability to thrive in uncertain times. Whether it's through sharing knowledge, offering emotional support, or challenging you to grow, adaptable individuals can be a source of constant inspiration and motivation. They remind you that the journey of adaptability is not about going it alone but about building a community that helps you rise above challenges and embrace the opportunities that come with change.

Ultimately, the people you surround yourself with have a profound impact on your own adaptability. By cultivating a network of mentors, peers, and friends who embrace change, resilience, and growth, you create an environment that nurtures your own development. This network provides both the inspiration and the tools necessary to navigate life's transitions with confidence, knowing that you have the support of those who understand the value of adaptability. Just as Hemant's circle of mentors and peers helped him navigate his journey, the people in your life can help you stay grounded, focused, and inspired, making the path of adaptability a shared experience—one that is enriched by the collective wisdom and strength of those around you.

These strategies don't just help in isolated situations—they lay the groundwork for a lifetime of resilience, growth, and positive change. By nurturing a growth mindset, expanding your comfort zone, practicing mindfulness, and surrounding yourself with people who value adaptability, you can build a foundation that empowers you to face whatever life brings with confidence and courage. Adaptability, as Hemant's journey demonstrates, isn't simply a skill—it's a lifelong philosophy that enables you to turn life's unexpected twists into opportunities for growth and fulfillment.

Conclusion

Adaptability is at the heart of Hemant's journey—a quality that has guided his choices, molded his career, and catalyzed his growth as an individual. In reflecting on his life, it becomes clear that adaptability is not just a skill or a reaction; it is a foundational mindset, a thread that connects each chapter of his story. It empowered him to leave behind the familiar and embrace a new path, one that led him from the stability of a corporate job to the uncharted territory of education and entrepreneurship. Through it all, his willingness to adapt enabled him to discover new dimensions of his potential, expand his sense of purpose, and make a meaningful impact.

As you navigate your own journey, consider that change is one of life's few constants. No matter how carefully you plan, life will always present unexpected shifts and turns. The ability to embrace change with an open heart and an open mind can transform these moments of uncertainty into gateways to growth. Adaptability is about trusting yourself enough to let go of the familiar when necessary and welcoming the unknown as a space of possibility. Like Hemant, you may find that each challenge, each pivot, and each leap into the unknown brings new insights and opportunities for fulfillment.

In the following chapter, we'll explore what it means to cultivate a mindset of readiness. Embracing uncertainty isn't always easy, but it's essential for staying adaptable and resilient. Keep your bags packed and your mind open, because the journey of adaptability is an ongoing adventure—one that continuously unfolds, taking you to places you may have never expected but are precisely where you need to be. The next adventure is always waiting, and with adaptability as your compass, you'll be ready for whatever lies ahead.

Chapter 7: Readiness for Change

In the dynamic rhythm of life, change is the one constant. Yet, many of us resist it—not because we don't understand its inevitability, but because we are often mentally and emotionally unprepared for it. Being ready for change goes beyond simply reacting to life's curveballs; it involves cultivating a mindset that actively seeks out new opportunities, embraces uncertainty, and uses change as a catalyst for growth.

In the philosophy of "Keeping Bags Packed," readiness for change is a central pillar. It's about being mentally equipped to handle life's unpredictable nature, emotionally resilient in the face of new challenges, and proactive in preparing for the next chapter of your journey.

Hemant's life story offers a rich exploration of what it means to be ready for change. His career, his decisions, and his personal growth all exemplify the importance of preparing yourself—emotionally, mentally, and practically—to not just accept change, but to actively seek it out. From leaving a stable job in a bustling city to embracing the uncertain world of teaching and entrepreneurship, Hemant's journey demonstrates that readiness is not about waiting for the "perfect moment"; it's about equipping yourself to make the most of whatever comes your way.

The Concept of Mental and Emotional Readiness for Change

Being mentally and emotionally prepared for change is not something that happens instantly; it's a gradual, transformative journey that moves us from a place of comfort to a space where uncertainty becomes something to welcome rather than avoid. Hemant's experience of leaving a secure job and stepping into the unknown offers a powerful example of what it takes to build this kind of readiness.

When Hemant first began to consider the idea of leaving his stable, well-paying job in Mumbai, he was flooded with doubts. The idea of leaving behind the familiar—a steady income, a respected position, and a clear path—felt like an enormous leap. His life in Mumbai had been one of structure and predictability, and the thought of venturing into a future filled with unknowns was, at first, overwhelming. Yet, as he spent time wrestling with this decision, he started to see the limits of his comfort zone. The security of his job, while reassuring, was also confining his potential. He began to ask himself difficult questions: Was he truly fulfilled? Was he growing? Was he making the impact he wanted to make?

As he gradually opened himself up to the possibility of leaving, Hemant realized that his comfort was holding him back. This shift in mindset—seeing change not as a disruption but as an opportunity—was the beginning of his mental readiness for a new path. This readiness did not come from a sudden epiphany but rather from a deliberate process of reflection and a willingness to let go of control. He allowed himself to imagine a future beyond his current reality, one that might be more aligned with his values and aspirations, even if it came with more challenges and less certainty.

Mental readiness for change requires a shift in perspective. It involves embracing the idea that the future is inherently unpredictable and that our potential is often found on the other side of fear. For Hemant, the turning point came when he accepted that he couldn't anticipate or control everything—and that was okay. Once he stopped clinging to the safety of the known and let go of his fear of the unknown, he found himself open to new possibilities and willing to pursue a life that aligned more closely with his evolving vision of success.

Emotional readiness, however, is just as vital as mental readiness. Where mental readiness is about embracing new perspectives, emotional readiness is about staying resilient and grounded through the turbulence that often accompanies change. Hemant's emotional resilience was not something that came easily; it was built gradually, often through moments of failure, self-doubt, and external judgment. Friends and family didn't always understand his choice to leave a well-paying job, and there were times when he questioned his own decision. But through these experiences, Hemant cultivated a deep sense of inner stability. He learned that embracing change wasn't about hoping everything would go smoothly—it was about accepting that setbacks were part of the journey and that each challenge was an opportunity for growth.

His emotional readiness was further strengthened as he accepted that success wouldn't come without discomfort. He learned to navigate the highs and lows without being thrown off course, finding ways to stay focused on his purpose even when things felt uncertain. By embracing the emotional rollercoaster of change, Hemant built a foundation of resilience that allowed him to face whatever challenges came his way.

Ultimately, mental and emotional readiness for change go hand in hand, allowing us to approach new paths with openness and strength. Hemant's journey shows that this readiness is not about eliminating doubt or fear; it's about learning to live alongside them, to view uncertainty as a teacher rather than an obstacle. It's about trusting that we have what it takes to handle the unknown and that the act of stepping into change is often what enables us to discover our fullest potential.

Hemant's Experiences Reflecting the Importance of Readiness

Hemant's journey offers valuable insights into what it means to be truly ready for change. His story reveals that readiness is about much more than planning or waiting; it's about a mindset that welcomes transformation, even when it means stepping into the unknown. Let's revisit some defining moments where Hemant's readiness for change guided his life in unexpected yet profoundly impactful directions.

Leaving a Stable Job for the Unknown

Hemant's decision to leave his well-paying, stable job in Mumbai was not just a physical relocation; it was a profound shift in his life's trajectory. Leaving behind the comforts of city life, a secure paycheck, and a predictable routine was an act of profound self-awareness and boldness. To most, a steady job in a metropolitan city would symbolize success, but Hemant saw beyond the immediate comfort. He understood that while the comfort of his corporate life offered financial security, it also limited his potential for personal and professional growth.

For Hemant, the choice to walk away from everything he knew was not a simple one. It required immense courage to step away from a career that many would consider the pinnacle of success, to face the vast unknowns that lay ahead. At the time of his decision, he had no roadmap—no clear path or concrete plan for his future. He wasn't sure where this leap would take him, or how long it would take to find a new purpose, but what he was certain of was that remaining in his comfort zone would never lead him to the growth and fulfillment he sought.

This pivotal moment exemplifies what it truly means to embrace the essence of readiness—an inner readiness to let go of the familiar in pursuit of something greater. Hemant understood that the journey ahead was filled with uncertainty, but he also recognized that real growth often requires stepping into the unknown. He knew that only by leaving behind the predictable could he begin to uncover new possibilities and discover talents and passions that had remained dormant. The very act of leaving a stable job symbolized his willingness to challenge the status quo and create a space where he could grow beyond the constraints of his previous life.

It wasn't just a physical transition; it was a mental and emotional recalibration. Hemant's decision to take the risk was driven by a deep belief that true success lies in the process of becoming—not in the security of maintaining the status quo. He embraced uncertainty, not as a threat, but as a gateway to new experiences and deeper fulfillment. His trust in himself, even in the absence of a clear plan, became the foundation of his resilience. It was this trust that allowed him to face each day without a fixed idea of the outcome, knowing that the act of stepping into the unknown was, in itself, a form of personal growth.

This transition also marked the beginning of Hemant's exploration into his deeper values and desires. In the corporate world, he had been defined by his role, salary, and responsibilities. In leaving it all behind, he was giving himself the chance to rediscover who he was, beyond the titles and financial success. He didn't know exactly what form his future would take, but he knew that it would be aligned with his personal values—values he hadn't fully explored while in the corporate grind.

Each day, as he navigated the uncertainties of his new path, Hemant learned that growth isn't always linear or easy. There were moments of doubt, moments when he questioned if he had made the right choice. But the very fact that he had chosen to leave the stability of his corporate job meant that he had already demonstrated the courage to keep going, even when faced with uncertainty. For Hemant, this decision wasn't just about pursuing a career change—it was about redefining his purpose, exploring his potential, and making a conscious choice to align his life with what he truly valued.

Leaving a stable job for the unknown isn't a decision most people are willing to make. It requires a level of faith—faith in yourself, in the process, and in the belief that life's greatest opportunities often lie just beyond the edge of your comfort zone. Hemant's willingness to take this leap is a powerful reminder that growth doesn't come from avoiding risks, but from stepping into them with an open heart and an open mind. By choosing the unknown, Hemant opened the door to a future that, while uncertain, would ultimately be more aligned with his passion and purpose. And in doing so, he became a living example of how embracing risk can lead to a more fulfilling and meaningful life.

In the end, Hemant's story reveals the profound truth that sometimes the most significant changes in life come not from finding a clear path, but from daring to create one. By releasing the familiar and stepping into the uncertainty of what's next, he found the space to redefine his life and chart a course that was uniquely his own. This decision—to embrace the unknown—wasn't just about leaving a job; it was about forging a new, richer life, one that would continue to unfold as he faced new challenges, seized new opportunities, and grew into the person he was meant to become.

Embracing Teaching and Entrepreneurship

When Hemant returned to his hometown, he found himself at a crossroads—facing a new chapter in life that would test his readiness to embrace the unfamiliar. His move from the bustling corporate world to a quieter, more grounded life was not a retreat; it was a deliberate step toward a new beginning. The opportunity that awaited him wasn't about financial security or prestige; it was about discovering a role that would allow him to give back, continue growing, and connect more deeply with his community. Hemant accepted a teaching position at a local engineering college, not because it was a step up in his career, but because it offered a platform for him to share his knowledge and mentor future generations.

Teaching, however, brought with it a new set of challenges—ones Hemant had not fully anticipated. As he settled into his new role, he quickly realized that the curriculum, while comprehensive, often felt disconnected from the practical realities of the industry. The gap between academic theory and real-world application was glaring, and Hemant found himself questioning the effectiveness of the system in preparing students for the challenges they would face in their careers. Rather than passively accepting this as an inherent flaw in the system, Hemant saw it as a call to action. He understood that the knowledge students were receiving needed to be enriched with real-world insights, hands-on experiences, and practical skills that would make them more effective and adaptable in their professional lives.

Ready for a new challenge, Hemant took matters into his own hands. He decided to fill this gap, not by merely complaining about the system, but by taking proactive steps to address it. This marked the beginning of his entrepreneurial journey. He founded his own coaching institute, a space where students could gain both theoretical knowledge and practical, real-world experience. The goal of this new venture was clear: to bridge the divide between academic learning and industry needs. Hemant wasn't just interested in imparting knowledge; he wanted to equip his students with the tools and mindset they needed to succeed in a rapidly changing world.

The transition from teaching to entrepreneurship was no small feat. It required Hemant to stretch beyond his comfort zone and acquire a completely new skill set. He had to learn the intricacies of running a business—managing resources, balancing budgets, understanding marketing strategies, and making critical decisions that affected the livelihood of his students and staff. This leap into entrepreneurship also meant assuming financial risks, something he had never done in his corporate career. Hemant wasn't simply shifting careers; he was starting from the ground up, navigating a new set of challenges that tested his adaptability and resilience.

But this shift wasn't about abandoning his roots in teaching; it was about finding a new way to merge his passion for education with his drive for entrepreneurship. Hemant's readiness to step into the unknown was the key to his success. The same mindset that had enabled him to pivot from the corporate world to academia now allowed him to embrace the challenges of running a business. He took his years of experience in industry and blended them with his teaching expertise to create a unique educational environment—one that emphasized both academic rigor and real-world applicability. This fusion not only enriched his students' learning experience but also brought a deep sense of fulfillment to Hemant's life.

The decision to launch his own coaching institute didn't just fulfill a personal ambition; it also served as a response to a pressing need in the educational system. Hemant's ability to identify a problem and take decisive action allowed him to create an institution that was not just another coaching center, but a transformative space for students. By adapting to the needs of the changing world and applying his insights as an educator and entrepreneur, Hemant built an organization that not only helped students gain knowledge but also nurtured their ability to think critically, solve problems, and apply what they learned in real-world situations.

In embracing both teaching and entrepreneurship, Hemant demonstrated the power of adaptability. His journey was a testament to the fact that true growth comes not from staying within the lines of one's comfort zone, but from blending diverse skills, perspectives, and experiences into a new, innovative path. Hemant didn't just adapt to the demands of the education sector; he reshaped it, finding a way to make his mark while simultaneously enriching the lives of his students. His story serves as an inspiration for anyone willing to take risks, embrace change, and follow their passion—showing that sometimes, the greatest opportunities lie in the willingness to merge your skills and passions into something entirely new.

Spending Time with Illiterate and Tribal Communities

Hemant's journey toward growth wasn't confined to the traditional realms of education and entrepreneurship; it also took him to places that were far removed from his everyday experiences. His readiness to grow and expand his understanding of the world led him to make a bold and life-changing decision: to spend 15 days walking through rural and tribal communities, places where access to education, healthcare, and basic resources was limited. This was not a project or a career move—this was a personal mission, a deliberate effort to immerse himself in the lives of people who faced challenges far beyond what most people in urban areas could imagine.

For Hemant, this was about more than just gaining knowledge—it was about truly understanding the realities of people living in conditions of extreme poverty and isolation. Stepping into the world of tribal communities, where modern conveniences and comforts were luxuries few could afford, was both humbling and eye-opening. He had spent years in urban environments, often surrounded by the relative privilege of education, opportunity, and access. But when he entered these communities, he was confronted by the stark contrast of life in rural areas. Here, education was not a given; it was a privilege many did not have access to, and basic necessities like clean water and healthcare were scarce.

The experience challenged many of Hemant's preconceived notions about the world. It was easy to assume that education and progress were universally valued or available, but his time in these communities revealed just how deeply entrenched the divide was. The people in these villages, many of whom had never attended school or learned to read and write, lived in a world where survival was the primary concern. Yet, despite their challenges, there was a deep sense of community and resilience, a quality that Hemant had come to deeply respect. The raw realities of these people's lives were difficult to process, but they also stirred a powerful sense of compassion and a desire to do more.

This immersion into rural life was transformative, reshaping Hemant's worldview. It wasn't just about witnessing hardship; it was about seeing the strength and dignity of people who had learned to live with far less than most. The emotional and intellectual impact of this experience was profound—it gave him an invaluable perspective on the educational divides in society, the systemic barriers that kept so many people from accessing even the most basic education, and the urgent need for sustainable, inclusive solutions.

During his time in the tribal villages, Hemant also had the opportunity to engage with community leaders, local educators, and the people themselves, hearing their stories and understanding their dreams. It became clear that while these communities had little access to formal education, they possessed an immense wealth of knowledge about survival, resourcefulness, and cultural preservation. Hemant was able to witness firsthand how a lack of formal education didn't mean a lack of wisdom or understanding. However, it also made him painfully aware of the opportunity gap—how education could open doors for these communities in ways that would fundamentally change their lives, if only they had access to it.

This experience not only deepened Hemant's empathy but also strengthened his resolve to make a meaningful difference in the education sector. He came to understand that true education wasn't about simply delivering academic content—it was about ensuring that people from all walks of life, regardless of their background, had access to the tools and opportunities that would allow them to thrive. Hemant's experience in the tribal villages cemented his belief in the power of inclusive education, one that didn't just cater to the urban elite, but reached across the divide to include the marginalized and underserved.

More importantly, Hemant's time spent with these communities gave him a renewed sense of purpose. He understood that the work ahead of him wasn't just about filling gaps in curriculum or creating new educational institutions. It was about addressing the systemic inequities that kept vast sections of society from accessing the transformative power of education. It was about creating sustainable, community-driven solutions that could meet people where they were, rather than expecting them to fit into a system designed for the privileged few.

In the years that followed, this experience would continue to guide Hemant's work, shaping his approach to education, his values as an entrepreneur, and his understanding of what it meant to truly make a difference. His readiness to step outside the boundaries of his own life, to immerse himself in a world so vastly different from his own, became a crucial part of his personal and professional evolution. It wasn't just about gaining knowledge; it was about gaining wisdom, perspective, and compassion—qualities that would enable him to build an education model that could address the unique challenges faced by marginalized communities.

Hemant's journey through these rural and tribal villages wasn't just a brief chapter in his life—it was a turning point, one that would shape his future endeavors. It reminded him of the importance of stepping outside one's own world to gain a broader, more inclusive view of society. This experience not only reinforced his commitment to creating opportunities for those who had been left behind but also inspired him to develop an education system that was grounded in the realities of life for all students, regardless of their socio-economic background. Hemant's time spent with these communities was a testament to the power of compassion, empathy, and the readiness to grow beyond the confines of one's own experiences.

Each of these moments demonstrates that true readiness for change is a combination of proactive decision-making, emotional resilience, and an open heart to unexpected opportunities. Hemant didn't passively wait for life to change around him; he embraced change with intention, seizing opportunities and trusting his ability to adapt. His story serves as a reminder that readiness isn't about having all the answers but rather about having the courage to seek them along the way. Through his journey, Hemant has shown that when we stay ready, we can turn even the most uncertain paths into a more purposeful, fulfilling life.

Practical Advice on Staying Proactive and Embracing Change

As we've explored through Hemant's story, readiness for change is not just a concept, but a way of life that can propel you towards new opportunities and growth. Now, let's delve deeper into practical strategies that you can adopt to cultivate readiness in your own life, making sure that you're always prepared to embrace change with confidence and proactivity.

Accept the Uncertainty of Life:

The foundation of readiness begins with an acceptance of life's inherent unpredictability. Hemant's decision to leave behind his comfortable job in Mumbai wasn't made from a place of certainty or security. Rather, it stemmed from his understanding that life is full of uncertainties and that these uncertainties shouldn't be feared—they should be embraced as part of the journey. Life's twists and turns are what make it rich with possibilities. By accepting that you cannot control every aspect of your future, you free yourself from the chains of overplanning and rigid expectations. Embrace the uncertainty, and you'll discover new horizons that would otherwise remain hidden. This mindset shift—seeing the unknown as an opportunity rather than a threat—can open doors to unexpected and rewarding paths.

Stay Proactive and Take Action:

Readiness isn't about passively waiting for the "right moment" or hoping for the perfect circumstances to arise—it's about actively creating your own opportunities. Hemant did not wait for an ideal job offer or a clear path to emerge. Instead, he actively shaped his future by seeking out new challenges and projects, such as teaching at an engineering college and starting his own coaching institute. This is the power of proactive action: it gives you the agency to determine your course. Taking the initiative in your own life—whether through gaining new skills, exploring different career paths, or tackling new challenges—ensures that you're always moving forward, creating momentum in the direction of your goals. If you wait for the perfect conditions, you might miss the opportunity to shape your own success.

Cultivate Emotional Resilience:

The road to change is rarely smooth, and setbacks are inevitable. What makes someone truly ready for change isn't the absence of obstacles, but the ability to navigate them with resilience. Hemant's journey wasn't free from moments of doubt, frustration, or fear of failure. But what set him apart was his ability to bounce back from setbacks and keep pushing forward. Emotional resilience is about maintaining composure during challenging times, not allowing disappointments to derail your progress. To build this resilience, practice mindfulness techniques, engage in regular self-reflection, and develop a support system of friends, mentors, or family who can help you through tough times. Emotional resilience enables you to recover quickly, learn from challenges, and continue your journey towards growth.

Continuously Learn and Evolve:

To be ready for change, you must commit to a mindset of continuous learning. Change, by its very nature, requires new skills, perspectives, and approaches. Whether you're advancing in your current field or pivoting to something entirely different, staying intellectually and emotionally engaged with your own growth is essential. Hemant's journey from a stable engineering career to teaching and entrepreneurship is a testament to the importance of learning and evolving. He never stopped gaining new knowledge—whether from formal education, practical experiences, or self-driven learning. To cultivate readiness for change, prioritize lifelong learning. This will not only keep you adaptable but will also ensure that you are constantly honing your skills and expanding your understanding of the world. The more you learn, the more confident and prepared you'll be for the changes life brings.

Let Go of the Past to Move Forward:

A critical part of embracing change is releasing attachments to the past. Often, we hold on to past successes, failures, or identities that no longer serve us. Hemant's willingness to leave behind his established career in engineering was not just about a change of profession—it was about letting go of the image he had built for himself in the corporate world. Holding on to the past, whether it's past achievements or regrets, can prevent you from moving forward. Embracing change requires an openness to let go of what no longer aligns with your growth and to trust that something better awaits. Letting go doesn't mean forgetting—it means choosing to prioritize what's next rather than clinging to what was. When you release the old, you create space for new opportunities, experiences, and growth.

Surround Yourself with Like-minded People:

Finally, one of the most powerful ways to stay proactive and embrace change is by surrounding yourself with a supportive network. Hemant's readiness to embrace change was reinforced by the mentors, peers, and friends who supported him throughout his journey. Surrounding yourself with like-minded people who inspire you, challenge you, and encourage you to grow can make all the difference. These individuals act as both sounding boards and sources of motivation, helping you stay on track when things get tough. Having a strong network can also provide you with fresh perspectives and ideas that you may not have considered on your own. Be intentional about the people you allow into your life; their influence can either propel you forward or hold you back.

By following these steps—accepting uncertainty, staying proactive, building emotional resilience, committing to continuous learning, letting go of the past, and surrounding yourself with supportive people—you can cultivate the readiness to embrace change in your own life. Change will always be a constant, and by remaining open, adaptable, and proactive, you can turn every change into an opportunity for growth and transformation.

Conclusion

Readiness for change lies at the heart of Hemant's story. His journey is a testament to the transformative power of embracing the unknown. From stepping away from the comfort of a stable job to venturing into the uncharted territory of teaching and entrepreneurship, Hemant demonstrated that the key to thriving in an ever-changing world is the ability to adapt. He didn't merely navigate change—he welcomed it as an opportunity to grow, to challenge himself, and to make a positive impact on the lives of others.

The foundation of his journey was mental and emotional readiness—the willingness to accept uncertainty and push through discomfort in pursuit of something greater. Hemant's story teaches us that readiness isn't about having everything figured out in advance; it's about the mindset that allows us to take action even in the face of doubt and uncertainty. His ability to move from one chapter to the next, without clear assurances of success, shows that readiness for change is not about perfect conditions, but about cultivating the courage and resilience to forge ahead.

Hemant's proactive approach to life—where he took ownership of his own path, sought out new opportunities, and turned challenges into stepping stones—was key to his success. He didn't wait for change to happen to him; he made it happen by staying open, staying engaged, and actively seeking out the next opportunity for growth.

As you reflect on your own readiness for change, remember that it's not about having all the answers or knowing exactly what the future holds. Life is unpredictable, and the road ahead is never clear-cut. What truly matters is your ability to stay open, proactive, and resilient when the inevitable changes come. When you're mentally and emotionally prepared for the journey, you'll be able to make the most of any opportunity that comes your way, no matter how uncertain or challenging it may seem.

Your path may not always be a straight line, and you may face obstacles along the way. But if you approach life with the readiness that Hemant exemplifies, the possibilities are limitless. The world is full of opportunities for those who are willing to step into the unknown with confidence and embrace change as a powerful tool for personal and professional growth.

So, as you continue your own journey, remember: readiness is not about predicting the future, but about embracing whatever comes with courage, determination, and a belief that every change holds the potential for a new and meaningful adventure.

Chapter 8: Non-Attachment to Outcomes

One of the most profound teachings in life comes from the concept of **non-attachment to outcomes**. In a world obsessed with results—be it in our careers, relationships, or personal endeavors—it's easy to fall into the trap of measuring success by what we achieve. Yet, true fulfillment and peace often lie in releasing the grip on specific outcomes and instead focusing on the process itself. Non-attachment doesn't mean being indifferent or careless about results—it means freeing yourself from the need to control them and trusting that the journey itself has inherent value.

In the philosophy of **"Keeping Bags Packed,"** this concept of non-attachment is critical. It's about finding balance between setting goals and not being overly fixated on their exact results. It's understanding that outcomes, while important, are often outside of our direct control. Hemant's journey is a perfect example of someone who embraced the essence of non-attachment, making decisions based on values and passion, rather than an obsessive pursuit of conventional success.

Let's dive into the power of detachment from outcomes and how we can apply it to lead a more meaningful life—one where the process becomes as rewarding as the end result.

The Power of Detachment from Specific Outcomes and Focusing on the Process

Non-attachment to outcomes doesn't mean abandoning goals or dreams; rather, it signifies a shift in perspective—an understanding that while we can aim for something, it is the journey, not just the destination, that holds the real value. When we become overly fixated on the end result, we risk losing sight of the process—the challenges, the growth, the lessons, and the self-discovery that shape us in ways we often don't anticipate. By focusing too intently on the outcome, we miss the opportunity to fully engage with the present moment, where true growth resides.

The power of detachment lies in realizing that while goals can guide us, they shouldn't define us. It's about recognizing that the act of pursuing something, the effort we put in, and how we engage with the process are what truly enrich our lives. The outcome may or may not align with our expectations, but the journey itself is always a rich source of growth.

Consider Hemant's bold decision to leave his well-established job in Mumbai and return to his hometown, a move that many would view as a backward step. From an external perspective, it seemed like a risky, uncertain choice. He was leaving behind financial security, career recognition, and the comfortable stability of city life. Yet, Hemant wasn't driven by the need for a specific financial or social outcome. He wasn't preoccupied with how this move would be perceived by others or whether it would lead to immediate success. Instead, his focus was on the process—on the personal growth, the learning, and the exploration of what lay ahead.

In choosing to leave his job, Hemant prioritized the journey of self-discovery over a predefined goal. He was ready to embrace uncertainty, to explore new opportunities, and to grow along the way. This mindset allowed him to release any pressure to succeed in a conventional sense. Hemant's ability to detach from the fixed expectation of what "success" should look like in terms of salary, social status, or traditional achievements freed him from unnecessary stress and anxiety. His focus shifted from what he might gain to what he could learn and experience.

When we let go of rigid expectations, we also let go of the fear that often accompanies them. We begin to see that life isn't just about achieving something specific; it's about the person we become as we work toward our goals. Whether we succeed or fail, the true value of our efforts often lies in the growth we experience during the process. Hemant's journey exemplifies this beautifully. It wasn't about reaching a particular point—it was about embracing the journey itself, staying open to the learning, and trusting that every step along the way added value, regardless of the final outcome.

This detachment from outcomes opens us up to unexpected experiences and joys that might not have been part of our original plan. By being present and invested in the process, we allow ourselves the freedom to explore new directions and opportunities that we might otherwise miss. Non-attachment doesn't mean we stop striving or setting goals; it means that we become more flexible, less rigid in our expectations, and more willing to embrace what the journey offers, even if it's different from what we imagined.

By focusing on the process, we learn to enjoy the present, engage deeply with our experiences, and cultivate a sense of peace, knowing that whatever the outcome may be, the journey itself has already made us richer. Whether in our careers, relationships, or personal projects, the path we take holds immeasurable value—often more than the destination itself. The richness of life lies not in what we achieve, but in how we navigate the pursuit of our goals, how we grow along the way, and how we learn to embrace the process rather than obsessing over a specific outcome.

Hemant's Decisions Reflect Non-Attachment to Conventional Success Metrics

Hemant's journey serves as a testament to the power of non-attachment to conventional measures of success. Throughout his story, he made decisions that defied the typical yardsticks by which society often judges a successful life—salary, prestige, recognition, and social standing. His ability to navigate these expectations with grace is a core theme that runs through his life.

One of the most striking examples of this is Hemant's decision to leave behind a high-paying, well-established job in the bustling city of Mumbai and move back to his hometown. For many, this would seem like a step backward—a rejection of the financial security and social status associated with a metropolitan career. In choosing this path, Hemant didn't base his decision on external factors like salary, job title, or the prestige of his role. He wasn't seeking validation from peers or society; instead, he listened to his inner calling. His focus was clear: it was about the process of teaching, the ability to connect with students, and the opportunity to shape the future of the young minds he would guide.

This decision reveals a deep level of self-awareness. Hemant was not swayed by the pressure to conform to traditional definitions of success, and as a result, he found fulfillment in areas that most people overlook. When he accepted the teaching job at the engineering college, he didn't waste time negotiating the terms of his salary or the perks of the role. His primary concern was the opportunity to teach and impact his students' lives in meaningful ways. This is a radical shift from the typical professional approach, where financial compensation and career advancement are often prioritized above all else. Hemant's satisfaction came not from the paycheck, but from the knowledge that he was offering something valuable—insight, mentorship, and inspiration to the next generation.

Even when Hemant ventured into entrepreneurship by founding his own coaching institute, he continued to demonstrate a non-attachment to conventional success metrics. Rather than immediately assessing success by the number of students enrolled or the amount of income the business generated, his focus was on creating a quality educational space. For him, success was defined not by quantitative measures but by the impact he could have on his students' critical thinking abilities, their personal growth, and their approach to learning. He sought to create an environment where students were not just taught to memorize lessons but were inspired to think differently, question the status quo, and approach problems creatively.

This approach is a powerful reflection of non-attachment to external outcomes. Hemant's decisions were guided not by a desire for external validation, but by his personal values and what he believed would be most meaningful. In this sense, his life and choices can be seen as an embodiment of what it means to live authentically—without being bound by the limiting definitions of success set by society. This detachment allowed Hemant to find true fulfillment, one that was not defined by societal standards, but by a deeper sense of purpose and a commitment to contributing to the lives of others.

By not anchoring his self-worth to the typical markers of success—like money, status, or accolades—Hemant was able to create something that was meaningful and aligned with his own values. This is the true power of non-attachment to outcomes: it frees us from the pressure to conform and allows us to create success on our own terms. It opens up the possibility of redefining what success truly means, and in Hemant's case, it led to a life rich in purpose, impact, and fulfillment.

Non-attachment to outcomes isn't about abandoning ambition or hard work; rather, it's about shifting the focus from external rewards to internal satisfaction. It allows us to prioritize the journey over the destination and gives us the freedom to pursue what truly matters without being tethered to the conventional markers that society often elevates. Hemant's story is a powerful reminder that true success is not measured by the material or social outcomes we achieve, but by the integrity with which we live our lives and the positive impact we make along the way.

Core Philosophy on How to Practice Non-Attachment in Life and Career

While non-attachment is a powerful concept, practicing it in real life can be challenging, especially in a society that glorifies success and outcome-based thinking. Here are some actionable insights on how to incorporate non-attachment into both life and career, taking inspiration from Hemant's journey.

Focus on the Process, Not the Result

One of the most profound ways to practice non-attachment is to shift our focus from the result to the process. It's easy to get caught up in the final outcome—the promotion, the financial gain, the accolades—but this focus on the result often leads to stress, disappointment, and frustration when things don't go as planned. Instead, by embracing the process, we learn to find fulfillment in the journey itself, in the small victories and the growth we experience along the way.

Hemant's early days as a teacher offer a perfect illustration of this mindset. When he started his teaching career, he could have easily set his sights on becoming the most successful or highly sought-after teacher in the region. He could have fixated on how many students would sign up for his classes or whether he would become a local celebrity in the education space. But Hemant chose a different path—he focused entirely on the process itself. His main concern was not how many students enrolled, but how he could improve as a teacher, how he could engage with each student meaningfully, and how he could make learning an enjoyable and enriching experience for them.

This mindset led Hemant to continually refine his teaching methods, to adapt to the needs of his students, and to remain curious about new approaches to education. Rather than focusing on becoming the best in terms of numbers or reputation, he poured his energy into mastering the craft of teaching. He read, he reflected, and most importantly, he listened—to his students, to his peers, and to himself. His dedication to the process of teaching meant that he didn't measure his success by the number of students who walked into his classroom or the accolades he received. Instead, he measured his success by his personal growth and the genuine connections he made with his students.

This approach was transformative. The result—his growing reputation as a respected and beloved teacher—followed naturally, but it was never the primary goal. It was simply a byproduct of his commitment to improving each day and learning through his experiences. By focusing on the journey rather than the destination, Hemant created a career that was not only successful in the traditional sense but also deeply fulfilling. The success came not because he obsessed over it, but because he had a genuine passion for the process itself.

When we focus solely on the outcome, we risk missing the beauty of the process. Whether we're working on a business idea, pursuing a creative project, or even learning a new skill, the joy lies in the work itself—the growth, the setbacks, the breakthroughs, and the moments of learning. By immersing ourselves fully in the process, we find fulfillment in the present moment, rather than waiting for the outcome to validate our efforts.

In Hemant's case, his journey as a teacher demonstrates how success is often a natural consequence of dedication and passion for the process. It reminds us that if we can let go of the obsession with results and instead immerse ourselves in the process, we can find joy in the work we do and trust that success will come in its own time.

Let Go of Control

One of the most profound aspects of non-attachment is learning to let go of control. It's a common human desire to want things to unfold according to our plan, to steer every moment in the direction we envision. But, as life so often teaches us, there are numerous factors beyond our control that shape the outcome of any situation. Trying to control everything can lead to frustration and stress, especially when things don't go as planned. Instead, practicing non-attachment means surrendering the need for control and trusting that life, or the universe, has a way of unfolding in ways we might not always understand. This trust allows us to remain open to the unexpected, knowing that every twist and turn holds value, even if it doesn't match our original vision.

Hemant's journey is a perfect illustration of this principle in action. When he began his career in engineering, it was with the clear goal of building a successful career in that field. He had a well-laid-out path, one that many would have considered predictable and stable. However, life had different plans. The moment he let go of the idea that engineering was the only path for him, his entire journey took an unexpected turn, leading him to teaching and entrepreneurship.

His decision to move away from his engineering career wasn't the result of a well-thought-out plan to switch fields, nor was it an attempt to control his future in any way. Hemant didn't rigidly control every step along the way; instead, he allowed his experiences to guide him, to shape his path. When he started teaching, he didn't approach it with the expectation that it would be a stepping stone to anything specific. He didn't force it to fit into his idea of success. He let go of the need for an immediate outcome and focused instead on the process of teaching itself.

Then, when the opportunity arose to start his own coaching institute, he didn't obsess over how it would succeed. Instead of forcing it to fit into a mold of what a successful business should look like, he embraced the uncertainty. He trusted that his experiences, along with the relationships he built, would guide him toward his true purpose. This willingness to let go of the need to control every aspect of his journey allowed him to remain flexible and open to unforeseen circumstances and unexpected opportunities.

This adaptability is key to Hemant's success. It's not that he didn't have goals or ambitions, but he didn't rigidly cling to a particular outcome. He recognized that life's trajectory is rarely linear and that the beauty often lies in its unpredictability. By surrendering the need to control every detail, he was able to embrace the opportunities that came his way—whether they seemed ideal at first or not—and use them to further his growth.

Letting go of control doesn't mean giving up on goals or ambitions. Rather, it's about trusting that life has a way of unfolding that may be better, richer, and more meaningful than what we originally imagined. It's about being open to the unexpected, to the experiences and lessons that come from letting go of rigid expectations. When we stop trying to control every aspect of our journey, we allow ourselves to flow with the rhythm of life, trusting that we will always be led toward what's meant for us.

In Hemant's case, his ability to adapt to new circumstances—whether it was shifting from engineering to teaching or embracing entrepreneurship—was a key factor in his success. His journey wasn't about having a fixed destination in mind; it was about allowing himself to grow, change, and learn along the way. By letting go of the need to control the outcome of each decision, he opened himself up to a world of possibilities, and in doing so, created a life that was fulfilling, meaningful, and uniquely his own.

Detach from External Validation

In today's world, it's easy to get caught up in the chase for external validation. Social media likes, professional accolades, financial achievements—these markers of success often become the yardstick by which we measure our self-worth. The more approval we receive from others, the more we feel validated and accomplished. But this external validation can also be fleeting and superficial. It's based on the opinions and judgments of others, which can shift and change in an instant. True fulfillment, however, comes from within. Non-attachment teaches us that our worth is not determined by the opinions of others or the external recognition we receive. Instead, it encourages us to focus on aligning our actions with our values, passions, and inner truth.

Hemant's journey is a testament to this principle. When he decided to start his own coaching institute, he wasn't motivated by a desire for fame or recognition. He didn't look at his decision as a way to gain accolades or climb the social ladder. In fact, he wasn't seeking the approval of others in any way. He had already let go of the need to conform to societal standards of success—such as earning a high salary, achieving professional status, or receiving external praise. For Hemant, the external measures of success were irrelevant. What mattered was that he was doing something meaningful and true to himself.

Hemant's decision was rooted in his inner drive to make a difference, not in the need for validation from the outside world. He wanted to create a space where students weren't just receiving lessons—they were being inspired to think critically, develop new skills, and approach life with a sense of purpose and direction. His focus was on shaping young minds, not on building a reputation or achieving external success. The impact he could make on his students' lives was far more important to him than any external measure of success.

In this process, Hemant found his true fulfillment. He didn't rely on the approval of others to feel validated. Instead, his sense of worth came from knowing that he was doing meaningful work—work that was aligned with his core values and beliefs. Whether his coaching institute grew quickly or slowly, whether he received awards or recognition, didn't matter to him. What mattered was the satisfaction of knowing that he was making a difference in his students' lives, helping them grow into thoughtful, capable individuals.

The fulfillment Hemant experienced from his work wasn't based on outside recognition; it came from within. He was able to detach from the need for validation and focus on what was truly important to him. This inner satisfaction is what fueled his continued growth and success. When you align your actions with your values, when you follow your passions and dedicate yourself to a purpose that resonates deeply with you, the need for external validation fades. You begin to realize that your worth is inherent, not something that can be given or taken by others.

This doesn't mean that external validation is bad—it's natural to feel good when others recognize our efforts. But when we rely too heavily on this external feedback for our sense of self-worth, we give away our power. We let other people's opinions dictate how we feel about ourselves. Non-attachment teaches us that true self-worth comes from within. When we detach from the need for validation and focus instead on the satisfaction of living in alignment with our values, we experience a deep, lasting sense of fulfillment.

Hemant's journey is a powerful reminder that when we stop chasing external validation and focus on doing the work that is meaningful to us, we create a life that is authentic and deeply fulfilling. By detaching from society's standards of success, we open ourselves up to a deeper sense of purpose and satisfaction—one that doesn't depend on the opinions or judgments of others, but rather on the alignment of our actions with our true self.

Embrace Failure as Part of the Journey

Failure is an inevitable part of every journey. No matter how much we plan or how carefully we try to avoid it, setbacks and failures are bound to happen. What often makes failure difficult to bear is the attachment we have to specific outcomes. When we are overly fixated on a particular result, failure can feel like a personal blow, shaking our confidence and making us question our abilities. However, practicing non-attachment allows us to see failure differently—not as an end, but as an essential part of the process, a stepping stone toward growth and improvement.

When we let go of the need to control every outcome, we can start to view failure as a teacher, not an enemy. Instead of seeing it as something to avoid at all costs, we begin to recognize its value. Failure is rich with feedback, offering insights into what didn't work, what needs to change, and where we can improve. It teaches us resilience, adaptability, and the importance of perseverance. In this way, failure becomes a powerful tool for learning, pushing us forward instead of holding us back.

Hemant's journey is a perfect example of how non-attachment to outcomes can transform failure into a catalyst for growth. Like anyone else, Hemant faced failures—both in his professional and personal life. There were moments when things didn't go as planned, when projects didn't succeed, or when he encountered obstacles that seemed insurmountable. But what set him apart was his ability to embrace these setbacks without letting them define him or derail his journey.

Instead of seeing failure as a sign that he wasn't good enough, Hemant saw it as an opportunity to reflect and learn. His non-attachment to the outcome of each failure allowed him to approach challenges with an open mind, willing to absorb the lessons they offered. Whether it was a failed business venture or a professional setback, he didn't let these moments of disappointment stop him from moving forward. Instead, he used them as stepping stones, drawing wisdom from each experience that helped him become more resilient, wiser, and more prepared for future challenges.

This mindset of seeing failure as a part of the journey is what helped Hemant grow stronger after each setback. When he faced difficulties, rather than sinking into self-doubt or frustration, he took the time to analyze what went wrong, what he could have done differently, and how he could improve.

This process of learning from failure enabled him to bounce back each time with greater clarity and determination.

Hemant's ability to embrace failure as a natural part of the journey helped him remain focused on his long-term goals. He didn't let short-term setbacks cloud his vision. Instead, he saw failure as an inevitable yet necessary element of progress, helping him refine his approach and stay committed to his purpose. By maintaining this perspective, Hemant was able to persevere in the face of adversity, ultimately achieving success in areas that mattered most to him.

The practice of non-attachment to outcomes gives us the freedom to fail without fear. It allows us to approach challenges with a sense of curiosity rather than dread, knowing that each failure carries valuable lessons that can propel us forward. When we detach from the need to achieve a specific result, we can be less harsh on ourselves and more compassionate toward our mistakes. Failure, in this context, is not a reflection of our worth but a tool for refinement and growth.

In the end, embracing failure as part of the journey frees us from the paralyzing fear of making mistakes. We start to understand that failure is not something to avoid at all costs but something that can make us better, stronger, and more capable. By practicing non-attachment and viewing failure as a teacher, we open ourselves up to new opportunities for learning, growth, and eventual success. Hemant's story teaches us that the true value of failure lies not in the outcome but in the lessons it offers along the way.

Cultivate Gratitude for the Present Moment

Non-attachment, while often associated with letting go of the future, is equally about embracing and appreciating the present moment. It's a practice of fully experiencing the here and now without constantly seeking more or better. In our fast-paced, goal-oriented world, it's easy to become fixated on what's next—the next promotion, the next success, the next achievement. This constant forward-looking mindset can make us forget that true fulfillment often comes from fully experiencing and appreciating the present moment. Non-attachment helps us to let go of the compulsive need for future outcomes and, instead, fosters a deep sense of gratitude for what we have right now.

Gratitude for the present moment is about recognizing the value in where we are, regardless of whether we are exactly where we want to be or not. It's about finding joy in the small, everyday moments—whether it's savoring a peaceful morning, enjoying a conversation with a loved one, or simply being present in whatever task we're engaged in. The key is to cultivate an awareness that every moment, in its own unique way, contributes to our journey and growth.

For Hemant, this practice of gratitude became an essential part of his life. Throughout his journey—from his days as an engineer to his transition into teaching and eventually starting his own coaching institute—he learned to appreciate the moments as they unfolded, regardless of where they fit into his bigger plans. For instance, while teaching, Hemant didn't just focus on the future potential of his students or the success of his career. Instead, he took the time to truly engage with the present, focusing on the quality of his interactions with students, enjoying the act of teaching, and being fully present in those moments of connection.

Hemant's appreciation for the present was not limited to his professional life. He also learned to value the time spent with his family, understanding that life's most meaningful moments often come when we're simply being with the people we care about. Whether it was a quiet evening at home, a spontaneous conversation with his loved ones, or sharing experiences with his family, Hemant found joy in these moments, recognizing that they were not just filler between big milestones but essential parts of the journey itself.

Even his time spent with the tribal communities, when he would take long walks, offered him valuable lessons in being present. These walks were not about reaching a specific destination or accomplishing something. They were about immersing himself in the beauty of the natural world, connecting with the people around him, and embracing the simplicity of life in that moment. Hemant understood that in those walks, in the quiet exchange of stories and experiences, there was a profound richness that often gets overlooked in our pursuit of more.

By cultivating gratitude for the present moment, Hemant found contentment and fulfillment, not just in the grand achievements but in the small, seemingly ordinary moments that often pass by unnoticed. This sense of contentment didn't mean he was complacent; it meant that he was at peace with where he was, appreciating the journey he was on, and trusting that everything would unfold in its own time.

Practicing gratitude for the present moment allows us to stay grounded, no matter where our journey takes us. It helps us remain connected to the now, rather than becoming overwhelmed by the weight of the past or the uncertainties of the future. When we are grateful for the present, we become more mindful, more aware of the beauty and richness around us, and more appreciative of what we have in the moment. This sense of appreciation enhances our overall well-being and deepens our connection to life itself.

Hemant's story teaches us that non-attachment isn't just about detaching from outcomes or the future—it's also about fully embracing and appreciating the now. The present moment, with all its simplicity and beauty, holds immense value. By cultivating gratitude for it, we unlock a deeper sense of fulfillment, peace, and connection, making the journey itself just as meaningful as the destination.

Conclusion

Non-attachment to outcomes is not about indifference; it's about a fundamental shift in how we approach life. It's not about abandoning goals or aspirations but about loosening the grip on expectations and learning to embrace the flow of life. Often, we're conditioned to think that success is defined by the end result—by the prize, the recognition, or the destination. However, true fulfillment comes not from the result, but from the journey itself. The process of growth, the lessons learned along the way, and the alignment of our actions with our deepest values are what truly define success.

Hemant's journey is a powerful illustration of this principle. His decisions—sometimes unconventional, often bold—were not made with a fixed outcome in mind. He didn't base his actions on the desire for external validation or societal approval. Instead, he focused on the process of learning, evolving, and contributing to something meaningful. From leaving behind a high-paying job to teaching in his hometown and later starting his coaching institute, each decision was less about the potential for fame or wealth and more about personal growth and impact. His story teaches us that success is not something you achieve at the finish line, but something you experience continuously through your efforts, growth, and the positive difference you make in the lives of others.

When we let go of the need for certainty, we open ourselves to the richness of life's experiences. We free ourselves from the stress of trying to control every outcome, allowing ourselves to be fully present in the process. Hemant's journey exemplifies this idea. His willingness to embrace uncertainty, to follow his passion even when the future was unclear, is a testament to the strength that comes from non-attachment. He didn't obsess over what would happen tomorrow or the next year; he focused on what he could do today to make the most of his situation and his calling. This kind of approach is what allows us to stay grounded, focused, and engaged in the present, rather than overwhelmed by the pressure of a distant, uncertain future.

As you continue on your own journey, remember that the most important thing is not where you end up, but who you become along the way. The challenges, setbacks, and unexpected twists are all part of the process. Embrace them, learn from them, and trust that every experience is helping you grow into a better, more aligned version of yourself. If you can remain focused on the journey and the person you are becoming, you'll find that success is already within your grasp.

Keep your focus on the process. Commit to your growth, invest in your values, and find joy in the act of living authentically. Let go of the need to control the outcome, knowing that life has its own way of unfolding. Trust in the path you're walking, even when it doesn't seem clear, and remember that each step—whether forward or sideways—is moving you closer to where you need to be. The beauty of non-attachment is that it helps us let go of the need for things to unfold in a specific way, so that we can be open to all the possibilities that life has to offer.

By focusing on the process, you allow yourself the freedom to live fully and authentically. Let go of the pressure to control every aspect of your journey, and instead, trust that the path you are walking will lead you exactly where you need to go. When you focus on becoming the best version of yourself, everything else will fall into place, and success will be measured not by the end goal, but by the person you become along the way.

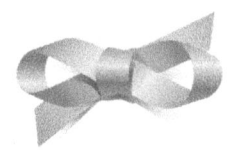

Chapter 9: Embracing Uncertainty

In life, one of the most powerful tools for growth and progress is the ability to embrace **uncertainty**. The very idea of stepping into the unknown, without the assurance of a clear outcome, can feel unsettling. Yet, it is through uncertainty that we unlock our deepest potential, discover hidden opportunities, and push beyond the limitations we impose on ourselves. It is not the absence of uncertainty but our relationship with it that defines how we grow.

In the context of **"Keeping Bags Packed,"** embracing uncertainty becomes a central theme. When we learn to accept that we cannot control everything, we free ourselves from fear and doubt. Instead, we open the door to endless possibilities. Hemant's journey is a remarkable example of this philosophy. His career trajectory, filled with unpredictable twists and turns, demonstrates how uncertainty—rather than being something to avoid—can become a catalyst for personal transformation.

Let's delve deeper into why embracing uncertainty is crucial, how Hemant's experiences exemplify this process, and how we can start to welcome the unknown with open arms.

Why Embracing Uncertainty is Necessary for Growth and Progress

Uncertainty is often seen as a threat, an unwelcome intruder that disrupts the calm of our familiar world. The unknown stirs discomfort, and it is human nature to resist it. We gravitate toward what feels safe and predictable, seeking the comfort of routines, known outcomes, and established patterns. However, the very thing that we fear the most—uncertainty—holds the key to true growth and transformation. It is through stepping beyond the familiar and into the unknown that we open ourselves to new possibilities, experiences, and insights.

The discomfort of uncertainty is not a sign that we are on the wrong path, but rather a signal that we are on the verge of change. It's a doorway to experiences we can't yet fully comprehend, ideas we haven't yet conceived, and breakthroughs that could reshape our lives. If we cling to certainty, we trap ourselves in a cycle of stagnation. Growth cannot occur in a space where everything is known, because growth requires movement—movement that challenges our assumptions, tests our limits, and pushes us beyond the boundaries of our comfort zone.

Uncertainty forces us to adapt, to rethink our approach, and to develop resilience. It challenges us to find creative solutions because we are no longer following predetermined scripts or relying on a set formula. When faced with the unknown, we are invited to innovate, to think outside the box, and to find new ways of navigating the world. It is in this space of unpredictability that we stretch our potential, unlocking new levels of capability and insight. Without uncertainty, there would be no need for problem-solving, no room for learning, and no opportunity for evolution. It's in those moments of uncharted territory that we discover our true strength, creativity, and capacity for growth.

Hemant's journey is a vivid example of how embracing uncertainty can lead to profound growth. Coming from a stable, well-paying job in the corporate world, he made the bold decision to leave behind the security of his career and venture into the world of teaching and later, entrepreneurship. At every turn, there was no clear blueprint for success. The risks were evident, and there were no guarantees. Yet, it was precisely this uncertainty that propelled him forward. He was willing to face the unknown, to take the leap despite not knowing how things would unfold. It was this courage to embrace uncertainty that allowed him to discover new opportunities, redefine his path, and ultimately align his life with his true passions.

Throughout his journey, Hemant encountered challenges, setbacks, and moments of doubt, yet each obstacle became an opportunity for learning and growth. His willingness to embrace the uncertainty of change allowed him to evolve professionally, personally, and spiritually. When he started his own coaching institute, for example, he had no certainty that it would succeed, but he understood that the journey itself was as valuable as the destination. The process of building something meaningful, of learning from his mistakes, and of growing through the challenges became the true reward. His story teaches us that embracing uncertainty is not about knowing exactly what will happen next, but about trusting that the experiences we gain along the way will shape us into the person we need to become.

Hemant was able to redefine success on his terms, free from the expectations of others or the pressure of societal norms. He made decisions not based on external validation, but from a deeper place of fulfillment, meaning, and purpose. His willingness to walk through uncertainty allowed him to build a life that felt authentic and true to his values.

Embracing uncertainty is not easy, and it requires a shift in perspective. Instead of fearing what we cannot control, we must learn to see it as an invitation to grow. When we are willing to let go of the need for certainty, we open ourselves up to endless possibilities. We learn that our path is not always linear, and that the unexpected twists and turns are not signs of failure but signs of progress. The true power of embracing uncertainty lies not in the outcome, but in the growth we experience along the way. It is through this willingness to step into the unknown that we discover what we are truly capable of achieving.

Hemant's Transition Through Various Careers and His Ability to Thrive in Uncertainty

Hemant's professional journey is a testament to the power of adaptability and the willingness to embrace uncertainty as a catalyst for personal and professional growth. His story is not just about career transitions but about the deeper changes in his mindset that allowed him to thrive despite the unpredictable nature of life. From working in a high-paying corporate job in a bustling metropolitan city to leaving it all behind and moving back to his hometown to become a teacher, Hemant's career path was anything but conventional. Each of these transitions was marked by a leap into the unknown—an act of stepping away from financial security, status, and the predictable trajectory of a corporate career in exchange for the uncertainties of a new field.

At first glance, his decision to leave the comfort and prestige of his corporate job might have seemed like a risky move. He was abandoning a well-established career path with clear benchmarks of success in favor of teaching at a small-town engineering college, a job that offered neither the same level of pay nor the same kind of social recognition. His decision to later open his own coaching institute was similarly fraught with uncertainty. There were no guarantees of success, no certainties about how his efforts would be received, and no assured financial return. It wasn't the kind of decision most would make when seeking a comfortable, predictable future. But for Hemant, it wasn't about the certainty of success—it was about the willingness to embrace the uncertainty of the journey and trust that the process itself would lead him toward something greater.

Each shift in Hemant's career was not driven by a need for external validation or by a concrete roadmap to success. Instead, he approached these changes with an open mind and a deep belief in the value of the process. Rather than focusing on outcomes like salary, prestige, or status, he committed himself to the growth and learning that each transition would bring. Moving from the corporate world to education was a significant leap, not just in terms of career but in his personal outlook on life. He stepped into a completely new arena—one that was unfamiliar and full of challenges. Yet, within that uncertainty, he found the opportunity to make a lasting impact.

For many, the idea of moving from a corporate job to a teaching role in a small-town college might have seemed like a "step down" in terms of social standing and economic rewards. But for Hemant, this new path became a springboard for deeper fulfillment. By shifting his focus from traditional markers of success to a sense of purpose, he discovered a new sense of meaning in his work. In the classroom, he was no longer merely exchanging his time for money; he was shaping the lives of future engineers, imparting knowledge, and inspiring critical thinking. It wasn't just about teaching textbooks—it was about guiding students toward their potential, helping them understand the power of learning, and nurturing their ability to think independently.

This leap into the unknown opened up a world of new opportunities for Hemant, both professionally and personally. He learned to navigate the challenges of the education sector, developed new teaching methodologies, and found joy in the intellectual growth of his students. His transition into entrepreneurship, starting his own coaching institute, was another example of embracing uncertainty. Again, there were no guarantees of success, no promise that his efforts would be financially fruitful or widely recognized. But through this uncertainty, he honed his business acumen, learned the ins and outs of running an educational institution, and, most importantly, stayed true to his core values.

Hemant's story is a powerful reminder that the most transformative growth often happens when we step into the unknown, when we leave behind the safety and familiarity of what we know and take a chance on something new. When we venture into uncharted territories, we are forced to rely on our inner resources—our resilience, creativity, and intuition. These qualities, which might have remained dormant had we stayed in our comfort zones, become essential in navigating the challenges that come with uncertainty. In the face of obstacles, Hemant's adaptability and willingness to learn allowed him to overcome setbacks and keep moving forward. His journey underscores a fundamental truth: true growth doesn't happen when things are easy or predictable; it happens when we allow ourselves to face the unknown and trust that, through the process, we will become stronger, wiser, and more aligned with our true purpose.

As Hemant's career path shifted from one stage to the next, he didn't just adapt to change—he embraced it fully. He found fulfillment not in the certainty of outcomes but in the journey itself, in the ongoing process of learning, evolving, and creating something that reflected his deepest values. His ability to thrive in uncertainty shows us that growth is not a destination but a continuous process. It is in the moments when we cannot predict the outcome that we discover our true potential and redefine success on our own terms.

How to Embrace Uncertainty and Find Opportunities in the Unknown

Embracing uncertainty is one of the most powerful ways to unlock new opportunities in life. While the unknown can often feel daunting and unsettling, it is within this very uncertainty that growth and innovation thrive. Instead of fearing the unknown, we can learn to see it as a canvas for new possibilities, a space where flexibility, creativity, and adaptability allow us to not only survive but thrive. By letting go of the need for complete control and embracing the unpredictability of life, we open ourselves to unexpected paths that can lead to personal and professional breakthroughs.

Shift Your Mindset from Fear to Curiosity

One of the most powerful ways to embrace uncertainty is by shifting your mindset. Often, when faced with the unknown, our instinct is to feel fear and apprehension. The unfamiliarity of a situation triggers our natural defense mechanisms, pushing us to retreat into what is safe and known. But what if, instead of fearing uncertainty, we viewed it as a space teeming with possibilities? What if we approached it not with hesitation, but with curiosity and an eagerness to explore the unknown?

This shift in perspective is crucial for growth and progress. When we face uncertainty through the lens of curiosity, we open ourselves up to a world of new opportunities and experiences. Rather than asking "What if I fail?" we begin to ask "What can I learn from this situation?" or "What new paths could this open up for me?" Instead of seeing uncertainty as a roadblock, we begin to see it as an adventure waiting to unfold. We become less focused on the potential risks and more excited by the unknown, trusting that whatever happens, we will grow from the experience.

Hemant's journey exemplifies this mindset shift. Throughout his career, he continually approached uncertainty with a sense of curiosity. For instance, when he decided to leave his high-paying corporate job and move back to his hometown to become a teacher, there was no clear road map. He wasn't guaranteed success, and the future was unpredictable. Many would have viewed this as a risky, uncertain move—one that might have led to failure. But Hemant, instead of fearing the change, saw it as an exciting new challenge. He wondered what he could learn from it, how it might reshape his perspective, and what new opportunities might arise.

When he transitioned from working in engineering to teaching in a small-town college, it was a major shift in his professional identity. He could have been afraid that the change would lower his status or lead to stagnation. But he chose to view the move with a sense of curiosity. He didn't see it as a setback, but as an opportunity to immerse himself in a completely different field. He asked himself: How can I make an impact on the lives of students?

What new skills can I develop as a teacher? How will this challenge my creativity and problem-solving abilities?

It was this openness to the unknown that allowed Hemant to adapt quickly and find new avenues for both personal and professional growth. Every step he took was an opportunity to learn something new. Moving into the world of education, and later starting his own coaching institute, were both steps into the unknown, yet Hemant was never deterred. His mindset remained focused on the potential for growth. Even when faced with obstacles, he reframed them as opportunities to learn and evolve.

This mindset shift—changing the perception of uncertainty from something to fear into something to explore—is transformative. It turns every challenge into a learning experience and removes the fear of failure. By cultivating a mindset of curiosity, we embrace the unknown with a sense of wonder and anticipation. We stop seeing uncertainty as a threat and start seeing it as a space full of possibility.

The ability to stay curious in the face of uncertainty not only allows us to remain adaptable but also fosters resilience. When things don't go as planned, instead of being discouraged, we remain open to what might come next. We begin to see setbacks as part of the process, not as indicators that we've failed. Hemant's story illustrates that by shifting our mindset, we don't just survive uncertainty—we thrive in it. Each step becomes a discovery, each challenge a lesson.

As you continue on your journey, try reframing uncertainty in your own life. Rather than being paralyzed by fear, ask yourself what could emerge from stepping into the unknown. Approach each new situation with an open mind and a heart full of curiosity. This mindset shift will not only help you embrace uncertainty—it will also propel you toward greater growth, fulfillment, and success.

Take Calculated Risks

Embracing uncertainty doesn't mean acting impulsively or recklessly. Instead, it calls for a willingness to take risks, but with careful consideration and a grounded approach. The difference between recklessness and calculated risk-taking is in the balance between instinct and insight. Taking risks is an inherent part of growth, but to be truly effective, these risks must be calculated—thoughtful decisions that stretch us outside of our comfort zones without leaping into the unknown without preparation. It's about trusting your instincts, applying your knowledge, and having faith that taking the first step, despite the uncertainties, will eventually lead you to clarity.

Calculated risks require us to analyze the situation, weigh the potential outcomes, and determine if the rewards outweigh the risks. These decisions aren't made on a whim, but rather from a place of awareness and trust in our abilities. While uncertainty surrounds every decision, the key is to avoid paralyzing fear. Instead of waiting for perfect conditions, we take that first step, knowing that the full picture will only become clearer as we move forward.

Hemant's decision to leave his secure corporate job and enter the field of education was a prime example of taking a calculated risk. At the time, it may have seemed like a leap of faith. The corporate world offered stability, financial security, and a clear trajectory for advancement. However, Hemant had something greater calling him—an unfulfilled desire to make a meaningful impact on people's lives. He knew that a career in teaching wouldn't offer the same financial rewards that his corporate job provided, but he believed that the opportunity to shape the minds of young individuals, to inspire them, and to be a catalyst for their growth was worth the risk.

He didn't make this decision recklessly; it was a well-thought-out choice. Hemant had already gained considerable experience in his field, and his passion for teaching had grown over time. He knew that, although there was uncertainty in the path ahead, the reward of making a difference in the world outweighed the potential financial setback. He understood that true fulfillment comes not from external rewards, but from aligning one's work with one's core values and passions.

This calculated risk paid off. By stepping into the world of education, Hemant found far greater fulfillment than he ever could have imagined in the corporate world. The impact he had on his students and the personal growth he experienced in the process were invaluable. Later, when he decided to start his own coaching institute, it was another calculated risk. He was well aware of the challenges and uncertainties involved in entrepreneurship, but his passion for education and his desire to create a platform that could reach more students drove him forward.

The success of Hemant's journey wasn't a result of blind optimism or luck; it was the outcome of calculated risks that pushed him to take bold steps without letting fear or uncertainty dictate his decisions. He trusted in his experience, his instincts, and his vision. With each calculated risk, he gained new insights, expanded his horizons, and found greater satisfaction in the work he was doing.

Taking calculated risks is about creating opportunities for yourself, even when the outcome isn't guaranteed. It's about recognizing that uncertainty is a natural part of growth and that, by making informed decisions, we can navigate the unknown with confidence. Every risk involves some level of uncertainty, but it's through these risks that we open doors to new possibilities. Hemant's story teaches us that, when guided by a sense of purpose and a willingness to act, the uncertain path can lead to profound growth and fulfillment.

As you consider the next steps in your own journey, ask yourself: What risks are you willing to take in order to align your actions with your values? By taking calculated risks, you will not only find greater personal satisfaction but also uncover opportunities that you might never have considered otherwise.

Trust the Process and Let Go of the Need for Immediate Results

One of the most challenging aspects of embracing uncertainty is learning to let go of the expectation for immediate results. In today's fast-paced world, we're constantly bombarded with messages that promote instant gratification. From the success stories we hear on social media to the fast-track programs promising quick wealth or fame, we've been conditioned to expect swift outcomes. However, when we embrace uncertainty, we enter a space where the journey is just as important—if not more so—than the destination. Trusting the process means relinquishing the urge for quick fixes and being comfortable with gradual progress.

It's tempting to seek immediate results, especially when we're venturing into uncharted territory. We want to see the fruits of our labor right away, and the longer it takes, the more difficult it becomes to stay committed. But in reality, true growth and lasting success often come from the consistency and patience we demonstrate over time. The process—the small, incremental steps—holds value beyond the immediate payoff. It's in these steps that we learn, adapt, and build the foundation for something truly sustainable.

Hemant's decision to start his own coaching institute was a clear reflection of this principle. Unlike ventures that promise overnight success, he knew from the outset that building his business would take time. His journey was not about achieving success in a matter of months, but about establishing a solid foundation for long-term growth. He had no illusions that everything would fall into place immediately. The road ahead would be filled with challenges, learning curves, and constant adaptation. Yet, Hemant chose to focus on the process rather than fixating on immediate results.

In the early days of his coaching institute, there were no guarantees. The student base was small, and the future was uncertain. However, Hemant trusted that the right opportunities would arise if he continued to put in the effort and remain committed to his mission of providing quality education. He didn't rush the process, nor did he allow setbacks to derail him. Instead, he focused on refining his teaching methods, improving the student experience, and building relationships with his students. Through this patient, methodical approach, his institute slowly grew, gaining more recognition and success over time.

It was this trust in the process that enabled Hemant to create something sustainable. He understood that success is not always about reaching the destination quickly; it's about cultivating a journey that is aligned with your values and goals. The patience required to build his institute, step by step, allowed him to create something that would last, and the rewards of that long-term commitment became evident as his institute gained a strong reputation in the community.

Trusting the process also meant letting go of the fear of failure. Hemant knew that there would be times when things didn't go as planned, when growth stalled, or when opportunities seemed scarce. But instead of being discouraged, he trusted that these challenges were simply part of the process. He gave himself the freedom to explore new strategies, learn from his mistakes, and adapt as needed. Each misstep became an opportunity to fine-tune his approach, rather than an obstacle to his success.

In our own lives, trusting the process requires us to let go of the need for validation or immediate recognition. It calls for patience and resilience, knowing that the efforts we put in today will yield results in the future. By focusing on the journey and trusting that each step is bringing us closer to our goals, we free ourselves from the stress of needing instant success. It's about cultivating the belief that our actions, no matter how small, are valuable and will eventually lead to meaningful outcomes.

Hemant's story teaches us that success is rarely instantaneous. It's the result of consistent effort, adaptability, and a willingness to trust that the right opportunities will unfold when the time is right. By embracing the process and letting go of the need for immediate results, we open ourselves to a more fulfilling and sustainable path of growth.

As you navigate your own journey, remind yourself that progress doesn't always look like rapid success. Sometimes, it's in the quiet, steady work that real transformation occurs. Trust the process, and know that with patience and perseverance, you'll build something that lasts.

Accept Failure as a Part of the Journey

Failure is often regarded as the opposite of success, but in reality, it is an integral part of any meaningful journey. When we step into the unknown, embracing uncertainty and taking risks, failure becomes an inevitable companion. It's easy to become discouraged when things don't go as planned, but true growth comes not from avoiding failure, but from learning how to navigate through it. Accepting failure as a natural part of the journey allows us to build resilience, refine our strategies, and ultimately reach our goals with a deeper sense of purpose and clarity.

When we set out on a new venture, whether it's in our personal life or our professional career, there's a certain level of uncertainty that we must accept. Not every decision will yield the desired outcome, and not every plan will succeed. The discomfort of failure often arises because we fear that it reflects our inadequacy or lack of capability. However, failure does not define us; it is simply feedback. It highlights areas that need improvement, invites reflection, and challenges us to adjust our approach. By embracing failure instead of shying away from it, we make space for growth, creativity, and innovation.

Hemant's journey into the world of education is a perfect example of how embracing failure can lead to long-term success. When he first ventured into teaching, it was not without its challenges. The shift from a corporate environment to a classroom setting was a significant change, and there were moments when Hemant wondered if he had made the right choice. The initial stages were filled with doubts and uncertainties. His teaching methods weren't always well-received, and the students didn't always engage as he had hoped. There were days when he felt like giving up, questioning whether his decision to leave behind the corporate world for education was a mistake.

However, Hemant chose to view these challenges and moments of failure as opportunities for learning rather than signs of defeat. Instead of allowing setbacks to discourage him, he took the time to reflect on his teaching style, the students' needs, and the gaps in his approach. He sought feedback, made adjustments, and embraced a growth mindset. He didn't see failure as something that would stop him but rather as a tool that would help him grow and improve. This perspective allowed him to adapt quickly, making the necessary changes to his approach and continuing to refine his skills as an educator.

With time, these initial failures began to transform into valuable lessons. Hemant realized that success wasn't about avoiding mistakes, but about how he responded to them. He understood that the real measure of progress wasn't in perfect outcomes, but in his ability to learn and evolve. Every failure, whether it was a lesson in teaching or in business, helped him become more adept at navigating the complexities of the education system. It taught him the importance of patience, flexibility, and resilience.

Moreover, his ability to embrace failure gave him the confidence to take bigger risks, such as starting his own coaching institute. The lessons learned from his earlier failures gave him the clarity to build a business that was aligned with his passions and values. He knew that the journey ahead would be filled with uncertainties and obstacles, but instead of fearing them, he saw them as opportunities to learn, innovate, and refine his approach.

Through this mindset, Hemant demonstrated that failure is not an end, but a beginning—a stepping stone that leads us to deeper understanding and greater success. Each failure becomes a lesson that guides us closer to our ultimate goals. His ability to embrace failure without being defeated by it allowed him to build something lasting and meaningful. As he continued on his journey, Hemant's resilience, built from his acceptance of failure, became one of his greatest assets.

For anyone navigating a path filled with uncertainty, Hemant's story serves as a reminder that failure is not a sign of personal inadequacy, but rather an opportunity to learn and grow. By accepting failure as part of the journey, we free ourselves from the fear of making mistakes and open ourselves to new possibilities. Each misstep becomes a stepping stone that propels us forward, refining our strategies and deepening our understanding. Ultimately, it's this acceptance of failure—and the lessons we take from it—that helps us develop the resilience necessary for long-term success.

Stay Flexible and Open to Change

One of the fundamental truths about life is that it is unpredictable. No matter how well we plan, things rarely go exactly as we anticipate. Uncertainty is a constant companion, and our ability to navigate through it largely depends on our flexibility. Flexibility isn't just about reacting to change when it happens; it's about staying open to new possibilities and adjusting our approach when the path we're on no longer serves our goals. In many ways, flexibility becomes a skill that empowers us to remain resilient and adaptable in the face of the unknown, ensuring that we continue moving forward no matter what obstacles or detours we encounter.

The journey of embracing uncertainty is not about rigidly holding onto a single vision or plan. Life rarely unfolds in a straight line; there are twists, turns, and unexpected detours. If we are too attached to one outcome or one way of doing things, we can miss out on new opportunities that arise. The key is to stay open, observe, and be willing to change course when necessary. Flexibility allows us to shift our mindset, reevaluate our situation, and respond to new circumstances with clarity and purpose. It is this ability to pivot and adapt that often determines how successfully we navigate uncertain and challenging situations.

Hemant's career provides a powerful example of the importance of staying flexible and open to change. His journey began in the engineering field, where he built a solid career and enjoyed the stability that came with it. Yet, as time passed, he realized that his true passions lay elsewhere—in education and, eventually, in entrepreneurship. This realization marked the first major shift in his professional life, and the transition was anything but simple. Leaving behind the comfort of a well-paying job and a defined career path to venture into the unknown of teaching was a significant leap.

But rather than viewing it as a risk, Hemant embraced it with flexibility, recognizing that it offered him a chance to make a deeper impact on others and align his career with his personal values.

However, the transition didn't end with teaching. As he settled into his new role as a teacher, Hemant faced yet another challenge: creating a sustainable and fulfilling future in the education sector. The path to becoming an educator wasn't straightforward, and Hemant quickly realized that teaching alone wasn't enough to fulfill his vision of making a real difference. He needed a way to expand his influence, reach more people, and create a lasting impact. So, he began exploring the idea of starting his own coaching institute.

Starting a business is never easy, and there were numerous obstacles and uncertainties along the way. Hemant didn't have a guaranteed road to success, and the landscape was filled with competition, financial risks, and logistical challenges. But his ability to stay flexible in the face of these challenges allowed him to move forward. He adapted to the changing needs of his students, adjusted his business strategies, and embraced new technologies and methods to enhance the learning experience. Each time an obstacle arose, he found a way to adjust his approach, seeing each challenge not as a setback but as an opportunity to refine his vision and move closer to his goal.

Hemant's story highlights how the ability to adapt and remain open to change is essential for growth, especially in uncertain times. His success didn't come from sticking rigidly to a plan, but from being willing to change direction when necessary and finding new ways to achieve his goals. Whether it was moving from engineering to education, or from teaching to entrepreneurship, Hemant's flexibility allowed him to thrive in an ever-evolving environment.

This adaptability not only helped Hemant professionally but also personally. In a world that is constantly changing, flexibility allows us to maintain balance and stay aligned with our values and aspirations. When we are open to change, we become more resilient and resourceful, better equipped to handle life's ups and downs. We learn to trust ourselves, to pivot when necessary, and to view obstacles as opportunities to grow and improve.

For anyone navigating uncertainty, whether in their career or personal life, Hemant's experience serves as a powerful reminder of the importance of staying flexible. The ability to adapt, learn from experiences, and embrace change is one of the greatest strengths we can cultivate. Life may not unfold exactly as we plan, but by staying open and flexible, we can shape it into something even better than we imagined. Flexibility allows us to navigate the unknown with confidence, knowing that no matter what comes our way, we have the ability to adjust, evolve, and continue moving forward with purpose.

Conclusion

Embracing uncertainty is not an instinctive or comfortable choice for most of us. It requires a conscious shift in perspective, especially in a world that often prioritizes stability, security, and predictability. Yet, uncertainty holds one of the most powerful keys to growth and progress. It is in the unknown that we find the space for discovery, innovation, and transformation. As challenging as it may seem, the willingness to step into uncertainty opens up a world of possibilities, and it is through this openness that we unlock opportunities that would have otherwise remained hidden.

At the core of embracing uncertainty is curiosity. When we approach the unknown with curiosity, rather than fear or hesitation, we free ourselves from the constraints of expectation and open our minds to new experiences and ideas. Curiosity fuels learning and creativity, allowing us to see beyond what is immediately in front of us and imagine what could be. It is this mindset shift that Hemant exemplifies in his own journey—a journey that constantly evolved, from his corporate career to education and entrepreneurship. Through each stage of his transition, Hemant's curiosity led him to see uncertainty not as something to avoid, but as a fertile ground for growth.

Taking calculated risks is another essential element of embracing uncertainty. While it may be tempting to play it safe, true growth often requires stepping outside of our comfort zones. Hemant's leap from a stable job into the world of teaching, and later starting his own coaching institute, was a calculated risk—one that required him to trust his instincts, his knowledge, and his vision for the future. The key, as demonstrated in

Hemant's story, is not about making reckless choices, but about taking informed actions that push us toward our potential, even without the certainty of success. It's through these calculated risks that we find new paths, learn valuable lessons, and expand our capabilities.

Equally important is trusting the process. In a world where instant gratification is the norm, we often expect immediate results. However, when we embrace uncertainty, we must also let go of the need for quick answers. The journey toward growth is rarely linear or immediate, and it takes patience, persistence, and faith. Hemant's decision to start his coaching institute wasn't driven by the desire for quick success, but by his belief in the process. He trusted that each step, no matter how uncertain, would bring him closer to building something meaningful. By focusing on the journey and not obsessing over the outcome, Hemant allowed himself the freedom to grow and adapt as opportunities arose.

Perhaps one of the most transformative aspects of embracing uncertainty is the ability to learn from failure. When we take risks and step into the unknown, we are bound to encounter setbacks. However, failure is not a dead end; it is simply a lesson in disguise. Every failure, as Hemant's journey shows, is an opportunity to adjust our approach, learn from our mistakes, and come back stronger. The fear of failure often keeps us from pursuing our dreams, but when we view it as an inevitable and necessary part of the process, it becomes a powerful catalyst for growth.

Hemant's story serves as a testament to the profound transformation that happens when we choose to embrace uncertainty. Instead of shying away from the unknown, he faced it head-on and allowed it to shape him into the person he is today. His journey teaches us that embracing uncertainty isn't just about surviving—it's about thriving. It's about moving forward, even when the path isn't clear, and trusting that the steps we take today will lead to a brighter future.

As we continue exploring the philosophy of "Keeping Bags Packed," we begin to understand that embracing uncertainty is not merely a survival tactic in a changing world—it is the very essence of thriving within it. The unknown is not a void; it is a space brimming with potential. When we welcome it with open arms and a willing heart, we set ourselves on a journey that is not limited by past experiences or conventional paths. Instead, we find ourselves in a perpetual state of growth, learning, and opportunity—ready to evolve with the times and shape our future, regardless of what lies ahead.

In this way, uncertainty becomes not something to fear, but something to embrace. The unknown is no longer a threat, but a door to endless possibilities. And it is by stepping through this door—curious, open, and ready for the adventure—that we unlock the true potential for growth and transformation. So, as we move forward, let us remember that embracing uncertainty is not just about taking risks, it's about embracing the very essence of life itself: a journey of constant change, evolution, and opportunity.

Chapter 10: Lifelong Learning and Growth

In today's fast-paced world, the only constant is change. As we journey through life, the challenges we face, the opportunities that come our way, and the technologies that shape our world all demand one thing from us: continuous **learning**. Lifelong learning is not just an academic pursuit, but a philosophy of life—one that keeps us open to new ideas, helps us grow in our personal and professional lives, and allows us to adapt to ever-changing circumstances.

At the core of the **"Keeping Bags Packed"** philosophy is the commitment to ongoing self-growth. In a world where knowledge and circumstances evolve constantly, the journey of growth is never truly complete. Embracing this journey means that we remain forever curious, always willing to evolve, and unafraid to reinvent ourselves in the face of new challenges.

Hemant's life and career serve as a testament to the power of lifelong learning and reinvention. His willingness to continually evolve, even when faced with uncertainty or drastic career changes, highlights the importance of staying open to new experiences and learning from every step along the way.

This chapter will explore why lifelong learning is essential for personal and professional growth, how Hemant's story reflects continuous learning, and how we can foster a mindset that embraces growth, especially during transitions.

The Importance of Lifelong Learning and Self-Growth

Lifelong learning is more than just an educational concept; it is a mindset and a way of life. It is the continuous, voluntary, and self-motivated pursuit of knowledge and skills throughout one's life. Unlike traditional education, which typically occurs within a fixed timeframe, lifelong learning is not confined to classrooms or formal degrees. It extends into every facet of life—whether we are picking up new skills, exploring new subjects, enhancing our existing capabilities, or simply adapting to the ever-changing world around us. This commitment to ongoing learning is essential because it enables us to remain agile, relevant, and capable in a world that is in constant flux.

In both our personal and professional lives, we are regularly confronted with new challenges and demands. These situations often require innovative thinking and a fresh perspective. The world of work is becoming more specialized, and industries continue to evolve with technological advancements, market shifts, and changes in social dynamics. In such an environment, staying stagnant is not an option. The need to learn and adapt has never been more crucial. Lifelong learning provides the tools necessary to not only survive but thrive in a fast-paced, interconnected world. As new technologies emerge, new fields open up, and old paradigms shift, lifelong learners are the ones who can harness these changes to their advantage.

Moreover, the value of lifelong learning extends far beyond professional development. It touches on every aspect of our being, contributing to emotional, spiritual, and personal growth. This holistic approach to learning means that we are constantly evolving and improving ourselves—not just our career prospects, but our relationships, our perspectives on the world, and our ability to cope with life's challenges. Engaging in continuous learning fosters curiosity, which in turn sparks self-reflection and personal insight. These qualities are essential for maintaining a balanced and fulfilled life, as they help us remain open-minded, compassionate, and adaptable in our daily interactions and decisions.

Lifelong learning also nurtures essential qualities such as resilience and creativity. In a world that is unpredictable and often overwhelming, the ability to adapt and think on one's feet is vital. By continuously acquiring new knowledge and skills, we develop a flexible mindset that allows us to face challenges with confidence. Furthermore, the exposure to diverse ideas and experiences enhances our creativity, giving us the tools to come up with innovative solutions when faced with obstacles. Lifelong learning, therefore, is not only about accumulating facts or achieving certifications—it is about cultivating the mental and emotional capacity to navigate an ever-changing world.

For Hemant, learning was not just something he did—it was an integral part of who he was. From the very beginning of his career, he understood that learning was a journey that didn't have a clear endpoint. It wasn't limited to the content he needed to master for his job but extended to everything in his life. Hemant's experiences—his transitions from corporate work to teaching, from teaching to entrepreneurship—were all deeply influenced by his commitment to learning. He saw each new challenge as an opportunity to expand his knowledge, whether through formal courses or the lessons embedded in real-world experiences.

Hemant's continuous self-education, both formal and informal, was the foundation of his personal and professional growth. He didn't just wait for knowledge to come to him; he actively sought it out, learning from every person he met, every obstacle he encountered, and every new environment he entered. His journey wasn't always easy, but his ability to learn and grow through each experience helped him adapt, evolve, and thrive in the face of uncertainty.

His story exemplifies how lifelong learning goes hand in hand with self-growth. It's not just about acquiring knowledge; it's about becoming the kind of person who is constantly curious, open to new ideas, and willing to reflect on one's own experiences to create a better future. Hemant's career is a testament to the power of lifelong learning in fostering personal evolution, proving that growth isn't a destination—it's a continuous process.

Through his example, we see that self-growth and lifelong learning are not merely optional—they are essential for navigating the complexities of today's world. By committing to ongoing learning, we empower ourselves to face the future with confidence, adaptability, and the resilience to overcome any challenge that comes our way. Whether in our careers or personal lives, the pursuit of knowledge, self-improvement, and reflection will always be the keys to sustained growth, success, and fulfillment.

How Hemant's Journey Reflects Continuous Learning and Reinvention

Hemant's journey is a powerful illustration of how continuous learning and the willingness to reinvent oneself can lead to profound personal and professional growth. His decision to leave a stable, successful career in industry and transition into teaching was not just a change in profession—it was an intentional step towards reinventing himself and embracing the unknown. The decision to leave behind the security of a corporate career, with its well-established trajectory, could have seemed like a risky, even backward move to some. However, for Hemant, it was an opportunity to grow in ways that he could not have anticipated at the time. This leap wasn't just about career change—it was about embracing the lifelong process of learning and evolving.

Throughout his career, Hemant has actively sought opportunities for self-improvement and reinvention. His initial decision to enter teaching was motivated by a deep desire to make a meaningful impact on others, but it also represented a commitment to his own growth. Teaching, Hemant realized, would allow him to not only impart knowledge to students but also learn from them in ways he hadn't anticipated. This realization marked a turning point in his professional journey—he understood that learning isn't just about absorbing facts but also about engaging with others, understanding their perspectives, and expanding one's own worldview. Each interaction with students, each question raised in the classroom, became an opportunity for Hemant to reflect on his own beliefs and methods.

This shift in perspective transformed Hemant's approach to education. What began as a one-way exchange of information quickly became a two-way process. As Hemant taught, he was also learning—about the challenges his students faced, the ways in which they processed information, and the diverse backgrounds they brought with them into the classroom. Through this exchange, Hemant gained new insights into the educational system, and his teaching methods evolved accordingly. He revisited his previous approaches, making them more inclusive, adaptive, and student-centered. This ongoing process of self-reflection and adaptation is what kept his teaching effective and relevant.

As Hemant continued to evolve, he reached another pivotal moment when he decided to open his own coaching institute. Again, he was stepping into uncharted territory, embracing a new chapter of his life. This was not just a continuation of his educational journey—it was a bold step into the world of entrepreneurship, which required an entirely new skill set. Hemant's decision to run an institute was not without its challenges, but he approached it with the same learner's mindset that had guided him throughout his career. He knew that running a business in education would require him to acquire new competencies in areas like leadership, management, marketing, and entrepreneurship. These skills were far outside his previous scope of knowledge, but he tackled them with the same enthusiasm and determination he had brought to his teaching career.

Moreover, Hemant's journey of opening and running the coaching institute was not just about learning new skills—it was about adapting to the ever-changing educational landscape. The field of education is constantly evolving, and Hemant had to stay ahead of these changes in order to meet the needs of his students. He had to stay informed about the latest technological advancements, educational trends, and student expectations. Through this ongoing learning process, Hemant was able to grow his institute, refine its operations, and create an environment where both students and faculty could thrive.

Hemant's story is a testament to the fact that growth is not a linear journey. Life, and career, often present new opportunities for reinvention. Sometimes, these opportunities may not come in the form we expect, and the next step may seem unclear or uncertain. But by staying open to learning and maintaining a mindset that views challenges as opportunities for growth, we can adapt and thrive in any situation. Hemant embraced uncertainty throughout his career, not as something to fear but as a space in which he could evolve. Whether it was transitioning from a corporate job to teaching or later starting his own coaching institute, each step was an opportunity for reinvention—a chance to grow, learn, and adapt to new challenges.

What is clear from Hemant's journey is that true growth and reinvention require an ongoing commitment to learning. It is not enough to simply rely on past knowledge or experience. To continue evolving, we must remain open to new ideas, be willing to unlearn outdated concepts, and embrace change as a natural part of the process. Hemant's career is proof that learning is not just for the young, or for those who are just starting out in their careers. It is a lifelong endeavor that requires humility, curiosity, and resilience. When we embrace this mindset, we allow ourselves the freedom to reinvent ourselves, adapt to new circumstances, and unlock the limitless potential for growth and fulfillment.

Insights on Fostering a Mindset of Lifelong Learning, Especially During Periods of Transition

Lifelong learning is the key to staying adaptable and relevant, especially during times of transition. When life changes, the urge to pause and reflect can be strong, but it's in these moments of uncertainty that the desire to learn becomes even more crucial. Embracing a mindset of continuous learning allows us to see each transition not as a setback, but as an opportunity to grow, adapt, and acquire new skills. Whether it's gaining new knowledge, developing fresh perspectives, or refining existing capabilities, the willingness to learn ensures that we remain resilient and capable of navigating any challenge life presents.

Cultivate Curiosity: The Key to Lifelong Learning

Curiosity is often the spark that ignites our desire for knowledge and growth. It's an intrinsic drive that compels us to ask questions, explore the unknown, and seek new understanding. This desire to learn isn't driven solely by external factors, but rather from an internal urge to better understand the world and ourselves. In the context of lifelong learning, curiosity becomes an essential tool that keeps us engaged and motivated in our personal and professional development. Without curiosity, we risk stagnation; with it, we open ourselves up to endless possibilities and growth.

Hemant's journey is a testament to the power of curiosity. Throughout his career, he remained curious, constantly seeking new avenues for learning and self-improvement. Whether he was transitioning from a corporate job to teaching, or later deciding to open his own coaching institute, curiosity was the underlying force that fueled each decision. His willingness to embrace the unknown and approach new challenges with an open mind allowed him to evolve continuously, despite the hurdles he faced.

In Hemant's case, curiosity was not just about acquiring knowledge for the sake of it—it was about deepening his understanding of the world, his work, and himself. As he moved through various phases of his life, he asked critical questions: What could he learn from his experiences? What new perspectives could he gain from the people he interacted with? And most importantly, how could he use these insights to adapt, innovate, and continue to grow?

Curiosity served Hemant well during times of transition—especially when he faced career changes or personal shifts. Instead of being overwhelmed by the uncertainty of those moments, he viewed them as opportunities to expand his skills and broaden his horizons. When he made the leap into teaching, for instance, he didn't just teach—he learned from his students, from the challenges of the classroom, and from the education system itself. This process of mutual learning helped him refine his approach and continually evolve.

Lifelong learning is inherently linked to the practice of staying curious. During transitional phases in life, whether they are personal or professional, curiosity serves as a grounding force. It encourages us to look at challenges not as roadblocks but as opportunities for growth. The key question during these transitions is not "How can I avoid difficulty?" but rather, "What can I learn from this phase?"

Curiosity allows us to recognize that every moment, no matter how challenging, is an opportunity to grow and develop. It compels us to ask questions and explore the unfamiliar, which in turn leads to new knowledge, new skills, and new insights. By embracing curiosity, we ensure that we are never static, even in times of uncertainty.

In Hemant's case, his curiosity led him to question conventional paths, explore new fields, and continuously reinvent himself. The process of learning became an ongoing journey, one driven by his intrinsic desire to explore, understand, and improve. As he navigated each transition—whether shifting careers or opening his own business—curiosity kept him open to new experiences and enabled him to thrive in new environments.

So, as we embark on our own journeys of growth and change, let us remember the importance of cultivating curiosity. It is the foundation that enables us to see the world not as a series of challenges to avoid, but as a vast landscape full of opportunities to explore. Ask yourself: What new skills can I develop during this phase of my life? What knowledge can I gain that will help me move forward? By embracing curiosity, we continue to evolve and expand our understanding, no matter where life takes us.

Embrace Adaptability and Flexibility: Navigating Life's Unpredictability

Adaptability and flexibility are two of the most vital components of lifelong learning, particularly when navigating life's inevitable changes. Life is inherently unpredictable, and the journey rarely follows a straight path. Whether in our personal lives, careers, or pursuits of knowledge, we often find ourselves at crossroads, facing transitions that challenge the plans we once set. It's in these moments that our ability to adapt and remain flexible is tested.

Hemant's career journey is a powerful example of how embracing adaptability can lead to success. His career path, like many others, was not linear. Moving from a corporate job in industry to teaching, and then transitioning to entrepreneurship by founding his own coaching institute, required continuous adjustments in both his mindset and skillset. At each of these critical junctures, Hemant's willingness to adapt to new challenges was central to his ability to thrive.

Throughout his career, Hemant demonstrated that growth doesn't always come from following a prescribed plan. Instead, it comes from the ability to embrace change and pivot when necessary. Each transition—whether it was shifting to a different profession or adapting to the evolving needs of his students—was an opportunity for him to acquire new skills and learn how to navigate uncertainty. By staying flexible and open to change, Hemant not only thrived in his various roles but also discovered new pathways to growth and fulfillment that he had never considered initially.

Adapting to change, however, is not always easy. It often requires stepping out of one's comfort zone and relinquishing the need for certainty. Many people naturally resist change because it involves stepping into the unknown, where there are no guarantees. But, embracing change is a fundamental part of personal and professional growth. Without the ability to adapt, we risk becoming stagnant, missing out on opportunities that may arise from new experiences, challenges, and roles.

In times of transition, it's essential to stay flexible and keep a learner's mindset. Rather than resisting change or clinging to past strategies, adaptability encourages us to view uncertainty as an opportunity for learning. Whether it's learning a new skill, acquiring fresh knowledge, or revising our approach to a particular challenge, being adaptable enables us to meet whatever comes our way.

For example, during transitions in Hemant's life, such as when he shifted from industry to teaching, he had to develop new competencies—whether it was mastering the art of teaching, adjusting his communication style to reach students, or gaining a deeper understanding of education as a system. When he later took on the responsibility of running his own coaching institute, he had to broaden his skills once again—this time in leadership, management, and entrepreneurship. Each of these changes required him to be flexible, to unlearn certain approaches, and to embrace new ways of thinking and working.

This flexibility isn't just about being open to professional growth. It also pertains to shifting our attitudes and perspectives. For example, adapting to new technologies, communication methods, or even changing cultural dynamics in the workplace requires us to continuously revise our thinking and practices. If we hold onto rigid ideas or resist new ways of doing things, we limit our ability to grow. Flexibility allows us to embrace challenges as part of the process, not as obstacles, and to respond creatively to the demands of our changing environment.

In today's fast-paced world, where new information, tools, and technologies emerge regularly, the need for adaptability is greater than ever. The workforce is increasingly dynamic, and industries are transforming rapidly. To stay relevant, we must be open to learning and willing to change our approaches. By embracing adaptability, we equip ourselves to face whatever the future holds, knowing that the key to survival and success lies in our ability to adjust and evolve.

In Hemant's case, he didn't just adapt once—he continuously embraced change, evolving along the way. This ongoing process of learning and reinvention helped him to build a successful career and contribute to the lives of many others. He was never afraid to pivot or take a different route when necessary. His journey exemplifies how adaptability, combined with a lifelong commitment to learning, can open up new opportunities and lead to a richer, more rewarding life.

As we look to the future, we must also adopt a mindset that welcomes change and uncertainty. Instead of seeing change as something to fear or resist, we should view it as a chance to adapt and grow. Life will not always follow a set plan, but by cultivating adaptability and flexibility, we can thrive in an ever-changing world. Just as Hemant's story shows, the path to growth is not always a straight line, but with the ability to adapt, we can find success and fulfillment in places we never expected.

Commit to Continuous Self-Reflection: The Key to Lifelong Growth

Self-reflection is an essential practice in the journey of lifelong learning. It's the process of looking inward to evaluate our thoughts, actions, and beliefs, and it plays a critical role in our ability to grow and evolve. Without this practice, we risk stagnation—remaining stuck in old patterns of thinking, acting, and responding. By committing to continuous self-reflection, we open ourselves up to new insights and opportunities for development.

Hemant's journey exemplifies the profound impact that self-reflection can have on both personal and professional growth. Throughout his career, he consistently took time to reflect on his teaching experiences, his interactions with students, and his personal evolution. This self-reflection wasn't a passive process; it was an active, intentional practice that allowed him to refine his approach and enhance his effectiveness in every role he undertook. Whether in the classroom or in the entrepreneurial world, Hemant continuously assessed his actions and beliefs, always seeking to learn from his mistakes and adapt his strategies moving forward.

In the classroom, Hemant was not just teaching but also learning. Each day, he reflected on his methods, his interactions with students, and the effectiveness of his teaching style. Did his students understand the material? Were his teaching methods engaging? Did he create an environment where students felt motivated and empowered? By reflecting on these questions, he was able to identify areas for improvement and make necessary adjustments. For example, if a particular teaching method didn't work as planned,

Hemant didn't view it as a failure but as a learning opportunity. He used it to evaluate what went wrong, refine his approach, and ensure better results in the future.

Self-reflection also played a significant role when Hemant transitioned from teaching to entrepreneurship. Opening his coaching institute was a huge shift from his previous role as a teacher, and this required a new set of skills and a different mindset. In this new phase of his career, he constantly reflected on his leadership style, his business decisions, and his ability to meet the needs of his students in a different capacity. This ongoing evaluation helped him make more informed decisions, develop better strategies, and ultimately build a successful institute. Each step of the way, Hemant used reflection to assess his progress and adapt to the challenges of entrepreneurship.

During times of transition—whether in a career change, a personal shift, or facing new challenges—self-reflection becomes even more important. It helps us make sense of what's happening, learn from our experiences, and figure out the best way forward. When everything seems uncertain or overwhelming, self-reflection provides clarity. It allows us to evaluate our past actions, determine what worked and what didn't, and then take deliberate steps toward improvement.

Self-reflection also fosters greater self-awareness. When we are reflective, we gain a deeper understanding of our own values, strengths, weaknesses, and motivations. This self-awareness is vital for personal growth because it helps us align our actions with our true goals. For example, when facing a challenge, reflecting on our beliefs and values can provide insight into how we should approach the situation. Are we acting in alignment with what we truly care about? Are our actions helping us move closer to our goals, or are they diverting us from what really matters? By answering these questions honestly, we can ensure that our decisions and actions are consistently in line with our values and long-term vision.

Moreover, reflection isn't just about evaluating past actions. It's also about anticipating future growth. By reflecting on our experiences, we can identify the lessons we've learned and apply them to the next phase of our journey. Self-reflection enables us to recognize patterns in our behavior, understand the reasons behind our decisions, and develop strategies for better outcomes in the future. Whether it's improving a skill, developing a new habit, or preparing for the next challenge, ongoing reflection helps us move forward with intention and purpose.

Taking the time for regular self-reflection is a practice that should be integrated into our daily routines. It doesn't have to be a formal process; it can be as simple as taking a few minutes each day to consider our experiences. For instance, after a meeting or a teaching session, we can ask ourselves: What went well today? What didn't work as planned? How can I improve tomorrow? By asking these kinds of questions, we set the stage for continuous learning and growth.

For Hemant, self-reflection was not just a method for improving his work, but a cornerstone of his personal development. It allowed him to evolve as a person, adjust his mindset, and continuously refine his approach to both teaching and business. It was through this practice of self-reflection that he was able to see his own potential, identify areas of growth, and adapt his actions accordingly.

As we continue our journey of lifelong learning, we must remember the importance of committing to regular self-reflection. It is through this practice that we gain the insights necessary for continual progress. Whether in moments of success or failure, during times of transition or stability, self-reflection helps us stay aligned with our true purpose and ensures that we are always moving toward greater personal and professional fulfillment.

In a world that's constantly changing, where challenges and opportunities arise unexpectedly, self-reflection serves as a compass, guiding us on our journey and helping us evolve with purpose and clarity.

Develop a Growth Mindset: Embracing the Power of Effort and Perseverance

At the core of lifelong learning lies the belief that our abilities and intelligence are not fixed traits, but qualities that can be developed and strengthened over time through effort, dedication, and perseverance. This belief forms the foundation of what is known as a growth mindset—a concept first introduced by psychologist Carol Dweck. With a growth mindset, we view challenges as valuable opportunities for learning and growth, rather than as insurmountable obstacles that hinder our success. This mindset transforms the way we approach life's difficulties, allowing us to embrace the journey of self-improvement with enthusiasm and resilience.

Hemant's journey throughout his career is a perfect example of how cultivating a growth mindset can lead to continuous transformation. From his early days in engineering to his shift into teaching, and later to his venture into entrepreneurship, Hemant demonstrated that success is not determined by inherent talent or circumstances, but by the willingness to learn, adapt, and grow at every stage of life. Each time he encountered a challenge, whether it was transitioning into a new career or adapting to a different work environment, Hemant approached it with the firm belief that he could evolve and master the necessary skills to succeed.

In his early career, Hemant could have easily seen the decision to leave a stable engineering job to become a teacher as a risk—a step away from a secure, well-established career. But instead of viewing the transition as a threat to his success, he embraced it as an opportunity to develop new skills and knowledge. The growth mindset allowed him to view the challenges of teaching not as barriers, but as stepping stones to greater expertise and fulfillment. He didn't view himself as someone locked into one path or role, but as someone with the ability to reinvent himself, adapt to new environments, and constantly evolve.

The beauty of a growth mindset is that it allows us to learn from failure, rather than seeing it as a sign of defeat. For Hemant, every setback, whether in the classroom or in his business ventures, was a valuable learning experience. He understood that failure is not an endpoint but part of the process of mastering new skills. Instead of becoming discouraged by challenges, he used them to sharpen his abilities and refine his approach. Each mistake or failure was a lesson that made him more resilient and resourceful in the face of future challenges.

In times of transition, nurturing a growth mindset becomes especially crucial. Transitions often come with uncertainty, and it's easy to feel disheartened when success doesn't come immediately or when the path ahead seems unclear. However, if we approach these transitions with a growth mindset, we can shift our focus from the discomfort of change to the potential for growth. When faced with a new challenge, we can ask ourselves:

What can I learn from this experience? What skills can I develop? How can I grow stronger and more capable through this process?

In many cases, success does not come overnight. Whether it's adapting to a new career, starting a new project, or learning a new skill, the journey is often long and filled with ups and downs. But with a growth mindset, we come to understand that the process of learning and evolving is just as valuable, if not more so, than the end result. It is through these periods of challenge and growth that we develop resilience, creativity, and the ability to overcome adversity. When we approach difficulties with the belief that we can improve through effort and persistence, we are empowered to keep moving forward, even when immediate success feels out of reach.

For Hemant, his willingness to reinvent himself multiple times throughout his life speaks volumes about the power of a growth mindset. Each new phase of his journey—whether it was teaching, running a coaching institute, or expanding his entrepreneurial ventures—was not just about achieving external success, but about deepening his own personal growth. By embracing the idea that he could always learn and improve, he was able to navigate various transitions with confidence and clarity.

A growth mindset also helps us to stay motivated and focused, even when faced with setbacks. It encourages us to view each challenge as an opportunity for improvement, rather than as a roadblock. This perspective fuels our desire to keep pushing forward, knowing that every step we take—no matter how small—brings us closer to our goal. It allows us to remain open to feedback, refine our approach, and continuously evolve into better versions of ourselves.

In the context of career transitions or significant life changes, a growth mindset becomes even more important. It helps us reframe uncertainty as a natural part of the learning process. Instead of seeing new challenges as threats to our success or identity, we can view them as an essential part of our journey—opportunities for growth that will ultimately lead us to greater success and fulfillment.

So, whether you are navigating a career change, learning a new skill, or stepping into uncharted territory, remember the power of a growth mindset. Embrace challenges as opportunities to learn, adapt, and grow. Recognize that the path to success is rarely linear, and the true value lies not just in the destination, but in the lessons we learn along the way. As you continue to evolve, trust that with perseverance, effort, and a commitment to lifelong learning, you will continue to grow stronger, smarter, and more capable of achieving your goals.

Invest in Learning New Skills and Knowledge: A Cornerstone of Lifelong Learning

One of the most effective ways to foster lifelong learning is through a proactive investment in acquiring new skills and knowledge. This process is not just about gathering information, but about continuously evolving and adapting to the changing demands of the world around us. The willingness to seek out new learning opportunities, whether through formal education, self-study, or hands-on experience, is a fundamental aspect of lifelong growth. This commitment to ongoing learning empowers us to stay relevant, adaptable, and prepared for the challenges and opportunities that come with each new phase of life.

For Hemant, investing in new skills has been a defining feature of his career and personal growth. His journey is a testament to the idea that no matter how accomplished or established we may be in our current field, there is always room for further development. Hemant's career trajectory shows how, from his corporate engineering background to his role as an educator, and later to his entrepreneurial endeavors, he actively sought opportunities to learn and evolve, each time enhancing his ability to face new challenges.

In the early stages of his career, Hemant's technical expertise was central to his work in the corporate world. He focused on honing his engineering skills, continually striving to improve and stay ahead in his field. However, as his career evolved and he transitioned into teaching, Hemant realized that his technical skills were no longer enough. To be an effective teacher, he needed to master new skills—like communication, pedagogy, and student engagement. Recognizing this, he invested time and effort into acquiring the teaching skills necessary to connect with his students and deliver impactful lessons.

Hemant's learning didn't stop at teaching. As he moved into entrepreneurship and opened his own coaching institute, he faced an entirely new set of challenges that required different skills. Running a business demanded that Hemant acquire knowledge in leadership, management, marketing, finance, and entrepreneurship—areas that he had not explored during his previous career. Rather than resisting the demands of his new role, Hemant embraced the need to learn these skills. He sought out resources, attended workshops, read extensively, and learned through hands-on experience in the business world.

Periods of transition, like career changes, personal milestones, or shifts in industry, often require us to develop new skills. These skills may not have been essential in the past but are crucial for progressing in our new environment. For example, moving from a technical job to a managerial role requires not just technical knowledge, but also leadership, emotional intelligence, and decision-making skills. Similarly, transitioning into a new industry or career path may require an understanding of different tools, technologies, or processes that are unfamiliar. It's during these moments of change that we must be proactive in seeking the skills we need to succeed.

The process of acquiring new skills can feel intimidating, especially when we step outside our comfort zone or confront areas in which we have little expertise. However, embracing this discomfort is key to growth. Hemant's example shows that being proactive about learning new skills can significantly accelerate personal and professional development. Whether it's mastering a new software tool, understanding a different market trend, or adapting to new technologies, every skill learned opens up new possibilities and avenues for growth.

One important aspect of investing in learning is the recognition that the process is continuous. Lifelong learning is not a destination but an ongoing journey. In today's fast-paced world, the need to keep learning is even more pressing. Technological advancements, changing industries, and global economic shifts constantly reshape the landscape. What was relevant a few years ago may no longer be sufficient today, which means we must remain committed to learning and adapting. Hemant's ability to evolve his career at different stages—whether it was transitioning from corporate work to teaching or from teaching to running a business—was only possible because of his commitment to continuously learning and upgrading his skills.

Furthermore, learning new skills doesn't always require formal education or structured courses. While these are certainly valuable, self-study and hands-on experience can also be incredibly effective ways of learning.

Hemant demonstrated this when he transitioned into entrepreneurship. Rather than relying solely on his formal education, he immersed himself in the business world, learning from mentors, peers, and real-world experiences. This practical learning allowed him to adjust to the nuances of running a business and adapt quickly to unforeseen challenges.

In times of transition, it's especially important to take a proactive approach to acquiring new skills. The natural response to uncertainty or change can be fear or hesitation, but embracing the need for new learning is key to thriving in these periods. Instead of waiting for opportunities to present themselves, seek out the skills you need to move forward. Identify areas where you feel unprepared or where you can enhance your knowledge, and take steps to address them. This could involve enrolling in courses, attending workshops, reading books, or seeking guidance from people with expertise in areas you want to explore.

Additionally, make time for reflection to evaluate the skills you've learned and identify those that are still missing. Often, we get so caught up in our daily tasks that we neglect to assess where we need to improve or how we can prepare for future challenges. Regular self-assessment helps ensure that we are on the right track and can help prevent stagnation. By keeping a growth-oriented mindset and continuing to invest in acquiring new skills, we position ourselves to not only survive but thrive in a world that is constantly changing.

In summary, investing in learning new skills and knowledge is a critical component of lifelong learning. By actively seeking out opportunities to learn—whether through formal education, self-study, or hands-on experience—we ensure that we stay relevant and adaptable in an ever-changing world. Hemant's journey underscores the importance of continually upgrading our skills, whether to navigate career transitions or to rise to new challenges. By committing to this process, we can turn every period of change into an opportunity for growth and evolution.

Conclusion: The Imperative of Lifelong Learning for Personal and Professional Growth

Lifelong learning is not a mere luxury or a passing trend—it is an essential cornerstone of both personal and professional growth. In a world that is constantly evolving, where industries, technologies, and social dynamics are in perpetual flux, the need to remain agile, adaptable, and informed is more important than ever. The journey of self-improvement doesn't have an expiration date or a final destination. It's a lifelong commitment to expanding our horizons, gaining new skills, and evolving into better versions of ourselves. Hemant's story perfectly exemplifies this truth. His journey underscores that the process of learning is not confined to the early years of life or limited to formal educational settings—it's an ongoing process that is central to navigating the complexities of adulthood and the professional world.

Hemant's ability to reinvent himself at multiple junctures in his career, transitioning from engineering to teaching and later to entrepreneurship, is a powerful testament to the transformative power of lifelong learning. Each phase of his life demanded new knowledge, skills, and approaches, and Hemant embraced every opportunity to learn, grow, and adapt. His story is not just about professional success but about the deeply personal satisfaction that comes from continuous self-improvement. Whether learning from his experiences in the corporate world, acquiring teaching methods, or mastering business leadership, Hemant's journey was defined by a commitment to learning at every stage. His success was not simply a result of luck or talent, but of his relentless pursuit of knowledge, his willingness to adapt, and his openness to reinventing himself when the circumstances called for it.

One of the key takeaways from Hemant's experience is the realization that learning doesn't stop once we reach a certain milestone. Life, particularly in the modern world, is full of transitions—whether they are career shifts, personal growth moments, or unexpected challenges. These transitions often require us to step outside of our comfort zones and embrace the unfamiliar. The mindset of lifelong learning provides us with the tools to approach such transitions with confidence and resilience. Instead of fearing the unknown, we can look at each challenge as an opportunity to learn something new and grow from it.

The philosophy of "Keeping Bags Packed" is a powerful metaphor for this mindset. Just as a traveler must be prepared for unexpected journeys and changes in plans, we too must remain ready to face the unknown with an attitude of flexibility and adaptability. "Keeping Bags Packed" is about staying prepared to evolve, about carrying a readiness to take on new challenges and embrace new opportunities. The willingness to learn and grow continually is at the heart of this approach—it's what allows us to navigate the uncertain paths that life inevitably presents. Hemant's journey reflects this philosophy beautifully, as he continually adapted to the twists and turns of his career, always prepared to face whatever came his way with the mindset of a learner.

Adopting a lifelong learning mindset is not just about acquiring technical skills or professional expertise. It's about nurturing curiosity, expanding our perspectives, and fostering personal growth. It means being open to new experiences, understanding that setbacks are a part of the learning process, and viewing each transition as a chance to develop. Hemant's ability to reflect, adapt, and apply new knowledge at various stages of his career serves as a blueprint for how we can approach our own growth journeys.

As we continue to explore the broader implications of "Keeping Bags Packed," it becomes clear that the willingness to learn and grow is fundamental to staying relevant in an ever-changing world. Embracing this mindset allows us to remain resilient, adaptable, and able to flourish, no matter what life throws our way. Life's transitions can be daunting, but by adopting the mindset of lifelong learning, we can approach each new challenge with curiosity, confidence, and a sense of purpose.

In conclusion, Hemant's story teaches us that success and fulfillment don't come from remaining static or comfortable. They come from the ongoing pursuit of knowledge, the continuous effort to evolve, and the willingness to embrace change. Lifelong learning is the tool that enables us to reinvent ourselves, rise to new challenges, and create a future that reflects our best potential. By committing to this journey, we can all continue to evolve, adapt, and succeed—on our own terms, at every stage of life.

Chapter 11: Purpose Beyond Material Success

In a world where career achievements, salary figures, and job titles often define success, it is easy to lose sight of a deeper, more meaningful purpose. From childhood, we are conditioned to think that happiness and fulfillment are closely tied to external measures of success—climbing the corporate ladder, earning a high salary, or attaining a prestigious job title. However, over time, many realize that true fulfillment does not lie in these material pursuits. The most profound sense of contentment often arises from living a life aligned with a deeper sense of purpose—one that transcends external success.

The **"Keeping Bags Packed"** philosophy teaches us that life is not solely about accumulating wealth, recognition, or status. It is about finding a sense of purpose that gives us a deep connection to who we are and what we truly value. In this chapter, we explore how to look beyond material success and focus on cultivating a sense of purpose that brings fulfillment.

Hemant's journey is a perfect illustration of this shift from external achievements to a deeper sense of inner fulfillment. His story reflects the realization that true success is not just about climbing the corporate ladder or achieving financial security. It is about finding joy in contributing to others' lives, discovering personal satisfaction in teaching, and embracing a calling that transcends conventional measures of success.

Exploring the Importance of Purpose and Fulfillment Beyond Salary and Job Titles

At the heart of true fulfillment lies a fundamental question: *What gives your life meaning?* It's a question that transcends the superficial markers of success that society often places on us. As human beings, we are naturally drawn to external validation—through material achievements such as high-paying jobs, prestigious awards, and well-recognized titles. These symbols of success can provide a temporary sense of accomplishment, but they rarely offer lasting happiness. The initial thrill of securing a coveted position or earning a significant paycheck tends to fade over time, leaving us feeling unfulfilled, no matter how much we may have gained in the material world.

The pursuit of material success, while important for meeting basic needs and achieving certain life goals, often diverts our attention from what truly gives our lives meaning—*purpose*. Purpose is the deeper force that guides us, shapes our decisions, and drives us toward greater achievements that are in alignment with our values and passions. It gives us direction and a reason to get out of bed each morning, energizing us to contribute to something greater than ourselves. Without a clear sense of purpose, even the most lucrative job or prestigious career can feel hollow, as if we're simply going through the motions without truly connecting to the work or the impact it may have.

Consider individuals who have reached the pinnacle of material success—CEOs, celebrities, and other high-achieving figures. Despite their outward accomplishments, many of them experience a profound sense of emptiness because they haven't found fulfillment beyond the tangible rewards of their careers. They may have millions of dollars or world-famous titles, but without a deeper connection to their core values or a meaningful reason for their work, they often struggle with feelings of being lost or disconnected from what truly matters.

On the other hand, a life that is centered around a deeper sense of purpose offers fulfillment that goes beyond the fleeting nature of material success. When our work, actions, and relationships align with our purpose, we feel a deep sense of satisfaction and joy that no paycheck or title can replace. Purpose-driven individuals often express a profound sense of contentment, knowing that their lives are making a positive difference, even if it's in ways that may not be immediately apparent or financially rewarding. This alignment of purpose with personal values fosters resilience, motivation, and a sense of meaningful accomplishment, providing a stable foundation for enduring happiness and fulfillment.

The journey toward discovering and embracing purpose begins with a shift in how we measure success. Instead of basing our self-worth on the size of our paycheck or the prestige of our job title, we need to focus on the impact we're making on others and the world around us. This shift in perspective is transformative. It invites us to stop chasing external markers of success and start seeking ways to contribute in ways that are meaningful to us and to those we serve. For some, this may involve redirecting their energy towards causes they are passionate about, helping others through mentorship or community service, or finding fulfillment through creative or humanitarian endeavors. The path toward purpose is highly individual, but it requires the courage to look beyond the conventional measures of success and evaluate our lives through a more holistic lens.

True fulfillment is found when we feel that we are living in alignment with our inner truth, contributing to a greater good, and pursuing our passions rather than simply meeting external expectations. The pursuit of purpose encourages growth, creativity, and a sense of deep connection to the world around us. It fosters a resilience that allows us to navigate challenges with a sense of meaning, even when external rewards are not immediately apparent.

This is not to say that material success or career achievements should be dismissed—they are important milestones that reflect hard work, dedication, and the ability to meet goals. However, when material success becomes the sole measure of our worth, we risk missing out on the deeper sense of fulfillment that comes from living with purpose. Achieving success without purpose can feel like a race with no finish line, while the pursuit of purpose adds richness and depth to every step we take, regardless of how fast or slow the journey may be.

In conclusion, lasting fulfillment comes not from the accolades we accumulate or the wealth we amass, but from the sense of meaning we derive from our daily actions, the connections we build, and the positive change we create. The journey of discovering and living our purpose is not always an easy one—it requires introspection, vulnerability, and sometimes a willingness to let go of societal expectations. However, the rewards are immeasurable. When we live with purpose, we find that every day holds the potential for joy, growth, and a sense of deep satisfaction that no paycheck or title can ever replace. By shifting our focus from external achievements to the internal fulfillment that purpose provides, we can truly experience a life that is rich, meaningful, and full of lasting happiness.

Hemant's Discovery of True Fulfillment in Teaching and Contributing to Others' Lives

For Hemant, the pivotal moment in his life came when he made the brave decision to step away from a successful corporate career, one that many would envy, to pursue a life of teaching and contributing to the development of others. Early on, Hemant's career was motivated by common societal aspirations—financial stability, job security, and the pursuit of respect and recognition in the professional world. Over the years, he checked off all the traditional markers of success: a well-paying job, financial security, a prestigious position in a respected company, and the kind of respect that often accompanies a successful corporate career. To many, his life seemed ideal, the embodiment of what most people strive for.

However, despite achieving all the external symbols of success, Hemant found himself feeling an unexpected emptiness. He had the financial resources and societal approval, but something was missing. The satisfaction that he had expected to find in climbing the corporate ladder and acquiring more wealth eluded him. The deep sense of fulfillment and purpose that he had hoped would come with his career never materialized. Instead, he often felt disconnected, as if he were simply playing a part in a bigger machine, without truly understanding the deeper meaning behind his work. It was a realization that material achievements, while important, were not enough to bring lasting happiness or a sense of fulfillment.

The decision to leave the corporate world was not easy for Hemant. It involved a significant shift in his priorities, a departure from the comfortable, predictable world he knew, and a leap into the unknown. He chose to transition to teaching, a field that seemed to offer more personal fulfillment, even though it came with financial and professional uncertainties. For many, this might have seemed like a risky move, especially when weighed against the security and status of a corporate career. But for Hemant, it was a move toward a deeper, more meaningful life.

As he embraced his new role as an educator, Hemant discovered a profound truth: the fulfillment he had been seeking was not found in external accomplishments but in the joy of helping others grow. Teaching became more than just a job for Hemant—it became his calling. It was an opportunity for him to make a direct, tangible impact on the lives of others, particularly his students, and to contribute to their development in a way that felt truly meaningful. Through teaching, he was able to shape young minds, guide them in their personal and academic growth, and contribute to their futures in ways that were far more lasting than any corporate achievement could provide.

In his work as a mentor and educator, Hemant found that true purpose lies not in what we accomplish for ourselves, but in the difference we make in the lives of others. As he worked closely with his students, watching them grow, face challenges, and ultimately succeed, Hemant experienced a sense of fulfillment that he had never encountered in the corporate world. The joy and satisfaction he derived from seeing his students develop into confident, capable individuals were far more rewarding than any financial success or professional recognition he had previously received. In this new chapter of his life, Hemant realized that purpose is not defined by the number of zeros on a paycheck or the prestige of a job title, but by the impact we have on others.

For Hemant, fulfillment was rooted in service—specifically, in teaching, guiding, and contributing to others' growth. His decision to leave a comfortable and secure corporate job, despite the risks involved, gave him a deeper understanding of what true success means. He realized that while material success can be fleeting, the impact we have on the lives of others has a lasting, immeasurable effect. The relationships he built with his students, the knowledge he imparted to them, and the guidance he provided all became more meaningful than any external accomplishment. In contributing to the development of others, Hemant found a sense of fulfillment that no salary or corporate title could ever replace.

In his journey, Hemant learned that purpose is often found in giving—not in receiving. Giving of our time, our knowledge, and our energy to those around us is where true fulfillment lies. It is in the selfless act of helping others grow, succeed, and find their own sense of purpose that we discover our own. This realization helped Hemant understand that fulfillment is not a destination but a process. It is not something that can be bought or earned through external achievements, but something that comes from within, through the contributions we make to the world around us.

Hemant's story serves as a powerful reminder that true fulfillment comes from living a life aligned with our deeper values and purpose. It is a life where the success of others becomes a reflection of our own success, and where the impact we make in the world creates a ripple effect that lasts long after we are gone. In teaching and mentoring, Hemant found the deep sense of meaning and satisfaction he had been seeking, proving that the greatest form of success is not measured by material wealth, but by the positive difference we make in the lives of others.

How to Identify and Cultivate Your Own Deeper Purpose in Life

Identifying and cultivating a deeper purpose in life is a journey that requires self-reflection, honesty, and courage. It's about asking the hard questions: What truly drives me? What do I want to contribute to the world? By tuning into our inner values, passions, and strengths, we can uncover a sense of purpose that resonates deeply within us. This purpose becomes our guiding force, helping us navigate challenges, stay motivated, and create a life filled with meaning. Cultivating this deeper purpose isn't a one-time discovery but a continuous process of growth, alignment, and action.

Reflect on What Brings You Joy

A critical and often overlooked step in uncovering your deeper purpose is to take the time to reflect on the activities, experiences, and moments that truly bring you joy, fulfillment, and a sense of pride. We often go through life in pursuit of external markers of success, but the most profound source of purpose comes from understanding what makes us feel alive, connected, and truly engaged with the world around us. For Hemant, this realization came when he reflected on his love for teaching and the impact it had on both him and his students. But for others, the source of joy might lie in creative pursuits, helping those in need, or solving intricate problems.

Understanding what brings you joy is not about searching for a singular, grand event; rather, it involves recognizing the patterns in your life that energize you. These moments of happiness are often rooted in the simplest of activities—the things that make you feel grounded and present. Take a step back to consider what activities give you a sense of purpose, whether it's working with a team, mentoring others, exploring new ideas, or even spending quiet time alone. These are all key indicators of where your true passions lie.

For some, joy comes from the act of creating, whether through art, writing, or invention. The process of making something new, expressing oneself, or bringing an idea to life can be an incredibly fulfilling experience. Others find joy in helping those around them—whether through teaching, volunteering, or offering support to friends and family. The satisfaction derived from positively influencing someone else's life can provide a deep sense of purpose.

Another source of joy might be found in problem-solving and analytical thinking—those who love to deconstruct complex challenges and come up with creative solutions often experience immense satisfaction in their ability to navigate and solve difficult problems. These moments of clarity and accomplishment offer valuable insight into the things that bring you fulfillment.

To discover what truly brings you joy, ask yourself: What are the moments in your life when you felt the most alive, excited, or engaged? What activities or interactions made you lose track of time, where you felt fully absorbed and connected to the task at hand? These moments often provide the clearest clues to your deeper purpose. It's important to spend time reflecting on these experiences, as they help shape a more profound understanding of what brings meaning to your life.

This process of reflection is a powerful tool for uncovering your true calling. It shifts the focus away from external pressures or expectations and redirects your attention inward, allowing you to assess what truly makes you feel connected to the world. By identifying these moments, you can begin to align your life with activities and pursuits that resonate deeply with your core values and passions, ultimately leading you closer to a life of true purpose and fulfillment.

Understand Your Values

Understanding your values is a critical step toward discovering your true purpose. Your values are the principles that guide your decisions, influence your behavior, and shape the way you interact with the world. They act as a compass, helping you navigate through life's challenges and ensuring that you stay aligned with what is most important to you. When you understand what you value deeply, you can make choices that resonate with your authentic self, leading you to a more purposeful and fulfilling life.

For Hemant, his journey was profoundly influenced by his core values of service and education. These values guided his career shift from a successful corporate job to a fulfilling life of teaching and mentoring. He found meaning in helping others grow, and his commitment to education became a driving force behind his decisions and actions. Hemant's story illustrates how aligning your career and personal life with your values can create a sense of purpose that goes beyond external achievements like titles or financial success.

To uncover your values, take time to reflect on what is truly important to you. Ask yourself: What principles guide my decisions in times of uncertainty? What do I want to prioritize in my life? Some people may value family and relationships above all, seeking to foster deep connections and build strong bonds with loved ones. Others may value innovation and creativity, constantly striving to explore new ideas, challenge the status quo, and bring something new into the world. Similarly, values such as service, compassion, or social justice may be at the heart of a desire to help others or contribute to the greater good.

Understanding your values also means recognizing what you don't value. In today's fast-paced world, it's easy to be swayed by external expectations, such as societal pressures or the pursuit of wealth and status. These external forces can often push you away from your true path, leading you to make decisions that don't align with who you truly are. By identifying what matters most to you and contrasting it with what others may expect from you, you can begin to carve out a life path that feels both true and fulfilling.

Once you have a clear understanding of your values, align your actions with them. Make decisions that reflect your beliefs, whether it's choosing a career, building relationships, or setting personal goals. When your actions are in harmony with your values, life becomes much more satisfying, as you are living authentically. Every step you take, whether big or small, reinforces your commitment to what matters most, ultimately leading you toward a deeper sense of fulfillment and a stronger connection to your purpose.

By understanding and living according to your core values, you can ensure that your journey is not only successful but also meaningful. When your work, relationships, and daily actions reflect what you deeply care about, you begin to live a life that feels right for you—a life driven by purpose, integrity, and authenticity.

Consider the Impact You Want to Have on the World

One of the most powerful ways to discover your purpose is by reflecting on the kind of impact you want to have on the world. At the core of a meaningful life is the question: *What kind of legacy do I want to leave behind?* The pursuit of purpose is not just about personal achievement or material success; it's about creating something larger than yourself—something that can inspire, uplift, or help others in a meaningful way.

For Hemant, his transition from the corporate world to teaching was rooted in this very realization. While his career in the corporate sector had given him financial security, professional success, and societal respect, he began to feel that the true value of his life's work would come from making a positive impact on others. He found his calling in education—an avenue through which he could influence the lives of many individuals, shaping their futures and helping them reach their potential. In helping others grow, Hemant discovered that the lasting fulfillment he sought could only be found in the impact he made, not in accolades or wealth.

To find your own sense of purpose, consider the ways you want to contribute to the world. What is the unique contribution you can make to those around you? What values do you want to pass on to future generations? Your impact might be in the form of mentorship, the work you do within your community, or how you use your skills to solve problems that benefit others. Purpose is often found in the difference you make in the lives of others—not in the pursuit of success for its own sake.

Think about how you can contribute to the greater good in your personal or professional life. Is there a cause you are passionate about that aligns with your skills and values? Do you have a desire to give back to your community, or help others in your field of work? Maybe you're drawn to creating a better world in some way, such as addressing social issues, improving education, advancing healthcare, or even promoting sustainability. Purpose often emerges from the desire to make life better for others, whether through direct action, spreading knowledge, or leading by example.

Reflect on your own legacy. How do you want to be remembered? Is it by the work you've done, the people you've inspired, or the relationships you've nurtured? When we think about legacy, we often envision the long-term effects of our actions, and how they ripple through time, touching people and circumstances in ways we may never fully understand. The positive influence you have, however small or large, can create a lasting impression and shape the world in ways that are meaningful to you and those around you.

Your legacy doesn't have to be monumental or globally recognized to be valuable. It can be found in the everyday contributions you make, whether it's by helping others learn, mentoring someone, supporting a cause, or simply living in a way that aligns with your values. Even small, consistent acts of kindness or service can leave a profound impact over time, creating a better environment for those who follow in your footsteps.

As you consider the impact you want to have, it's important to remember that purpose is not just about what you can achieve for yourself, but about how you use your abilities and resources to make the world a better place for others. This perspective shifts the focus from personal gain to collective well-being and helps create a more fulfilling, meaningful existence. By thinking about the lasting impact you want to leave behind, you can align your actions with your deeper sense of purpose, contributing positively to the world and creating a legacy that resonates far beyond your lifetime.

Take Small Steps Toward Your Purpose

Once you have identified your purpose, the next crucial step is to actively pursue it. The path to fulfillment does not happen in an instant. It requires consistent effort, patience, and a series of thoughtful actions, each building on the last. The key is to start small. Often, people delay pursuing their deeper purpose because they feel overwhelmed by the magnitude of the change it might require. They may think that they need to make drastic shifts in their lives immediately, but in reality, true progress often begins with incremental steps.

Hemant's journey is a perfect example of how slow, deliberate action can lead to profound transformation. While his decision to leave a successful corporate career and enter teaching may seem like a bold, life-altering choice, it wasn't something he did hastily. He took the time to reflect on his desires and then set a course toward fulfilling them—gradually, with patience and dedication. Hemant didn't dive straight into teaching full-time. He first explored different educational avenues, gained relevant experience, and learned how to effectively connect with students. By breaking down his larger goal into manageable steps, Hemant was able to transition thoughtfully into a career that truly fulfilled him, without the pressure of immediate success or change.

Similarly, when pursuing your own purpose, don't feel the need to make sweeping changes right away. Instead, start with small, deliberate actions that bring you closer to your goal. If you are passionate about helping others, perhaps you could start by volunteering your time to mentor or assist in local community projects. If you are drawn to education or public speaking, begin by taking small teaching opportunities, whether through tutoring, leading workshops, or speaking at local events. Taking on small projects can help you build confidence and experience, allowing you to test your passion and refine your skills.

Learning is also an essential part of this process. If you are pursuing a new career, a new cause, or a personal goal, seek out resources—whether books, courses, or mentors—that can help you deepen your knowledge in that area. You don't need to master everything overnight; the goal is continuous growth. Each small step of learning gets you closer to understanding the deeper nuances of your passion and strengthens your ability to make an impact.

Small steps are powerful because they create momentum. Each positive action, no matter how small, will give you a sense of progress, which will keep you motivated. These steps also allow you to refine your approach over time. When you begin small, you allow yourself the space to adjust your plans as needed, to evaluate your journey, and to learn from your experiences. This gradual progress ensures that your pursuit of purpose is both realistic and sustainable, while minimizing the pressure to achieve perfection or instant results.

Moreover, these small steps allow you to stay connected to your values and passions without feeling overwhelmed by the bigger picture. Rather than getting caught up in the end goal, which may seem distant and unattainable, focusing on small, tangible actions helps you stay grounded. Each step brings clarity and confidence, allowing you to adjust your course along the way as your understanding of your purpose deepens.

Remember that the journey toward living a life aligned with your purpose is not about making immediate, large-scale changes but about gradually building the life you want, step by step. By committing to taking consistent action, no matter how small, you will begin to notice shifts in your mindset, your habits, and your environment. Over time, these small steps accumulate, leading to the larger transformation you desire. The key is to stay patient and persistent, trusting that every small effort you make brings you closer to a life that feels authentic, meaningful, and fulfilling.

Embrace the Journey, Not Just the Destination

Finding your purpose is not a one-time event or a destination that you simply reach and then stop. It is an evolving process that spans your entire life, a journey that is as meaningful as the goal itself. It is easy to get caught up in the idea of a final destination or to think that once you achieve your purpose, you will have all the answers. However, the reality is that discovering and living out your purpose is a continuous process of growth, learning, and adaptation. Just like Hemant's ongoing evolution in his career, your purpose will continue to unfold as you go through different phases of life. It will change as you accumulate more experiences, meet new people, face new challenges, and achieve new milestones.

Hemant's journey exemplifies this beautifully. He didn't find his true calling in teaching and mentoring all at once. Instead, his purpose gradually revealed itself over time. He embraced the idea that finding fulfillment is a dynamic, ongoing process that requires openness to change and growth. Throughout his life, his purpose evolved—shifting from his corporate career to teaching, from focusing on his own success to contributing to the success of others. His willingness to adapt to new opportunities and challenges allowed him to continue aligning his work with what brought him the greatest satisfaction.

Similarly, your journey toward fulfilling your purpose will not look the same at all times. There may be moments of clarity, where you feel confident about your direction, but there will also be periods of uncertainty, where you may feel lost or unsure about your next steps. Embrace these moments of doubt as part of the process. They are opportunities for growth and reflection, helping you refine and redefine your purpose. Every success and failure, every high and low, is a crucial part of your personal development. They provide valuable lessons that shape your future decisions and guide you closer to a life aligned with your true values and passions.

Living with purpose means accepting that the path is rarely linear. You might go through periods of doubt, face setbacks, or find yourself questioning the direction you're heading. These moments of struggle are not failures—they are part of the journey. They help you become more resilient, more self-aware, and more attuned to what truly matters. In fact, the detours and challenges often lead to the most meaningful growth, providing the experiences and insights that help you refine your goals and move closer to the life you desire.

It is also important to recognize that your purpose may evolve as you change. As you acquire new skills, meet new people, and explore different aspects of life, your understanding of your purpose may expand or shift. What feels important to you today may be different in the future. That's okay. The key is to stay open to the journey, knowing that purpose is not a static point but a dynamic, evolving force that continues to shape your life's narrative.

Rather than focusing solely on reaching a destination or achieving a singular goal, embrace the beauty of the process itself. Every step of the journey contributes to your growth, and each experience, whether positive or negative, is part of what makes you who you are. The joy of discovering your purpose lies not in having it all figured out, but in the continual pursuit of it—growing through experiences, learning from each chapter, and evolving into the person you are meant to become.

Ultimately, by embracing the journey, you shift your mindset from a narrow focus on the end goal to a more holistic view of your life. This mindset allows you to appreciate the small victories, the lessons learned, and the connections made along the way. It fosters a sense of fulfillment that comes from living authentically, not simply from achieving a specific outcome. The journey itself becomes an integral part of your purpose, making it a rich and fulfilling experience that can last a lifetime. By staying present, open, and committed to continual growth, you will find that the pursuit of purpose is just as rewarding as the destination itself.

Let Go of External Expectations

In today's society, there is a constant barrage of messages about what success should look like. From a young age, we are taught that success is defined by financial wealth, prestigious job titles, and social status. These external markers of success are often held up as the ultimate goal, and we are made to believe that they are the true indicators of a fulfilling life. We are conditioned to measure our worth based on material possessions, career accomplishments, and public recognition. However, the reality is that these external expectations and achievements are not universal, and they do not necessarily lead to genuine fulfillment or lasting happiness.

Letting go of these external expectations is a crucial step in discovering your authentic purpose. When you begin to define success on your own terms, rather than by society's standards, you open yourself to a deeper sense of fulfillment and meaning. Too often, people chase external validation, seeking approval or admiration from others, without ever considering whether those goals align with their inner desires and values. They find themselves living someone else's version of success, never truly satisfied, because the goals they are striving for do not resonate with their own soul.

Hemant's journey offers a powerful example of how letting go of external expectations can lead to true fulfillment. Early in his career, Hemant was deeply embedded in a corporate world that emphasized financial success and status. He achieved the milestones that society typically celebrates: a stable job, financial security, and a respected position in his industry. However, despite outwardly appearing successful, he began to feel a growing sense of emptiness. The external markers of success that society held in high regard were not providing him with the sense of purpose he was truly seeking.

When Hemant made the bold decision to leave his corporate career behind and pursue teaching, he made a conscious choice to let go of society's expectations and follow a path that resonated with his inner desires. Teaching allowed him to focus on making a real, tangible impact on the lives of others—something far more meaningful to him than accumulating wealth or prestige. Hemant found fulfillment in helping others grow, guiding them toward their potential, and contributing to their future success. By focusing on what brought him joy and aligning his actions with his values, he found a deeper purpose that was uniquely his.

In the pursuit of purpose, it is essential to recognize that success is not a one-size-fits-all concept. What brings you joy, fulfillment, and meaning might look very different from what society tells you should bring those things. If you are constantly measuring your life by external standards, you will likely find yourself chasing something that never truly satisfies you. Letting go of these external pressures allows you to reconnect with your inner self and make choices that align with your personal values, passions, and vision for your life.

Take a step back and reflect on what truly matters to you. Is it financial success? Prestige? Social status? Or is it something deeper—perhaps a sense of connection, purpose, or service to others? By focusing on what resonates deeply with your soul, you can shift your mindset from one of external validation to one of internal fulfillment. When you let go of the need to meet society's expectations, you free yourself to follow your true path—one that may not always align with the conventional idea of success, but will undoubtedly lead to a life that feels authentic and meaningful to you.

Letting go of external expectations also involves shedding the fear of judgment. Often, we avoid pursuing our true passions or dreams because we fear how others might perceive us. The fear of being labeled as unsuccessful or unconventional can hold us back from living fully. But once you release that fear and trust in your own journey, you gain the freedom to explore and follow what truly fulfills you. Whether it's a career change, a new hobby, or a different approach to life, embracing your uniqueness can bring an immense sense of joy and purpose.

Moreover, by letting go of external expectations, you create space for personal growth. You begin to make choices based on what aligns with your core values rather than what you think is expected of you. This shift allows you to grow into a more authentic version of yourself, one that is not constrained by the opinions of others or societal pressures.

The journey toward finding your purpose is personal and unique. It is not about following a pre-determined path set by others but about creating your own. By letting go of external expectations and embracing your true self, you open the door to discovering a sense of purpose that is deeply fulfilling. This authentic purpose, aligned with your values and passions, will bring you a sense of joy and satisfaction that no external marker of success ever could.

Conclusion

The pursuit of material success is deeply ingrained in our society and is often viewed as a primary goal. After all, achieving financial stability, securing prestigious job titles, and accumulating wealth are milestones that many aspire to reach. However, while these external markers of success may bring temporary satisfaction, they are not sufficient to provide lasting fulfillment or true happiness. Material success alone can only take us so far; it's the deeper sense of purpose that transforms our achievements into a meaningful and satisfying life.

True happiness arises when we align our actions with a sense of purpose that goes beyond titles, salaries, and social status. Purpose is the thread that connects our passions, values, and aspirations. It is what fuels us to wake up every day with energy, excitement, and clarity about why we are doing what we are doing. When our efforts are driven by purpose—whether it's helping others, contributing to a cause, or pursuing something that brings us joy—we experience fulfillment that cannot be measured by the size of our paycheck or the prestige of our job title.

Hemant's journey offers a powerful example of this shift from seeking external validation to discovering internal fulfillment. He moved away from a successful corporate career—a career that had all the outward markers of success—because he realized that the true satisfaction he longed for wasn't in titles or financial achievements. What he craved was the ability to make a real impact on the lives of others. His decision to become a teacher allowed him to do just that. Through teaching, he discovered the joy of contributing to others' growth, guiding them toward their potential, and helping shape their futures. This new path brought him a sense of fulfillment that far surpassed anything he had ever experienced in the corporate world.

By aligning his life with his core values—service, education, and personal growth—Hemant was able to achieve a sense of satisfaction that was both deep and enduring. His journey illustrates that fulfillment doesn't come from external accomplishments but from living in accordance with one's true purpose. This shift in perspective is what made his journey so powerful. It's a reminder that we are not meant to live merely for material gains but to seek a deeper meaning in our work, relationships, and contributions.

As we continue to explore the philosophy of "Keeping Bags Packed," we are reminded that life is a journey, not a destination. It's about continuous growth, learning, and evolving. The process itself holds more value than any end goal or external achievement. Life is not just about accumulating success—it's about finding and nurturing purpose in the everyday moments. By living with intention, focusing on what truly matters to us, and contributing to the lives of others, we create a life that feels rich and fulfilling, regardless of the external markers of success.

The real measure of a successful life is not in what we acquire or achieve but in how we contribute to the world around us. It's in how we grow—emotionally, spiritually, and intellectually—and how we live with intention and authenticity. True success lies in the ability to make a meaningful difference, to align our actions with our deepest values, and to continuously evolve into the person we are meant to become. When we focus on purpose over external validation, we unlock the potential for a life that is truly rewarding, where fulfillment arises not from what we have, but from who we are and what we give to others.

Chapter 12: The Importance of Being Present

In a world where distractions are constant and the pace of life only seems to accelerate, the concept of **being present** has never been more crucial. With the constant pressure to achieve, succeed, and manage multiple roles simultaneously, it's easy to become consumed by future goals, past regrets, or external pressures. We often lose sight of the **present moment**, which is the only time where real change and growth can occur. **Mindfulness**, the practice of being fully engaged with the here and now, is an antidote to this stress.

In this chapter, we explore the transformative power of being present and how it can help us find peace and balance in a fast-paced, often overwhelming world. The **"Keeping Bags Packed"** philosophy encourages us to embrace the present with a sense of clarity and focus, as it is only by being rooted in the moment that we can adapt, grow, and thrive amidst life's chaos.

Hemant's journey, marked by a series of transitions and challenges, offers an insightful lens through which we can understand the true importance of presence. His life reveals how **being present**, despite external demands and internal distractions, can lead to greater clarity, peace, and fulfillment. As we unravel this chapter, we will reflect on practical strategies for staying present, mindful, and grounded in today's rapidly moving world.

Living in the Moment and Being Mindful Amidst the Chaos of Life

In today's fast-paced world, where productivity is praised and the constant chase for success is the norm, it's easy to become disconnected from the present moment. Society often celebrates multitasking, achievement, and forward momentum, encouraging us to constantly be on the move. We fill our days with a whirlwind of tasks, to-do lists, and future plans, all the while leaving little space to truly experience the world around us. The paradox is that while we're busy chasing external success, we often neglect our internal well-being. This lifestyle, though seemingly productive, can lead to burnout, anxiety, and a sense of detachment from life itself.

We become so focused on what's next—on our goals, our ambitions, or the mistakes of the past—that we forget to fully engage with the present. The moments that make up our lives pass us by unnoticed. We may even find ourselves looking back, wondering where the time went, wishing we had savored more of the here and now. This constant running leaves us feeling exhausted and disconnected, as though we are merely going through the motions, rather than living life in its full depth.

This is where mindfulness comes in. At its core, mindfulness is the practice of living in the moment. It's about being aware of our thoughts, emotions, and surroundings without judgment or distraction. Mindfulness teaches us to let go of the pressures of what has already happened or what is yet to come, and simply focus on what's unfolding right in front of us. In doing so, we allow ourselves to experience life more fully, in its raw and unfiltered form.

For Hemant, mindfulness became an essential tool in his journey of self-discovery and personal growth. As he transitioned from the high-stress demands of the corporate world to the more fulfilling but challenging role of a teacher, he felt the weight of constant pressure. He was still adjusting to his new life, grappling with the expectations of his students, the responsibilities of his new role, and the general pace of his new career. Yet, in the midst of all this, he began to realize something important: in order to thrive, he needed to shift his mindset and focus on the present.

The pressure to perform, meet deadlines, and manage his various responsibilities often left Hemant feeling overwhelmed. There were days when the anxiety of trying to juggle everything took a toll on his well-being. But when he started to embrace mindfulness, he discovered that it wasn't about eliminating these pressures or wishing them away. Instead, it was about how he responded to them. By practicing mindfulness, Hemant learned to immerse himself fully in each moment, instead of being consumed by what was next or the weight of past actions. When he was teaching, he focused solely on the students in front of him, giving them his undivided attention. When he spent time with family, he wasn't thinking about work or future responsibilities; he was present, appreciating the moments he had with them.

This shift in perspective brought a sense of peace to Hemant's life. He realized that by being present in the moment, he wasn't only improving his emotional resilience, but also enhancing his overall well-being. Mindfulness allowed him to respond more thoughtfully to stress, to find joy in simple experiences, and to approach each task with greater clarity. Whether it was teaching a lesson, enjoying a cup of coffee, or having a conversation, Hemant learned that true fulfillment comes not from the endless pursuit of what's next, but from deeply engaging with what's happening right now.

By living in the moment, Hemant discovered a profound sense of peace amidst the chaos of life. He was no longer a passenger in his own journey, drifting from one task to the next without truly experiencing them. Instead, he was an active participant in his life, savoring each moment for what it was. This practice of mindfulness became his anchor, helping him find balance even during the most hectic of days.

In a world that constantly pushes us to strive for more, to be constantly busy, and to keep moving forward, the simple act of being present can be a revolutionary shift. Mindfulness invites us to slow down, breathe, and reconnect with what really matters. It offers us the freedom to experience life as it unfolds, rather than being caught up in the whirlwind of constant striving. Hemant's journey teaches us that true peace and fulfillment are not found in the rush of achievement but in the quiet presence of living in the moment.

Hemant's Journey to Finding Peace and Balance in the Present, Despite External Pressures

Throughout much of his career, Hemant found himself trapped in the relentless cycle of external pressures that constantly demanded his attention. Like many in his position, he spent his early years chasing after external validation—climbing the corporate ladder, earning accolades, and securing financial success. These markers of achievement became the benchmarks by which he measured his worth. As a result, his focus was perpetually pulled in multiple directions, with little room to pause and reflect. He was driven by the idea that the next promotion, the next financial milestone, or the next career step would finally bring him the satisfaction he sought. Yet, despite his outward accomplishments, there was always a lingering sense of unease, a feeling that something was missing—an emptiness that could not be filled by titles, paychecks, or status.

The pressure to keep advancing, to constantly move forward and reach the next goal, became a heavy weight. Hemant realized that in his pursuit of external success, he had become disconnected from his own sense of fulfillment. His life had become a checklist, and no matter how many items he ticked off, it never felt like enough. The constant striving left him feeling exhausted and unfulfilled, despite achieving the very things society tells us will bring happiness. He recognized that he was caught in a cycle of perpetual dissatisfaction, where the joy of accomplishment was fleeting, replaced quickly by the hunger for the next success.

It was only when Hemant began to shift his focus toward being fully present in each moment that he started to feel a deep sense of peace. This change didn't happen overnight, and it wasn't easy. The external pressures, the expectations, and the relentless demands of modern life were still very much part of his world. But Hemant realized that instead of obsessing over what might come next—whether that meant preparing for a future promotion or worrying about the next career milestone—he needed to shift his energy toward the present moment.

He began with small, intentional changes. Rather than worrying about the next big task or outcome, he made a conscious effort to invest his energy fully into whatever he was doing at the time. Whether it was preparing a lesson for his students, having a deep conversation with a colleague, or simply spending quality time with his family, Hemant made an effort to let go of distractions and be present in each of those moments. The shift was subtle at first, but the impact was profound. For the first time in a long while, he experienced a sense of calm that wasn't dependent on achieving the next goal or reaching the next milestone.

This change wasn't without its challenges. Hemant had spent years building his identity around external success, and letting go of that mindset was difficult. The pressure to achieve, the cultural norms that told him his worth was measured by his job title and salary, didn't disappear overnight. But with time, he learned to embrace the simple but powerful practice of living in the present. He discovered that the key to peace and balance wasn't found in the relentless pursuit of more, but in the quiet satisfaction of fully engaging with the present moment.

For Hemant, balance came from recognizing that life is made up of moments, and that each of those moments, if lived with intention and awareness, could contribute to a life well-lived. By focusing on being present, he was able to invest his energy into what truly mattered to him—his students, his family, and his own personal growth. No longer preoccupied with the pressure of what he had to achieve next, Hemant found the freedom to fully appreciate the richness of the life he had already built.

The moment-to-moment mindfulness that Hemant embraced allowed him to feel more grounded and connected to the world around him. It was in the quiet moments of teaching, the casual conversations with friends, and the unhurried time spent with loved ones that he found a deeper sense of fulfillment. Hemant's journey was not about rejecting external achievements or goals; rather, it was about recognizing that true peace doesn't come from achieving more, but from finding contentment in the here and now. In letting go of the constant striving for validation and success, he discovered that fulfillment lies not in what's next, but in fully engaging with what's happening right in front of us.

Ultimately, Hemant's experience teaches us that balance and peace are not about escaping the pressures of life, but about shifting our mindset. Life will always have its demands, but the choice to be present in each moment gives us the ability to navigate those demands with a sense of calm, clarity, and purpose. By focusing on what truly matters in the present, we can find peace amidst the chaos, and cultivate a life that feels balanced, meaningful, and deeply fulfilling.

Practical Steps for Staying Present and Mindful in a Fast-Paced World

Being present in today's world is no small feat. Our lives are filled with constant noise and distractions. However, there are practical steps we can take to bring mindfulness into our daily lives:

Start with Focused Breathing:

In the midst of life's hectic pace, it's easy to feel scattered, pulled in different directions, and overwhelmed by the weight of responsibilities. One of the most effective tools for reconnecting with the present moment—and alleviating the stress that often accompanies it—is focused breathing. This simple yet powerful technique serves as a grounding practice that allows us to pause, reset, and center ourselves when external pressures threaten to overwhelm us.

At its core, focused breathing involves paying attention to the rhythm of your breath, consciously slowing it down, and breathing deeply into your lungs. This practice might seem basic, but its effects are profound. When we breathe deeply and mindfully, we activate the parasympathetic nervous system, which helps to counteract the body's natural stress response. This leads to a reduction in heart rate, lower blood pressure, and a sense of calm and relaxation. Focused breathing doesn't just help calm the body; it also soothes the mind by breaking the cycle of anxiety and overthinking.

Hemant, like many others, found that his days were often filled with constant tasks, meetings, and expectations. He was frequently pulled in various directions, constantly thinking about the next deadline, the next meeting, or the next challenge. This created a state of mental clutter that left him feeling anxious and drained. It was during these times of overwhelming pressure that Hemant turned to focused breathing to help regain a sense of clarity.

Whenever Hemant felt his stress levels rising, he would take a moment to close his eyes, inhale deeply, and exhale slowly. He would repeat this several times, allowing himself to let go of the swirling thoughts that filled his mind. By focusing solely on his breath, he redirected his attention away from distractions and into the present moment. This practice of mindful breathing became a way for him to "reset" his mind, giving him the space to step back and approach challenges with a fresh perspective.

The beauty of focused breathing lies in its simplicity. It can be done anywhere, at any time, without the need for special equipment or preparation. Whether he was sitting at his desk, preparing for a class, or even walking from one meeting to the next, Hemant learned to incorporate deep breathing into his routine. It became a mental tool he could rely on to ease anxiety and sharpen his focus when he needed it most.

The benefits of focused breathing go beyond merely calming the mind in the moment. With consistent practice, Hemant found that it helped him stay more grounded throughout his day. Rather than getting swept away by the demands of work and life, he was able to maintain a sense of composure and clarity, even in stressful situations. This, in turn, allowed him to approach challenges more effectively, without being overwhelmed by them.

Incorporating focused breathing into your daily life can also create a ripple effect that positively impacts your mental, emotional, and physical well-being. Over time, it helps you build resilience to stress, improves emotional regulation, and enhances your ability to remain present and engaged with whatever you are doing. Just as Hemant used deep breathing to refocus and calm his mind, you too can use this simple practice to reconnect with the present moment, reduce stress, and find clarity amidst the chaos.

Practice Mindful Listening:

In today's fast-paced world, we often find ourselves distracted, even when in conversation with others. Whether it's planning our response, thinking about our next task, or letting our minds wander, our attention is rarely fully focused on the person speaking. This lack of engagement can lead to misunderstandings, missed insights, and weakened connections. Practicing mindful listening is a way to counteract these tendencies, fostering deeper relationships and enriching our understanding of those around us.

Mindful listening is the art of being fully present in a conversation. It means quieting our own thoughts, setting aside our judgments, and focusing solely on what the other person is saying. We listen not to respond but to truly hear, understand, and empathize. When we practice mindful listening, we create a space for others to feel seen and valued, which strengthens bonds and enhances trust.

For Hemant, mindful listening became a transformative tool in his journey toward meaningful engagement. In his teaching career, he was responsible for guiding his students through both academic challenges and personal growth. Initially, he found himself falling into the common habit of thinking ahead during conversations—planning his responses or solutions rather than fully absorbing his students' words. However, he soon realized that by not fully listening, he was missing out on important cues and insights into his students' perspectives and needs.

Determined to make a change, Hemant began practicing mindful listening with his students and colleagues. He focused on clearing his mind of distractions during conversations, making eye contact, and nodding to signal his attentiveness. He paid close attention to both the words spoken and the emotions behind them, allowing himself to connect more deeply with the other person. Through this approach, he was able to better understand his students' challenges, fears, and aspirations, which helped him become a more effective and compassionate mentor.

Mindful listening had a profound impact on Hemant's relationships with those around him. His students felt more comfortable approaching him with their concerns, knowing that he would listen without judgment and offer guidance that was rooted in understanding rather than assumption. His colleagues, too, noticed the shift, and conversations in the staff room or during meetings became more collaborative and supportive. By being fully present in these interactions, Hemant created an environment of trust and respect that enriched his relationships.

The benefits of mindful listening extend beyond individual relationships; it also enhances our own sense of fulfillment and connection. When we listen deeply, we become more attuned to others' perspectives, broadening our understanding of the world and deepening our empathy. Mindful listening allows us to step outside of ourselves, temporarily setting aside our own thoughts, opinions, and agendas. This shift can be liberating, as it encourages us to let go of the need to control or steer the conversation and instead embrace the experience of simply being present with another person.

Practicing mindful listening is a skill that, like any other, takes time to develop. To start, try setting an intention before each conversation to listen with full attention. Avoid interrupting, refrain from forming responses while the other person is speaking, and focus on the emotions conveyed alongside the words. Body language, facial expressions, and tone of voice all provide valuable context and can deepen our understanding of the speaker's message. After the conversation, take a moment to reflect on what was shared and consider how it aligns with or challenges your own perspective.

Just as Hemant's relationships improved through mindful listening, we too can find greater connection and understanding by fully engaging in the conversations we have each day. Mindful listening is not only a gift to those we interact with; it's also a way for us to enrich our own lives, fostering deeper, more meaningful relationships that can support us in both personal and professional growth. When we listen with intention, empathy, and presence, we create a foundation of trust, respect, and mutual understanding, transforming ordinary interactions into moments of genuine connection.

Limit Multitasking:

In our fast-paced world, multitasking has become a badge of honor. Juggling multiple tasks at once often feels necessary to meet the demands of our busy lives, and it can give us a fleeting sense of productivity. However, studies have shown that attempting to handle multiple tasks at once can reduce our effectiveness and lead to a scattered mind, ultimately leaving us feeling drained and unfocused. The effort required to switch rapidly between tasks depletes our mental energy, making it difficult to do any single task well.

Limiting multitasking allows us to redirect our energy toward focused, intentional work. By concentrating on one task at a time, we can enter a state of "flow," a highly productive mental state in which we're fully immersed in what we're doing. This deep focus helps us work more efficiently and, surprisingly, often allows us to accomplish more in less time. Concentrating on one activity at a time not only improves the quality of our work but also contributes to a sense of accomplishment, which is often lost when we scatter our focus across multiple tasks.

For Hemant, limiting multitasking became a crucial part of his journey toward mindfulness and intentionality. As a teacher and mentor, his responsibilities were many—preparing lessons, grading assignments, meeting with students, and attending staff meetings. Initially, he would try to tackle these tasks simultaneously, responding to emails while planning lessons or discussing student progress in between grading papers. However, he soon realized that this approach left him feeling rushed and overwhelmed, and his work lacked the depth and care he wanted to bring to it.

Hemant made a deliberate decision to prioritize single-tasking. When preparing lessons, he gave his full attention to the material, ensuring his teaching plans were thorough and engaging. When he met with students, he set aside his other responsibilities to focus entirely on the conversation, allowing him to connect on a deeper level and understand their needs. In each task, he immersed himself fully, bringing a sense of dedication and care that enriched his work and allowed him to truly engage with his role as an educator.

This shift had a noticeable impact on both his productivity and his sense of fulfillment. Focusing on one task at a time enabled Hemant to approach his responsibilities with clarity, purpose, and greater creativity. Not only did his work improve, but he also found that he had more energy and fewer feelings of burnout. By setting aside the habit of multitasking, he was able to experience a sense of flow, where his tasks became more satisfying and his outcomes more meaningful.

Limiting multitasking can be a challenge, especially in environments that demand constant responsiveness and adaptability. However, there are small steps we can take to support focused work. For instance, try blocking out time for specific tasks, setting aside interruptions like email notifications, and taking breaks between activities. Each time you focus on a single task, remind yourself of the benefits of undivided attention—greater efficiency, enhanced creativity, and a deeper sense of satisfaction.

As Hemant discovered, embracing single-tasking over multitasking can lead to a profound shift in how we experience our daily work. By devoting ourselves fully to each task, we not only improve our performance but also cultivate a calmer, more fulfilling approach to our responsibilities. In a world that constantly urges us to do more and move faster, choosing to focus on one thing at a time can be a powerful way to reconnect with the present and truly value the work we do.

Be Aware of Your Surroundings:

In the rush of modern life, it's easy to move through our days on autopilot, barely noticing the world around us. This habit of "tuning out" happens naturally; with our minds focused on to-do lists, upcoming events, or thoughts about the past, we often miss out on the richness of our immediate surroundings. By making a conscious effort to observe and connect with the environment around us, we can experience a greater sense of grounding, clarity, and appreciation in the present moment.

Awareness of our surroundings means actively engaging with the small details of daily life that are often overlooked. It can start with something as simple as observing the scenery during a walk. Instead of rushing to your destination while lost in thought or scrolling on your phone, take a few minutes to notice the landscape around you: the colors of the trees, the sound of birds, the feel of the breeze. Each of these sensory details offers a new perspective on the beauty of the everyday, grounding us in the present and fostering a sense of connection with the world outside ourselves.

Another way to cultivate awareness is by savoring small routines, like drinking your morning coffee or tea. Instead of rushing through this daily ritual, try to fully experience each step. Notice the aroma, the warmth of the cup in your hands, the taste with each sip. These small moments, when fully appreciated, can bring unexpected joy and calm, creating a sense of mindfulness that carries into the rest of the day.

Hemant embraced this practice of awareness during his transition to a more mindful, intentional way of living. Initially, he, like many of us, had a tendency to be constantly preoccupied with his responsibilities and goals. However, by intentionally observing his surroundings—whether in the classroom, at home, or outdoors—he began to feel a deeper connection to the present moment. When he walked through the school hallways, he took the time to notice students laughing and talking, or the sunlight streaming in through the windows. When he prepared his lessons, he paid attention to the details of his work environment, grounding himself in the space he occupied. This practice helped him feel more engaged with his surroundings, enhancing his sense of calm and presence.

In the classroom, Hemant found that this awareness also positively impacted his teaching. By being fully present and aware of his students' expressions, body language, and engagement levels, he could adapt his teaching methods to better meet their needs. This shift allowed him to connect more deeply with his students and create a learning environment that was more supportive and responsive. Awareness of his surroundings helped him remain in tune with what was happening in the moment, reducing stress and improving his sense of fulfillment.

To cultivate this type of awareness, start by choosing one part of your day to focus on. For example, if you commute to work, take a few moments to observe the world outside—notice the colors, sounds, and activities around you. Or if you're at home, practice awareness by tuning into the rhythm of your environment, whether it's the warmth of a cozy room, the laughter of family members, or even the hum of appliances. As you become more accustomed to noticing your surroundings, you'll find that these small, seemingly simple observations bring a refreshing sense of calm and presence into your daily life.

Developing an awareness of your surroundings can also open you up to new insights and experiences. When we slow down to truly observe, we often notice things we might otherwise miss—a smile from a stranger, the beauty of a sunset, or the peace in a quiet moment. This practice isn't about ignoring responsibilities or avoiding the tasks ahead, but about reclaiming moments of mindfulness and recognizing that life happens in the present.

In a world where it's easy to feel disconnected and overwhelmed, learning to be aware of your surroundings can bring a powerful sense of balance and grounding. By tuning into the richness of your environment, you allow yourself to experience the world more fully, cultivating a life that is not only productive but also deeply fulfilling. Hemant found that by being aware of his surroundings, he was able to enjoy each day more fully, finding peace and satisfaction in the small, beautiful details that often go unnoticed.

Embrace Moments of Silence:

In our busy, noise-filled lives, silence is often a rare and uncomfortable experience. With constant alerts, conversations, and demands on our attention, it's easy to shy away from quiet moments, filling them with distractions out of habit or unease. Yet, silence can be one of the most powerful tools for cultivating mindfulness and reconnecting with ourselves. Taking time each day to embrace silence, even for a few minutes, offers a space to reflect, reset, and regain a sense of inner peace.

Silence isn't just the absence of noise; it's an opportunity to turn inward and observe our thoughts without interruption. When we sit in silence, we create a space where we can acknowledge and process what we're feeling. In these moments, we can let go of the day's mental clutter and focus on what's truly important. For some, it might mean setting aside time in the morning to start the day with a clear mind, or it might involve taking a few minutes of stillness before bed to unwind and release the stresses of the day.

For Hemant, moments of silence became a vital part of his daily routine, especially as he transitioned from a high-energy corporate career to teaching. In his previous role, silence was rare, with each day full of meetings, phone calls, and tasks demanding his immediate attention. The constant noise left little room for reflection or personal peace, and he realized that this pace had distanced him from his own thoughts and feelings. As he shifted into his new role, Hemant discovered the value of taking time at the end of each day to sit in silence. Whether he spent a few minutes in his classroom after students had left or found a quiet corner at home, this time allowed him to reflect on the day's events, release any tension he'd accumulated, and refocus on what mattered most to him.

Silence also gave Hemant the chance to observe his thoughts without judgment. Without distractions, he could address anxieties or lingering thoughts, making it easier to let go of what wasn't serving him and to gain a fresh perspective on what was. These small moments of quiet created a space for insight and helped him reconnect with his values, grounding him amidst the challenges and noise of everyday life. This practice allowed him to return to the present moment, more centered and prepared to approach his work and relationships with clarity and calm.

To incorporate silence into your own life, start by dedicating just a few minutes each day to a quiet moment with no specific goals or tasks. You don't need a particular setting—whether it's a few minutes at your desk, sitting outside, or lying in bed, all that matters is the intention to be still. During this time, focus on your breath, allowing your thoughts to settle without trying to control or analyze them. This simple practice can help bring a sense of peace and stability, even on the busiest of days.

Over time, as you grow comfortable with silence, these moments can serve as a retreat—a place where you can reconnect with your inner self.

Embracing silence can also help foster creativity and problem-solving skills, as it gives your mind the space to explore ideas freely without the interference of external stimuli. It's in these quiet moments that we often find new solutions, fresh perspectives, or a deeper understanding of our own needs and aspirations.

In a world filled with constant noise and pressure, taking the time to embrace moments of silence is a gentle but powerful way to cultivate mindfulness. Hemant found that his quiet moments helped him process his thoughts and reconnect with his sense of purpose, reminding him of why he chose to teach and guiding him in how he wanted to approach each day. By embracing silence, we allow ourselves to step back from the rush of life, creating a space for self-awareness, calm, and a renewed connection to the present moment.

Practice Gratitude:

Gratitude is a powerful tool that can transform our perspective, shifting our focus from what we lack or what isn't going well to an appreciation for what we already have. It's easy to get caught up in life's challenges and lose sight of the everyday blessings that surround us. By intentionally practicing gratitude, we create space to recognize the value in even the smallest experiences, helping us feel more grounded and present.

Practicing gratitude doesn't have to be complicated. It can begin with a simple moment of reflection each day, focusing on one or two things you are genuinely thankful for. This could be anything—a peaceful morning, the warmth of a family gathering, the satisfaction of completing a project, or even something as simple as a kind gesture from a friend. These moments of appreciation help to cultivate a mindset that finds value in the present, fostering contentment rather than constantly chasing the next big achievement or worrying about what's lacking.

For Hemant, practicing gratitude became a meaningful part of his daily life, especially as he transitioned from a corporate role to teaching. Initially, he struggled with the change in pace and the shift from a high-powered career to a quieter but more personally fulfilling role. However, by consciously choosing to acknowledge small moments of positivity, Hemant found himself more connected and engaged in his new journey. Each day, he would take a few minutes to recognize something he was grateful for.

Whether it was a productive class, a student's breakthrough, or a meaningful conversation, these small "wins" became pillars of support, grounding him in the present and reminding him of the purpose behind his work.

Over time, Hemant noticed that this simple practice of gratitude began to influence his entire outlook on life. Rather than focusing on pressures or worries about the future, he found himself more attuned to the positive aspects of each day. This shift in mindset helped him stay content, allowing him to approach his work and relationships with a renewed sense of purpose and calm.

You, too, can integrate gratitude into your daily life by setting aside a few minutes each morning or evening to reflect on what you appreciate. Consider keeping a gratitude journal, where you jot down one or two things that made you feel grateful each day. This could be a moment of laughter, a new insight, or the support of a friend. Over time, you'll build a collection of positive memories that remind you of the richness in your life, even during difficult times.

Practicing gratitude also encourages mindfulness. When you take a moment to be thankful, you're actively pausing to acknowledge and appreciate the present. This can be especially powerful in today's fast-paced world, where it's easy to overlook the simple joys in the rush of daily life. By regularly expressing gratitude, you strengthen your connection to the present, enhancing your overall well-being and emotional resilience.

Hemant's journey shows us that gratitude isn't about ignoring life's challenges; rather, it's about choosing to focus on what brings fulfillment and joy. His gratitude practice helped him stay centered, despite external pressures, and served as a gentle reminder of why he chose to teach. Each small moment of gratitude reinforced his commitment to his work and fostered a sense of inner peace.

Ultimately, gratitude is a mindset that empowers us to embrace life as it is, recognizing that each day brings unique opportunities to appreciate, learn, and grow. By practicing gratitude, we open ourselves up to a more balanced, fulfilling life—one where we acknowledge not only our achievements but also the beauty of everyday moments. This shift in focus can make a profound difference, helping us find contentment and purpose right here in the present.

Accept Imperfection:

Striving for perfection can often pull us away from experiencing the richness of life in the present. Perfectionism keeps us fixated on an ideal—whether it's achieving flawless work, making no mistakes, or avoiding any failures. While it's natural to want to excel, holding ourselves to impossible standards can create stress, disappointment, and a relentless focus on what we think *should* be rather than what is. Accepting imperfection, on the other hand, allows us to live more freely and fully, appreciating each moment for its real, unpolished beauty.

Learning to accept imperfection is, in itself, a journey. For Hemant, this was a hard but transformative lesson. In his early career, he was driven by high standards and a desire to excel. This drive pushed him to succeed, but over time, it also began to drain him, as he constantly sought to meet ever-rising expectations. Mistakes felt like failures, and he often found himself revisiting past decisions, wondering if he could have done things differently or better. This cycle of self-criticism prevented him from enjoying his accomplishments and made him feel disconnected from his own life.

But over time, Hemant began to understand that life's imperfections—its unplanned moments, flaws, and missteps—were not obstacles but integral parts of the journey. Embracing this reality brought him a new sense of peace. He realized that waiting for the "perfect" moment was futile; perfection didn't exist in the way he imagined. Instead, he learned to focus on the here and now, allowing things to unfold naturally. This shift in mindset enabled him to let go of rigid standards and open himself to the beauty of each moment, even when things didn't go as planned.

Accepting imperfection also allowed Hemant to build resilience. Rather than letting mistakes or failures throw him off course, he began to see them as valuable learning experiences. When a lesson didn't go perfectly or a student struggled, he stopped dwelling on his perceived shortcomings and instead looked at how he could grow from the experience. This new approach made him a more compassionate and effective teacher, as he was able to connect with his students on a deeper level and encourage them to embrace their own imperfections.

If we can learn to embrace imperfection, we too can experience life with a greater sense of freedom. By accepting that no day, interaction, or experience will be flawless, we can start to appreciate each moment for what it is. It's in these imperfect, unguarded moments that we often find joy, connection, and meaning. Mistakes remind us that we're human, while imperfections remind us that life is dynamic and full of surprises.

Practicing self-compassion is a key part of this journey. Rather than criticizing ourselves when things go wrong, we can remind ourselves that mistakes and setbacks are a normal part of life. Allowing ourselves to be human—flawed, learning, growing—frees us from the constant pressure of perfectionism. This mindset shift can be especially liberating in a world that often pressures us to appear perfect on the surface, whether in our work, our relationships, or even our personal lives.

Hemant's story shows us that life's beauty lies not in its perfection but in its imperfections. By accepting life as it comes, he was able to let go of the exhausting pursuit of flawless achievements and embrace a sense of peace and contentment. This acceptance allowed him to approach his work and relationships with a more genuine, open heart, free from the burden of unrealistic expectations.

When we embrace imperfection, we grant ourselves permission to live more fully and authentically. We open ourselves to the beauty of each moment, knowing that life, with all its messiness and unpredictability, is far richer than anything we could imagine. Embracing imperfection allows us to savor the present and discover that true fulfillment is found not in chasing an ideal but in accepting ourselves—and our lives—just as they are.

Conclusion

In the "Keeping Bags Packed" Philosophy, the Present Moment as a Sacred Space

The "Keeping Bags Packed" philosophy calls on us to treat the present moment as a sacred space—a unique realm where genuine growth and deep transformation take place. This approach isn't about disregarding the future or dwelling on the past; it's about fully inhabiting the here and now. It encourages us to recognize, respect, and appreciate each moment with all its layers, complexities, and endless possibilities.

Being present requires mindfulness—an active, intentional engagement with our lives as they unfold. It doesn't mean ignoring our aspirations or forgetting past lessons, but rather approaching them from a place of grounded awareness. In doing so, we gain the capacity to respond to life's challenges with clarity, resilience, and purpose.

Hemant's journey exemplifies this approach. As he moved from a high-stakes corporate role to a more meaningful career in teaching, he discovered that true peace and fulfillment didn't come from accumulating accolades or climbing the career ladder. Instead, he found them within, through the simple but profound practice of grounding himself in the present. By dedicating himself to his work in each moment—whether he was mentoring a student, preparing a lesson, or simply spending time with family—Hemant was able to let go of the distractions that had once consumed him. This shift allowed him to experience life more deeply, to connect with those around him more authentically, and to feel a profound sense of purpose that wasn't reliant on external validation.

When we embrace the present moment, we start to see life with a new level of clarity. We become attuned to the small yet significant details that often go unnoticed in our rush to get to the next thing. The scent of fresh morning air, the warmth of a smile, or the satisfaction of a job well done—all these seemingly small experiences become sources of real contentment. By rooting ourselves in the present, we begin to view life not as a series of goals to accomplish, but as a flow of experiences to appreciate and learn from.

This perspective also helps us let go of the things that distract us from what truly matters. The constant pull of notifications, the pressure to meet others' expectations, the fear of missing out—all of these distractions lose their hold on us when we're fully engaged in the moment. By focusing on what is right in front of us, we begin to cultivate a deeper sense of peace that isn't easily shaken by the highs and lows of external circumstances.

The present moment is the only space in which we can truly act, grow, and find fulfillment. When we ground ourselves here, we free ourselves from the regrets of the past and the anxieties of the future, allowing us to experience life in its fullest form. Hemant's story reminds us that lasting satisfaction comes not from achievements or future successes, but from a conscious engagement with life as it is right now. It's a profound realization that brings a quiet but powerful contentment—the understanding that our lives, in this moment, are enough.

As we move forward with the "Keeping Bags Packed" philosophy, let us hold this truth close: that the present is a gift. Each moment is an opportunity to connect with ourselves, engage with others, and find meaning in our actions. When we cultivate this awareness, we're able to approach life's challenges with greater grace and resilience, knowing that whatever comes next, we have the strength to handle it from a place of presence and purpose.

Ultimately, this approach to life is about finding peace and balance, not in some distant goal or future achievement, but in the here and now. It reminds us that real fulfillment doesn't come from reaching an ideal destination but from appreciating the journey, moment by moment. The present, then, is more than just a point in time—it's where our lives happen, where purpose is found, and where we can find ourselves, over and over again.

Chapter 13: Building Resilience through Adversity

Resilience is one of the most powerful qualities a person can cultivate, yet it often emerges not in times of comfort, but through the toughest of circumstances. It is born from the challenges and adversities we face and is defined not by the avoidance of difficulty but by our ability to endure, adapt, and grow through it. The **"Keeping Bags Packed"** philosophy teaches us that life is unpredictable, and resilience is key to navigating its ups and downs. Resilience is not a trait we're born with, but a skill that can be nurtured through experience, perseverance, and self-awareness.

In this chapter, we explore the role adversity plays in shaping resilience, the strength that comes from facing hardship, and how these experiences can build a foundation for future growth. By examining Hemant's journey, we see how his personal struggles, setbacks, and failures were not obstacles to his success but stepping stones that shaped his inner strength. Resilience, as we'll explore here, is not simply bouncing back after a fall but using adversity as an opportunity to **transform** and emerge stronger.

How Facing Adversity and Challenges Builds Resilience

Adversity often arrives in our lives unannounced, like an unexpected storm, disrupting our plans, causing pain, and challenging our sense of stability. Yet, it's precisely these difficult moments that reveal who we are and shape us into who we can become. Challenges have a way of exposing our limitations, yet they also stretch our capabilities, guiding us to discover strengths that would remain hidden during times of ease. Through adversity, we uncover a sense of resilience, strength, and tenacity that would otherwise remain dormant.

Everyone encounters challenges, whether it's navigating a career setback, coping with a personal loss, managing financial strains, or dealing with health issues. Adversity is a universal experience, something that connects all people, regardless of background or life circumstances. Yet, what sets resilient individuals apart is their response to these moments. Resilient people face difficulties head-on, confronting pain and discomfort rather than shying away from them. Rather than allowing setbacks to define or limit them, they use adversity as a catalyst for growth and transformation.

Resilience is forged in the crucible of hardship. It's not about avoiding difficulty or preventing challenges from arising, but rather about responding to them with a determination to push through. Each time we confront adversity and refuse to surrender to it, we add a layer of strength, patience, and understanding to our character. These experiences build on one another, creating a foundation of resilience that we can draw upon whenever new challenges arise. Over time, we develop a mindset equipped to handle life's storms with greater grace and endurance.

Hemant's journey is a powerful example of resilience shaped by adversity. Early in his career, he faced numerous setbacks that could have easily derailed his dreams. He encountered a string of difficulties—from failed business ventures and financial struggles to the emotional toll of unmet career expectations. Each setback brought him to a crossroads, leaving him questioning his choices and reconsidering his path. However, Hemant did not see these challenges as the end of his journey. Instead, he chose to view each obstacle as an opportunity to become stronger, wiser, and more adaptable.

Hemant's outlook transformed his approach to adversity. Rather than allowing failure to discourage him, he saw these moments as stepping stones toward a deeper understanding of himself and his purpose. Each setback became a lesson, each struggle a new chance to redefine his goals and recommit to his values. With every difficult decision and moment of uncertainty, Hemant learned to embrace discomfort and confront his fears. He discovered that resilience wasn't just about enduring hardship but about growing through it, about using challenges as a means to build character and refine one's direction.

As Hemant navigated these challenging times, he began to see adversity not as a barrier but as an essential force that would ultimately shape his journey. Each trial was an invitation to build a stronger version of himself, to expand his capacity for persistence, and to deepen his understanding of what truly mattered to him. The setbacks became turning points—moments when he could choose to either retreat or move forward with greater conviction. Through these experiences, Hemant grew comfortable with the discomfort of uncertainty, understanding that each challenge carried within it the potential for growth.

Over time, Hemant's resilience became his greatest asset. He developed a mindset rooted in courage and adaptability, qualities that allowed him to face whatever life threw his way. His journey teaches us that resilience isn't something we are simply born with; it's a quality built through the act of facing hardship, learning from each experience, and continuing forward with newfound strength. Adversity, rather than being an unwelcome guest, becomes a teacher that helps us grow into the most resilient versions of ourselves.

Hemant's Personal Struggles and How They Shaped His Inner Strength

Hemant's journey was one shaped by trials that, at first glance, appeared overwhelming. His early years were marked by the bold decision to leave a stable career behind and pursue the uncertain path of entrepreneurship. Excited by the prospect of building something from scratch, he threw himself into his new business venture. Yet, despite his best efforts, reality proved more challenging than he had anticipated. The business struggled to take off, and Hemant soon found himself facing not only financial setbacks but also the emotional weight of unmet expectations and self-doubt.

The aftermath of this failure was difficult for Hemant. He had to confront the painful realization that success wouldn't come as easily as he had hoped. But rather than withdrawing from the challenges in defeat, he chose to face them head-on. He began to understand that resilience isn't about achieving a flawless success story but about persevering through obstacles. Hemant learned that true strength lay in his willingness to keep moving forward, even when circumstances were less than ideal.

This period of his life taught Hemant that resilience wasn't merely about financial or professional recovery. The deeper strength he gained came from an emotional resilience that allowed him to embrace failure as a learning process, not a final verdict on his abilities. He came to see setbacks as opportunities to better understand his own limitations, fears, and untapped potential. By allowing himself to fully feel the disappointment and navigate the uncertainty of his next steps, he gradually transformed his experience of loss into a tool for personal growth. He learned to approach challenges with a sense of curiosity and to view mistakes as stepping stones toward self-discovery.

A defining moment for Hemant came when he reached a low point after another major setback. Feelings of doubt and insecurity crept in, casting shadows over his confidence and sense of purpose. In this moment of vulnerability, he began to question the metrics by which he had been measuring his self-worth. For so long, he had associated his value with professional success and external achievements. Yet, at his lowest point, he realized that his true worth was rooted not in accomplishments but in the resilience and insight he had gained through adversity.

This realization was transformative. Hemant recognized that his identity was not bound to his career but was instead defined by the strength he had built through the challenges he had faced. His focus shifted away from seeking external validation and toward cultivating a sense of inner peace and fulfillment. By embracing this new perspective, he found a renewed sense of purpose and direction in his life.

Actionable Insights on How to Build Resilience in Your Own Life

Building resilience is not something that happens overnight—it is a gradual process that requires consistent effort and a mindset shift. Here are some actionable insights based on Hemant's journey and the **"Keeping Bags Packed"** philosophy that can help you develop resilience in your own life:

Embrace Challenges as Opportunities

Building resilience starts with a shift in perspective—seeing challenges not as roadblocks but as essential experiences that foster growth. When faced with adversity, it's natural to feel overwhelmed or defeated. However, by reframing challenges as opportunities, we open ourselves up to learn and evolve in ways we may never have anticipated. This approach allows us to look beyond immediate discomfort and recognize that each difficulty we encounter has something valuable to offer.

For Hemant, this shift in mindset was transformative. By choosing to embrace challenges rather than shy away from them, he began to see them as stepping stones toward greater personal and professional growth. The setbacks that once seemed daunting became moments that tested his resolve, developed his problem-solving skills, and pushed him to expand his capabilities. Each time he faced a new challenge, he built resilience, becoming more adaptable and better prepared for whatever lay ahead.

Embracing challenges doesn't mean minimizing their difficulty; rather, it's about acknowledging that growth often comes from discomfort. When we lean into adversity, we develop a stronger sense of self and a deeper understanding of our strengths and limitations. By adopting this mindset, you, like Hemant, can discover new levels of confidence and adaptability, transforming life's trials into opportunities that shape a more resilient, capable, and empowered version of yourself.

Develop a Growth Mindset

A growth mindset is the belief that abilities and intelligence are not fixed traits but can be cultivated and expanded over time with effort, learning, and perseverance. This mindset encourages individuals to embrace challenges, learn from criticism, and see failure as an integral part of the learning process, not as an indication of personal inadequacy. When you adopt a growth mindset, you understand that success is not dependent on innate talent alone but on your willingness to work through difficulties, persist in the face of obstacles, and continuously improve.

For Hemant, this mindset was crucial in his personal and professional evolution. In moments of failure, rather than viewing them as signs of defeat, he saw them as valuable lessons and opportunities for growth. Each challenge or misstep became a chance to refine his approach, acquire new skills, and ultimately become more resilient. Hemant didn't allow setbacks to define his capabilities; instead, he used them as stepping stones to further his development. Every time he faced adversity, he reminded himself that learning, not immediate success, was the true goal.

This perspective allowed Hemant to remain focused on long-term growth rather than getting discouraged by temporary obstacles. He understood that growth doesn't happen overnight and that persistence, hard work, and reflection are key to overcoming challenges and building resilience. By continuously embracing challenges with a growth mindset, Hemant became more capable, adaptable, and prepared to tackle future hurdles with confidence.

In adopting a growth mindset, you too can shift your view of setbacks and difficulties. Instead of feeling defeated by them, you can see them as essential moments for growth—opportunities to strengthen your skills, improve your character, and push beyond your perceived limits. This perspective not only helps you build resilience but also cultivates a deeper sense of fulfillment as you focus on your continuous journey of personal development.

Cultivate Emotional Resilience

Emotional resilience goes beyond simply recovering from physical challenges; it involves developing the ability to navigate and thrive through emotional hardships. Life inevitably brings moments of fear, disappointment, frustration, and stress. How we respond to these emotions can either strengthen or weaken our emotional fortitude. Building emotional resilience is about learning to acknowledge and process our emotions without letting them overwhelm or define us.

For Hemant, cultivating emotional resilience was a pivotal aspect of his journey. When faced with setbacks, he didn't suppress his feelings of fear or frustration; instead, he allowed himself to feel them fully, without judgment. By recognizing these emotions, he was able to understand the underlying causes and avoid letting them dictate his actions or perceptions. Hemant learned that emotional experiences, though painful, were temporary and often provided valuable insights into his personal growth. Instead of letting emotions control his responses, he developed the ability to step back, reflect, and manage them thoughtfully.

To build emotional resilience, Hemant practiced various emotional regulation techniques. Mindfulness was one tool he found especially useful. By staying present in the moment and observing his thoughts and feelings without attachment, Hemant was able to distance himself from the emotional intensity of the situation. This helped him maintain clarity and respond rather than react impulsively. Journaling was another practice that Hemant embraced. Writing down his emotions allowed him to process them more deeply and gain perspective on the challenges he faced. It also helped him track his emotional progress, which encouraged personal growth.

Hemant also found that emotional resilience wasn't just about managing negative emotions—it was about fostering positive emotions like gratitude and hope, even in tough times. By consciously focusing on what he could control, such as his mindset and responses, he was able to stay grounded, despite external pressures. This practice of emotional regulation allowed him to navigate through stress, uncertainty, and fear with a calm and composed demeanor.

For anyone looking to build emotional resilience, the key lies in recognizing that emotions, while powerful, do not have to dictate your actions. By acknowledging your feelings, practicing mindfulness, journaling, or using other emotional regulation techniques, you can cultivate the inner strength needed to navigate even the most turbulent times. Emotional resilience doesn't mean being unaffected by adversity; rather, it means being able to face and process emotional challenges in a way that helps you grow and continue moving forward.

Focus on What You Can Control

During difficult or uncertain times, it's easy to feel overwhelmed by circumstances beyond your control. Whether it's an unforeseen setback, a personal loss, or external challenges, it's common to fixate on things you can't change. The reality is, life is unpredictable, and not everything falls within our grasp. However, instead of allowing this sense of helplessness to take over, focusing on what you can control can be a powerful tool for maintaining clarity, resilience, and a sense of agency.

For Hemant, this was a crucial realization during the various difficult moments in his life. He understood that while he had no control over external events—such as the failure of his business venture, the unpredictability of the job market, or unforeseen personal challenges—he had complete control over his reactions to those events. He couldn't always change the outcomes of certain situations, but he could decide how to respond, what mindset to adopt, and what actions to take. This shift in perspective was transformative.

Focusing on controllable aspects like thoughts, actions, and responses allowed Hemant to regain a sense of agency. He realized that while external forces might dictate some of the conditions in his life, he held the power to shape his internal world. Hemant learned to direct his attention to what he could influence—his mindset, his work ethic, his personal growth, and his responses to the challenges in front of him. Instead of spending energy on the uncontrollable, he poured his efforts into making choices that aligned with his values, purpose, and long-term goals.

By focusing on what he could control, Hemant found a greater sense of peace and stability. When faced with a crisis, rather than feeling paralyzed by what he couldn't change, he took action in areas where he had influence. For example, when business setbacks occurred, he worked to improve his skills, refined his approach, and focused on what he could do to turn things around, instead of dwelling on external factors he had no power over. This proactive attitude made him feel more empowered and less vulnerable to the stress and chaos that often accompany life's challenges.

This approach also extended to his emotional and mental well-being. Hemant took control of his mindset by practicing self-awareness, reframing negative thoughts, and engaging in practices that enhanced his resilience. For instance, he learned to turn moments of self-doubt into opportunities for reflection and improvement. He worked on developing a mindset that embraced challenges as growth opportunities and refrained from wasting energy on lamenting past mistakes or worrying about the future.

Focusing on what you can control doesn't mean ignoring external circumstances; it means shifting your attention from what's beyond your influence to what is within your grasp. It helps you regain a sense of purpose and direction, even in the most turbulent times. Hemant's journey exemplified this approach: by taking charge of his internal reactions, mindset, and actions, he was able to maintain a clear path forward. In doing so, he demonstrated that the most empowering thing in any situation is recognizing the power you hold within yourself to shape how you respond, no matter the challenges life may present.

Build a Support System

Resilience doesn't mean going through life's challenges alone. In fact, one of the most critical aspects of building resilience is recognizing the importance of a solid support system—people who can offer guidance, encouragement, and a sense of belonging when the road gets tough. Whether it's family, friends, colleagues, or mentors, having a network of individuals who genuinely care about your well-being can make all the difference in how you navigate adversity.

For Hemant, his journey through personal and professional setbacks wasn't a solitary one. At times, when the weight of failure and disappointment felt overwhelming, he found solace in the people around him. Hemant understood that resilience wasn't just about internal strength—it was also about leaning on others when necessary. He learned that reaching out for support didn't signify weakness, but rather, it was a powerful way to stay grounded and to find clarity when things seemed uncertain.

Hemant's support system played an instrumental role in his resilience. Family, for instance, offered unwavering emotional support during times of personal struggle, reminding him that his worth wasn't defined by his failures but by his ability to learn and grow from them. His friends provided a sense of camaraderie, allowing him to express his frustrations without fear of judgment. Their empathy and understanding helped him release the burden of trying to handle everything on his own. Through conversations with trusted colleagues, he gained valuable perspective on his professional challenges, which often gave him new insights and fresh approaches to his problems.

Moreover, Hemant recognized the importance of surrounding himself with people who lifted him up—those who believed in his potential even when he didn't believe in himself. Their faith in him was often the spark he needed to keep going, especially when self-doubt crept in. These relationships provided not just emotional comfort but also practical advice, which helped him regain focus and stay motivated during hard times.

Building a support system isn't just about having people to lean on in difficult moments; it's also about actively nurturing these connections. For Hemant, maintaining open lines of communication with his support network was vital. He regularly reached out for feedback, shared his progress, and expressed gratitude for the support he received. This mutual exchange not only helped him stay resilient but also deepened his bonds with those around him.

Additionally, Hemant's support system wasn't limited to just close family or friends. He also understood the value of professional mentors and peers who could offer guidance from an objective standpoint. These mentors helped him reframe challenges and offered practical strategies for overcoming obstacles. By tapping into a broader network of support, Hemant was able to approach problems with a well-rounded perspective, knowing he had a diverse group of people who cared about his success and well-being.

In moments of vulnerability, Hemant learned that it was okay to admit when he was struggling. Vulnerability in these relationships often led to deeper, more meaningful connections and enabled him to gain insights that would have been difficult to reach on his own. He realized that relying on others didn't diminish his own strength; rather, it enhanced his ability to bounce back from setbacks with more resilience.

In times of adversity, building a robust support system is not just a safety net, but a key pillar of emotional well-being. It provides the encouragement and wisdom needed to navigate challenges with resilience. Hemant's story highlights that, while we all have the ability to build resilience within ourselves, there's no harm in leaning on others when we need it most. Surrounding yourself with those who believe in you and support you can help you develop the inner strength to face life's obstacles head-on and emerge stronger on the other side.

Take Small, Consistent Steps

Resilience is not something that is built overnight. It's a process—one that requires patience, commitment, and a series of small but deliberate actions over time. The journey toward resilience is like building a muscle: it grows stronger with consistent, mindful effort, even when progress feels slow. Hemant understood that resilience wasn't about making huge leaps in a short period; rather, it was about showing up every day, taking small steps, and making incremental improvements, no matter how challenging the circumstances.

For Hemant, the key to his transformation lay in his ability to focus on small, manageable actions each day. He didn't wait for a grand moment of change or for everything to align perfectly. Instead, he took one step at a time, knowing that every small effort would compound over time. Whether it was making time for self-care, setting clear intentions for the day, or breaking down a large, overwhelming task into smaller, more achievable actions, Hemant recognized the power of gradual progress.

This approach became especially important during times of personal and professional setbacks when the path forward felt unclear or difficult. When Hemant faced moments of doubt, he focused on what he could do right now, rather than worrying about the future or the long road ahead. It wasn't about solving every problem at once; it was about taking a step, however small, that moved him forward. If it was a challenging day at work, he'd take a few minutes for deep breathing or a short walk to reset his mind. If a personal issue seemed insurmountable, he'd break it down into smaller conversations or actions to make it more manageable. This ability to focus on small victories helped him avoid the overwhelm that often comes with major challenges.

Hemant also understood that building resilience meant being kind to himself. He didn't expect perfection from himself or expect immediate results. On difficult days, when the progress felt slow, he gave himself permission to acknowledge the effort and recognize the courage it took to face the day. This self-compassion played an essential role in his ability to stay consistent, even when the road felt long or the outcomes uncertain.

Small steps also allowed Hemant to confront his fears one at a time. Whether it was facing a difficult conversation, tackling an intimidating project, or challenging his own self-limiting beliefs, Hemant didn't rush into everything at once. Instead, he gradually stepped outside of his comfort zone, taking on challenges in manageable pieces. Each small victory, whether it was completing a task or confronting a fear, built his confidence and prepared him for even greater challenges ahead.

In times of hardship, Hemant found that it was easy to become disheartened when progress wasn't immediate. But by focusing on the daily, incremental steps, he found that progress came naturally, even in the face of setbacks. He embraced the philosophy that resilience is about staying in motion, no matter how small the steps may be. Over time, these small, consistent actions accumulated and resulted in significant growth. Hemant's ability to maintain a steady pace of action—even when the results weren't immediately visible—was one of the factors that helped him build resilience over time.

Consistency was the key. Every day was an opportunity to build resilience, and Hemant embraced each day's challenges as an opportunity to grow. By focusing on what he could control and taking small steps toward his goals, he found that his resilience grew naturally. His journey wasn't about grand transformations; it was about committing to small, daily efforts that gradually shifted his mindset, strengthened his resolve, and ultimately allowed him to bounce back stronger after every setback.

In the end, Hemant's story is a reminder that resilience isn't about dramatic, overnight change. It's about showing up, taking small actions, and trusting that every step counts. Whether it's through practicing self-compassion, setting achievable goals, or facing fears one at a time, these incremental steps can help build a foundation of inner strength that will carry you through the toughest of times. Through consistent effort, the seemingly small steps will eventually lead to great strides forward.

Learn from Setbacks, Don't Dwell on Them

Setbacks are a natural part of life, and no one is immune to them. Whether they come in the form of a missed opportunity, a failed project, or an unexpected personal or professional challenge, setbacks can feel discouraging and disheartening. However, the way we respond to these setbacks has the power to shape our future success. Rather than allowing setbacks to define us or hold us back, we can choose to view them as valuable learning experiences that contribute to our growth.

Hemant's journey was filled with numerous setbacks, but his ability to approach each one with a mindset of learning rather than defeat set him apart. Every challenge became an opportunity for self-reflection and improvement, rather than something to regret or resent. When faced with failure or disappointment, Hemant didn't allow himself to get stuck in negative thoughts or feelings of inadequacy. Instead, he asked himself the crucial question, "What can I learn from this?"

This shift in perspective allowed Hemant to break free from the trap of dwelling on his mistakes. He learned to focus not on the emotional weight of failure, but on the lessons embedded within it. For instance, after a failed business venture, instead of lamenting the financial loss or the perceived "wasted" time, Hemant took stock of what he had learned from the experience—what strategies worked, what didn't, and where he could improve in the future. By approaching setbacks with curiosity and a willingness to learn, Hemant was able to turn each setback into a building block for future success.

This mindset of continuous learning was a cornerstone of Hemant's resilience. He recognized that setbacks didn't mean the end of the road; they were simply detours that provided new insights and perspectives. The ability to ask reflective questions, such as, "How can I do better next time?" and "What did this teach me?" helped him avoid becoming mired in regret. Instead of seeing a setback as a personal failure, Hemant reframed it as a valuable part of his journey—an opportunity to fine-tune his approach, sharpen his skills, and increase his understanding of what was needed to succeed.

This willingness to learn from setbacks, rather than being defeated by them, made Hemant's path to resilience a transformative one. Each mistake or failure became a lesson that fueled his growth. Whether it was reevaluating a decision he made, refining his strategies, or simply gaining a better understanding of his own limits, Hemant used every setback as a stepping stone. He understood that no experience, no matter how difficult, was ever wasted if he could learn from it.

For Hemant, setbacks were also a chance to test his emotional resilience. Rather than reacting impulsively or letting frustration take over, he practiced emotional regulation. This allowed him to step back and analyze the situation objectively, instead of letting negative emotions cloud his judgment. By taking a more measured approach to setbacks, Hemant was able to maintain a sense of control over how he responded, which ultimately helped him grow stronger in the face of adversity.

Additionally, Hemant's ability to learn from setbacks helped him develop a sense of self-compassion. He understood that no one is perfect, and that setbacks didn't make him a failure—they simply made him human. This compassion toward himself allowed him to avoid the paralyzing effects of self-criticism and instead focus on constructive actions that would lead to improvement.

The key takeaway from Hemant's approach is that setbacks are inevitable, but they do not have to define us. How we respond to them is what truly matters. By embracing a mindset of continuous improvement, we can use setbacks as opportunities for growth and self-discovery. This approach doesn't just help us bounce back—it helps us evolve, becoming more resilient, more adaptable, and better equipped to handle future challenges.

In life, setbacks are not the end; they are merely the beginning of a new chapter. By learning from each experience and making it a stepping stone toward progress, we can turn what initially seems like a failure into the foundation of future success. Hemant's ability to extract lessons from his setbacks and apply them to his future endeavors is a powerful reminder that resilience is not about avoiding failure, but about how we choose to learn and grow from it.

Find Purpose in Adversity

Adversity, in all its forms, can often feel like a heavy burden—something that weighs us down and makes it difficult to see beyond the immediate hardship. However, one of the most transformative ways to build resilience is by finding purpose within adversity. By shifting our focus from the pain or difficulty to the meaning behind the experience, we can uncover deeper lessons and find the strength to move forward.

Hemant's journey illustrates the profound impact of finding purpose in the face of hardship. Early on, when faced with personal and professional struggles, he could have easily succumbed to feelings of hopelessness or resentment. The challenges he encountered, from business failures to personal losses, could have defined his future in negative ways. But Hemant chose a different path. Rather than allowing adversity to cripple him, he looked for meaning in every struggle he faced. He realized that hardship wasn't just a test of endurance—it was an opportunity for growth, reflection, and transformation.

One of the most powerful ways Hemant found purpose was by reframing his struggles as opportunities to learn and serve others. After enduring his own setbacks, he shifted his focus to teaching. His struggles became the foundation of his passion for education, and his desire to help others avoid the same pitfalls became his guiding force. Hemant found purpose not only in overcoming his own obstacles but in using his experiences to empower and uplift others. By helping students navigate their own challenges, he found a sense of fulfillment that gave deeper meaning to his journey.

In adversity, Hemant discovered a new layer of his character. It was in the difficult moments, the times when he felt most vulnerable, that he learned about his own resilience and inner strength. Instead of succumbing to self-doubt or frustration, he embraced the discomfort of his situation and allowed it to refine him. Each challenge became an opportunity to deepen his character and develop qualities like patience, empathy, and persistence. These were the traits that would not only help him overcome his difficulties but would also make him a better teacher, mentor, and individual.

Another key aspect of finding purpose in adversity is using hardship as a means to connect with others. Hemant found that by sharing his struggles with those around him—family, friends, and colleagues—he was able to build stronger relationships and create a sense of community. His vulnerability in the face of adversity became a source of inspiration for others, demonstrating that even in the hardest times, it is possible to find strength and purpose. By opening up about his challenges, he connected with people on a deeper level and gained support from those who understood his journey. In this way, adversity became a bridge to greater connection and mutual support.

Additionally, Hemant discovered that by helping others through their own struggles, he was able to find a sense of meaning that transcended his personal challenges. As a teacher, he had the opportunity to share his wisdom and experiences with students who were going through their own difficult times. By providing guidance and encouragement, he was able to turn his own pain into a source of empowerment for others. This process of giving back not only helped him heal but also reminded him of the broader purpose of his life: to contribute to the growth and success of others.

Finding purpose in adversity also involves a shift in how we view our own hardships. Instead of seeing challenges as random or meaningless, Hemant chose to view them as stepping stones that would eventually lead him to a more meaningful life. Every setback became a part of a larger narrative—a journey of self-discovery and contribution. This perspective allowed him to maintain hope and stay focused on the bigger picture, even when the immediate situation felt overwhelming.

Moreover, Hemant realized that through adversity, he was being prepared for something greater. The lessons he learned from his challenges gave him the wisdom and perspective needed to make a deeper impact in the world. His struggles, rather than being obstacles to his success, became the tools he used to make a lasting difference in others' lives. He began to see that the purpose of his life was not just to achieve personal success, but to help others along the way—whether through teaching, mentoring, or simply being a source of support and encouragement.

For those facing their own difficulties, Hemant's story serves as a powerful reminder that adversity does not have to be meaningless. By finding purpose in hardship, we can turn challenges into opportunities for growth, connection, and service to others. When we look for the meaning in our struggles, we tap into a deeper well of strength and resilience, allowing us to overcome even the most difficult circumstances with grace and determination.

In finding purpose, adversity becomes not just something to endure, but a catalyst for transformation. It opens the door to personal growth, greater compassion, and a deeper connection to others. As we navigate the ups and downs of life, let us remember that every challenge, no matter how difficult, carries within it the potential for meaning, growth, and a greater sense of purpose.

Conclusion

Building resilience through adversity is not a quick or easy process, but it is one of the most transformative journeys we can undertake. In life, we are all bound to face challenges—those moments that push us to our limits, make us question ourselves, and sometimes even make us doubt our ability to continue. Yet, it is often in the most difficult of circumstances that we uncover our greatest strength. The very obstacles that seem to stand in our way can, over time, become the stepping stones toward personal growth, wisdom, and resilience.

The act of bouncing back from setbacks is not merely about returning to a previous state of normalcy; it is about transforming our response to adversity. Each setback is an opportunity to learn more about ourselves—our fears, our limits, and our true potential. Through perseverance and a willingness to learn from the process, we are able to turn challenges into powerful lessons. By embracing the discomfort of hardship, we ultimately unlock a deeper understanding of our own resilience and strength. This process of growth and transformation is not linear or predictable, but it is a crucial part of building lasting emotional and mental strength.

Hemant's journey is a perfect example of how resilience can be developed through hardship. His struggles were not merely obstacles to be overcome; they were catalysts for personal growth, providing him with the tools and mindset necessary to continue moving forward. What started as a series of setbacks in his life eventually shaped him into a person capable of embracing adversity with courage and determination. He learned to see each failure as an opportunity for self-improvement and a chance to deepen his character. His journey exemplifies how adversity, when approached with the right mindset, can transform us in ways we never thought possible.

As we move through our own lives, it is important to remember that resilience is not about avoiding life's challenges, nor is it about wishing that adversity would never come our way. Life's challenges are an inevitable part of the human experience, and rather than trying to escape them, we must learn to face them head-on. Resilience is about embracing the struggles that life presents with courage and openness, learning from them, and, through that process, becoming stronger and more capable individuals. The challenges we face are not merely obstacles; they are opportunities for growth and transformation, pushing us to become more than we were before.

The power of resilience lies not just in the ability to survive difficulties, but in our capacity to thrive because of them. By developing the mindset that challenges are not barriers but invitations for growth, we can approach life with a sense of curiosity and purpose, rather than fear or resistance. In doing so, we become more adaptable, more focused, and more attuned to the deeper lessons that each challenge holds. Hemant's story is a testament to this truth, showing that through persistence, reflection, and a willingness to grow, adversity can become the very force that propels us toward a more fulfilling and resilient life.

Chapter 14: The Wisdom of Letting Go

The act of letting go is often perceived as an act of surrender, an admission of defeat, or the relinquishing of control. In truth, it is one of the most powerful tools for **personal transformation** and growth. The paradox is clear: in order to move forward, we must first let go of the things that are no longer serving us—whether it's outdated beliefs, unhelpful attachments, or past identities. The wisdom of letting go lies not in weakness, but in recognizing the truth that sometimes, the **path to the future requires the courage to release the past**.

In this chapter, we explore the profound philosophy behind letting go, how it has played a critical role in Hemant's life, and how it can be a key practice in anyone's personal and professional growth. Hemant's story reveals how the decision to let go of old identities, past successes, and previous versions of himself has allowed him to reinvent his journey time and again. We'll also offer actionable insights for you to begin practicing letting go in your own life, unlocking the power of **new beginnings**.

The Paradox of Letting Go in Order to Move Forward

At first glance, the idea of letting go might seem counterintuitive. After all, we are often taught to hold on tightly to our dreams, our past achievements, and the identities we've built over time. These things give us a sense of security, a way to define ourselves in a world that is constantly changing. Our past accomplishments, career milestones, and even the roles we play in society are what anchor us, providing a foundation of stability. So, why would we be asked to let go of them?

Letting go, in this context, can feel like an incredibly difficult and emotionally charged decision. It's not just about releasing physical possessions, but about relinquishing the very parts of ourselves that we've worked so hard to build. The thought of letting go can make us feel as though we are giving up, losing our footing, or abandoning everything we've worked for. It can feel like a loss, even though it may ultimately be the key to moving forward. However, the deeper paradox lies in the truth that the more tightly we cling to our past, the more we risk stifling our own potential for growth. When we hold on too tightly—whether it's to outdated beliefs, old habits, or past successes—we inadvertently close ourselves off to new opportunities. Like a clenched fist that cannot grasp anything else, our refusal to release the old prevents us from embracing the new.

It's within this paradox that the wisdom lies: in order to move forward, we must first make space by letting go of what no longer serves us. This doesn't mean erasing or disregarding the past—it's about accepting it for what it was, learning from it, and then gently allowing it to take a backseat, making room for new possibilities to emerge. Letting go involves recognizing that while our past shaped us, it does not have to define us. The act of releasing isn't about forgetting; it's about creating the mental and emotional space necessary for fresh experiences and growth to enter our lives.

Hemant's journey beautifully illustrates the transformative power of letting go. Over the years, he has had to release many of the things he once thought were integral to his identity. In his early career, Hemant was deeply rooted in the engineering field. However, when he decided to pursue entrepreneurship, he had to let go of his identity as an engineer and step into an entirely new role. Despite the challenges and the eventual failure of his business, he continued to let go of his past notions of success. He had to release the idea of being a "successful entrepreneur" in the traditional sense and redefine success on his own terms. In each of these transitions, Hemant faced the internal struggle of letting go, yet each time, he found that releasing the old made space for new opportunities and personal growth.

Whether it was stepping away from his previous career, transitioning between business ventures, or even letting go of his attachment to a specific definition of success, Hemant realized that every time he released something from his past, he allowed for more room in his life for what was yet to come. Through each act of release, he unlocked new opportunities for exploration, learning, and reinvention. He was able to redefine who he was, not by holding tightly to past identities or successes, but by embracing change, growth, and the constant evolution of his journey.

It is often in the moments of release that we find the most powerful transformation. Hemant's story reminds us that growth often requires us to shed layers of our former selves, to let go of things that no longer serve us, and to trust that new experiences, perspectives, and opportunities will emerge in their place. Letting go is not an act of surrender, but an act of faith in the process of growth—a belief that when we create space, life will fill it with something even better than we could have imagined.

The act of letting go is not easy, nor is it a one-time decision. It is a continual process of recognizing when we are holding on too tightly and making the conscious choice to release. It's about acknowledging that growth, innovation, and new beginnings often come from creating space, both mentally and emotionally, for what is yet to come. Just like Hemant's journey, when we let go of our attachments to the past, we open ourselves up to the limitless potential of the future.

How Hemant's Ability to Let Go of Old Identities and Past Successes Helped Him Find New Beginnings

Hemant's journey is marked by several key turning points, each involving a conscious decision to release something he had once identified with deeply. These decisions weren't made in moments of desperation or weakness; rather, they were the result of a clear recognition that certain aspects of his life had become limiting, preventing him from evolving into the person he needed to be. His ability to let go, to release the old, created space for new possibilities and opportunities that would have otherwise remained out of reach.

One of the most significant moments in Hemant's life was when he transitioned from a well-established career in industrial engineering to the field of education and coaching. This was not simply a career change—it was a profound shift in identity. Hemant had spent years building a reputation as a skilled industrial engineer. His career was marked by professional success, respect from colleagues, and a sense of stability. At the time, he could have continued down that familiar path, enjoying the fruits of his past hard work and accomplishments. However, Hemant realized that his growing passion for teaching and coaching was no longer aligned with the life he had built in the engineering world. His attachment to the identity of "industrial engineer"—the title, the recognition, the status—was beginning to feel restrictive. It was holding him back from pursuing his true calling.

The decision to let go of this well-established identity was not easy, but it was necessary for his growth. Hemant didn't simply walk away from his job; he also walked away from the version of himself that was tied to that role. This was a key moment in his journey: he let go of the identity of "engineer" and embraced the unknown. This act of releasing his attachment to past successes, the ones he had worked so hard to achieve, allowed him to redefine success in his own terms. It was a leap of faith into a new world, one filled with uncertainty and doubt, but also with new potential and opportunities.

This shift opened the door to a fulfilling career in education and coaching—one that not only aligned with his evolving sense of purpose but also brought him a deeper sense of satisfaction and meaning. Had he remained attached to his previous career and the identity tied to it, he may never have discovered the true impact he could have as a teacher. This wasn't just a job change; it was a fundamental transformation in how he saw himself and his role in the world. The decision to let go of his old identity was a powerful catalyst that propelled him into a more purposeful life.

The next turning point in Hemant's journey came when he faced setbacks in his entrepreneurial ventures. Like many entrepreneurs, he encountered failures that challenged his beliefs about success and his own abilities. It would have been easy for Hemant to let these failures define him, to let them reinforce the belief that he wasn't cut out for entrepreneurship. However, Hemant took a different approach. He chose to let go of the fear of failure and the shame that often accompanies it. Instead of viewing failure as a reflection of his worth, he chose to see it as a valuable lesson. Every failure, every setback, became an opportunity for growth—a chance to learn, adapt, and improve.

Hemant's ability to embrace failure without letting it hold him back was crucial. He didn't allow the weight of past mistakes to define his future. Each failure became a stepping stone, not a roadblock. By letting go of the fear of failure, Hemant was able to move forward with a greater sense of confidence, resilience, and clarity. He learned that failure was not an endpoint; it was merely a part of the process, one that could ultimately lead to greater success. This mindset shift allowed him to keep moving forward, unencumbered by past disappointments.

But it wasn't just about letting go of tangible things, like career roles or business ventures—it was also about releasing outdated mindsets and beliefs. Hemant recognized that, in order to grow, he needed to challenge the deeply ingrained notions of success, failure, and his own worth that had guided him in the past. The idea that success was always linear, that failure was something to be avoided at all costs, and that his value was tied to external achievements—these were beliefs that no longer served him. He had to release these limiting thoughts and embrace a new perspective that allowed him to see the world and his place in it with more flexibility and openness.

Letting go of these old ways of thinking enabled Hemant to fully embrace his evolving purpose. It allowed him to approach each new chapter of his life with an open mind and heart, ready to learn and adapt without being tethered to outdated beliefs. The process of letting go was not a one-time event; it was a continual practice of reassessing what served his growth and what needed to be released. This ongoing process of shedding old identities and outdated beliefs has been essential for Hemant's personal evolution, allowing him to navigate new beginnings with a sense of clarity, purpose, and empowerment.

Ultimately, Hemant's story highlights the power of letting go—not as a form of loss, but as a necessary step toward growth and new beginnings. His ability to release his attachments to old identities, past successes, and limiting beliefs has allowed him to discover and embrace new opportunities that align with his true purpose. This practice of letting go has been instrumental in helping him reinvent himself time and again, proving that sometimes, in order to move forward, we must first create space by letting go of what no longer serves us.

Actionable Insights on How to Practice Letting Go in Your Own Life

Letting go can feel uncomfortable, but it is an essential practice for personal growth and transformation. Here are some actionable insights to help you practice letting go in your own life:

Recognize the Need for Change

The process of letting go begins with the critical step of recognizing that something in your life is no longer serving you. This awareness is often the most challenging part, as it requires a level of honesty with yourself that can be difficult to face. Sometimes, we remain in situations, relationships, or mindsets simply because they are familiar or comfortable. However, staying in these situations can prevent us from reaching our full potential and achieving the personal growth we are capable of. Recognizing the need for change means acknowledging that something in our lives has become stagnant or limiting, and that in order to move forward, we must let go of it.

For Hemant, this realization came at different points in his life, each marked by a sense of inner unrest or dissatisfaction. At one stage, he recognized that his career in industrial engineering, which had once brought him fulfillment and success, was no longer aligning with his evolving passions and goals. Hemant had built a solid foundation in his career, earned recognition, and gained expertise in his field. Yet, he began to feel a sense of emptiness in continuing along the same path. This was not due to failure or dissatisfaction with his work itself, but rather because he had outgrown the role it had played in his life. His passions had shifted towards education, coaching, and helping others grow—realizing this need for change became the catalyst for his decision to transition into a completely different career.

Recognizing the need for change can be an uncomfortable realization because it often requires us to confront the fact that we've outgrown something we once held dear. It may be a job that no longer challenges us, a relationship that drains us, or even a belief system that no longer resonates with who we are becoming. This recognition often comes after a period of reflection, sometimes triggered by an event or a pattern that can no longer be ignored. Hemant's recognition of the need for change was driven by a deep sense of self-awareness—he had come to understand that in order to evolve, he could no longer hold on to old versions of himself or the roles that defined him in the past.

This realization did not come easily. Hemant's decision to let go of his past career wasn't a sudden, rash choice. Instead, it was the result of careful self-reflection and an understanding of his deeper values and long-term goals. He had to ask himself difficult questions: Was he truly fulfilled by his work? Was he using his talents in a way that matched his personal growth and purpose? The answers to these questions led him to acknowledge that staying in his current path was preventing him from pursuing a more meaningful and aligned future. Once he had recognized that his career in engineering no longer served his true aspirations, the process of letting go naturally followed.

This process of recognizing the need for change isn't just about acknowledging external circumstances; it's also about examining internal feelings. Often, we find ourselves in situations that no longer serve us because we are afraid to confront the emotional discomfort that comes with change. Whether it's fear of failure, insecurity, or the discomfort of leaving behind the familiar, these emotions can prevent us from seeing the truth about what we need. However, Hemant's journey shows us that recognizing the need for change requires courage to face these emotions head-on and to allow ourselves to evolve, even when it feels uncertain or risky.

When we recognize the need for change, it's also important to understand that this realization is not a sign of failure—it's a sign of growth. It means that we are becoming more attuned to our inner needs and are willing to make the necessary adjustments in order to align ourselves with our authentic purpose. For Hemant, acknowledging that his old career no longer served him was an empowering act of self-awareness that allowed him to move forward and explore new opportunities.

Recognizing the need for change also involves accepting that change is a continuous process. Hemant's career transitions didn't end with one decision to let go; rather, each stage of his life required a fresh awareness that something had to shift in order for him to continue growing. Whether it was the realization that his business endeavors weren't fulfilling his purpose or the acknowledgment that he needed to let go of limiting beliefs about success, Hemant continually recognized that change was necessary for his development. This ongoing process of self-assessment and adaptation became a foundational aspect of his resilience and ability to reinvent himself over time.

Ultimately, recognizing the need for change is about being willing to listen to yourself—your desires, your inner voice, and the subtle signals your life is sending. It's about understanding that change is a natural part of life's evolution and that, in order to grow and thrive, we must be open to releasing what no longer serves us. Hemant's ability to see the need for change and take action is a testament to his willingness to embrace discomfort in order to unlock new opportunities and directions for his life.

Release Old Beliefs and Identities

Throughout our lives, we often build identities around the roles we play, the titles we carry, and the achievements we accumulate. These identities become the lens through which we view ourselves and the world, offering us a sense of security, belonging, and validation. Whether it's being a "successful professional," a "devoted parent," or a "reliable friend," these identities can provide us with a clear sense of purpose and place in the world. However, as time passes, these identities can become restrictive, preventing us from evolving or adapting to new circumstances and aspirations.

The difficulty of letting go of old identities arises from the deep connection we form with them. They can become so ingrained in our self-concept that the idea of releasing them feels like losing a part of ourselves. We may fear that without these identities, we will no longer be worthy, valuable, or recognized. This fear of change often leads us to cling tightly to these roles, even when they no longer serve our growth or align with our true desires. But the reality is that our identities are not fixed—they are fluid and can evolve with us as we grow.

To practice letting go of old beliefs and identities, the first step is to examine the roles you have taken on throughout your life. Start by reflecting on the various identities you have adopted over time. These could be professional identities like "doctor," "engineer," or "entrepreneur," or personal identities such as "caregiver," "provider," or "leader." Each of these identities may have served a specific purpose at one point in your life, helping you navigate challenges, gain recognition, or fulfill responsibilities. However, as you grow and change, these roles may no longer reflect who you truly are or where you are headed.

Ask yourself: Does the identity I've been holding onto still align with my values, my passions, and my evolving goals? Does it help me become the person I want to be in the future, or is it keeping me stuck in the past? For example, someone who has built their entire career around being an executive may reach a point where they feel unfulfilled or disconnected from their original purpose. The title of "CEO" may no longer excite them, yet they may fear the loss of status or the unknown future. In such a case, recognizing that this identity is no longer serving their growth can open the door to embracing a new identity—perhaps as a mentor, educator, or creative entrepreneur.

The next step in releasing old identities is to give yourself permission to evolve. You are not defined solely by the roles you've played in the past, and letting go of an outdated identity does not diminish your worth. In fact, it can be a courageous act of self-liberation, creating space for you to explore new possibilities and discover the deeper aspects of who you truly are. Hemant, for example, had to release his identity as a successful industrial engineer and entrepreneur in order to step into a new role as an educator and mentor. He realized that his purpose had shifted and that the skills and knowledge he had gained in the past were still valuable—but he needed to let go of the limiting identity that no longer resonated with his true self.

Releasing old identities also requires challenging the beliefs that have been attached to them. Often, the identities we hold are supported by certain beliefs we have about ourselves and the world. For example, the belief that "success" equals financial wealth, power, or societal status might have been ingrained over time through societal pressures or family expectations. These beliefs can create an inner conflict when we desire something different, like a fulfilling career in a creative field, or a simpler, more balanced life. In order to release old identities, we must also examine and reframe the beliefs that support them.

Ask yourself: What beliefs am I holding onto that no longer serve me? Are they based on fear, insecurity, or outdated societal expectations? Letting go of these beliefs can be just as liberating as shedding an old identity. For example, Hemant had to let go of the belief that success only comes from traditional career paths or material achievements. He had to redefine success on his own terms, based on personal fulfillment and the positive impact he could make in the lives of others.

Another key aspect of releasing old identities is embracing the discomfort that comes with change. When you let go of an identity, you might initially feel uncertain or even lost. You may wonder who you are without the roles you've played for so long. This feeling of ambiguity is normal, and it's a natural part of the transition process. However, rather than clinging to the familiar, it's important to lean into this discomfort. It's in this space of uncertainty that new possibilities begin to emerge. It's where you can reinvent yourself and explore new aspects of your personality and purpose.

Remember, you don't have to have all the answers right away. The process of releasing old identities and beliefs is gradual. It's about giving yourself the freedom to experiment with new ways of being and to discover new roles that better align with who you are now. Allow yourself to be open to the journey of reinvention, knowing that with each step forward, you are getting closer to a truer version of yourself.

Letting go of old identities also means forgiving yourself for any guilt or regret that may arise during the process. It's easy to feel as though you've failed by leaving behind a role or belief that you once held dear. But it's important to remember that change is a sign of growth, not failure. Every phase of life serves a purpose, and every identity you've taken on has been valuable in its own right. It's simply time to release it to make room for the next phase of your personal evolution.

Ultimately, releasing old beliefs and identities is an act of self-liberation. It allows you to embrace who you are becoming and to step into new roles and possibilities that align more closely with your evolving purpose. As you let go of outdated versions of yourself, you make space for new opportunities, greater fulfillment, and a life that is truly reflective of your authentic self. Hemant's journey is a testament to the power of letting go—the release of old identities, beliefs, and attachments—that opens the door to new beginnings and allows for deeper personal growth and transformation.

Forgive Yourself and Others

One of the most powerful and often most difficult steps in letting go is the act of forgiveness—both towards ourselves and others. When we carry resentment, regret, or anger from the past, it can weigh us down emotionally and mentally, keeping us trapped in a cycle of hurt and bitterness. These unresolved emotions act as a barrier to personal growth, hindering our ability to move forward and embrace new opportunities. Letting go in this context means forgiving ourselves for our past mistakes and releasing grudges against others who may have hurt us.

Forgiving ourselves is often the hardest part of the equation. We all make mistakes, and at times, we might feel deeply regretful for decisions we've made or actions we've taken that have negatively impacted our lives or the lives of others. It's natural to feel guilty or disappointed in ourselves when things don't go as planned. However, when we cling to these feelings of guilt and regret, we create emotional baggage that drags us down, preventing us from growing and moving forward.

The key to self-forgiveness is to accept that, as humans, we are not perfect. We will make mistakes, but those mistakes do not define who we are or our potential for the future. Forgiveness begins with acknowledging our shortcomings and understanding that we acted based on what we knew or understood at the time. As Hemant experienced in his own journey, there were moments where he felt regretful about decisions made in his past, whether it was related to his career path, business ventures, or personal life. However, he understood that holding onto these regrets would only keep him anchored to the past, preventing him from embracing the opportunities ahead.

Letting go of regret is about viewing mistakes as opportunities for learning rather than as defining moments of failure. Instead of continuously punishing ourselves for what went wrong, we can ask ourselves: *What did this teach me? How can I use this lesson to grow and improve in the future?* Hemant learned to embrace his failures as part of his personal growth. He saw them not as permanent stains on his character, but as stepping stones that helped him evolve into a better version of himself.

On the other hand, forgiving others is equally important in freeing ourselves from emotional weight. Holding onto grudges or resentment toward others can be emotionally exhausting. It's easy to justify anger or hurt, especially when we feel wronged by someone's actions. However, when we hold onto these feelings, we allow the other person's behavior to continue affecting our lives long after the event has passed. The act of forgiveness, in this case, is not about excusing the behavior of others or letting them off the hook—it's about releasing the power that their actions have over our emotional well-being.

For Hemant, forgiving those who had wronged him in the past allowed him to heal emotionally and regain control of his own life. He no longer let their actions dictate his feelings or hold him back from moving forward. Forgiving others allowed him to release the negative energy he had been holding onto, creating space for new relationships and positive experiences.

Forgiveness doesn't necessarily mean reconciliation or forgetting. It means choosing to let go of the anger, resentment, or sadness that is keeping us stuck. It is a conscious decision to release the grip of past wounds so that we can heal and grow. When we forgive others, we free ourselves from the emotional burden of carrying grudges and grievances, which can often manifest in physical or mental stress. Holding onto anger only perpetuates suffering, while forgiveness allows for the restoration of inner peace.

An essential part of this process is understanding that forgiveness is not a one-time event but a continuous practice. There may be moments when old wounds resurface, and we may find ourselves feeling anger or regret again. In these instances, it's important to remind ourselves of the work we've done to let go and to reaffirm our commitment to healing. This ongoing practice of forgiveness, both toward ourselves and others, is a vital step in our personal development journey.

In Hemant's case, his ability to forgive not only allowed him to emotionally detach from his past but also cleared the path for him to embrace his true calling. By releasing past emotional baggage, he made room for new beginnings—fresh opportunities that aligned with his purpose. When we forgive, we open ourselves up to the possibility of new experiences, relationships, and achievements. Forgiveness is ultimately about creating emotional space for healing and renewal.

Forgiving others also helps break the cycle of blame and victimhood, empowering us to take control of our own lives. It is an act of strength rather than weakness. By letting go of resentment and embracing forgiveness, we choose to take ownership of our own happiness and peace, instead of allowing past hurts to continue affecting our emotional state.

When we forgive, we take back our power. We allow ourselves to move forward, undistracted by the emotional chains of the past. The process may not always be easy, and it may take time, but with each act of forgiveness—whether it's forgiving ourselves or others—we move closer to a state of emotional freedom, healing, and personal growth.

In essence, forgiveness is an essential part of letting go. It is the key to breaking free from the emotional baggage that can keep us stuck in a cycle of negativity. It provides us with the emotional clarity and space to embrace new opportunities, cultivate meaningful relationships, and live a life aligned with our evolving purpose. Just as Hemant's ability to forgive both himself and others played a pivotal role in his journey, so too can forgiveness be the catalyst for transformation in our own lives. It's not just about moving on—it's about creating the emotional freedom necessary for personal growth, healing, and the emergence of new possibilities.

Embrace Uncertainty

One of the most challenging aspects of letting go is the need to embrace uncertainty. For many, uncertainty can be uncomfortable, even terrifying. We live in a world that often values predictability, control, and stability, and letting go of something familiar—whether it's a job, a relationship, or an old belief system—can feel like stepping into a void. The idea of releasing the known and stepping into the unknown may initially seem like a leap of faith, but it is precisely this willingness to face uncertainty that often leads to profound growth and transformation.

When we hold onto the familiar, we do so because it feels safe. The comfort of the known provides a sense of security, a feeling that we are in control of our circumstances. However, by remaining attached to what we know, we limit ourselves to the possibilities that are already within our grasp, closing ourselves off from the potential of something greater, something new. Growth doesn't happen in the comfort zone. It happens when we step outside the boundaries of the familiar and enter the unknown. Embracing uncertainty means allowing ourselves to venture into new territory, where there are no guarantees, but where there is also the potential for infinite possibilities.

Hemant's journey exemplifies this principle. Throughout his life, he faced many situations that required him to step into the unknown, often without a clear map of what the future would hold. Whether it was transitioning from a successful career in industrial engineering to the world of teaching and coaching, or starting new ventures in business, Hemant consistently demonstrated a willingness to embrace uncertainty. Each time he did, he encountered challenges, but he also discovered new opportunities and paths that he would have never found had he clung to the familiar.

Embracing uncertainty is not about being reckless or abandoning caution; it's about accepting that change is an inherent part of life and that, without change, there can be no growth. It's about trusting that even though the future may be unclear, it holds immense potential for new beginnings. The process of change is often messy and unpredictable, but it's in that uncertainty that we find the space for creativity, innovation, and reinvention.

Many times, we are paralyzed by the fear of the unknown. We worry about making the wrong decision, about failing, or about encountering obstacles we can't overcome. However, it's important to recognize that uncertainty doesn't equate to failure. It's a natural part of the process of growth. In fact, it's often the very act of embracing uncertainty that allows us to discover our true potential. It's through uncertainty that we build resilience, learn new skills, and develop the strength to overcome challenges we may never have imagined.

Hemant's ability to embrace uncertainty was a cornerstone of his reinvention. He didn't allow the fear of what he didn't know to prevent him from pursuing what he felt was right. Instead, he saw uncertainty as an opportunity for personal and professional growth. His willingness to step into unfamiliar territory allowed him to redefine success on his own terms, pursue a career that aligned with his passions, and ultimately create a life that was more fulfilling and meaningful.

The key to embracing uncertainty lies in cultivating a mindset that views change as an opportunity rather than a threat. When we view uncertainty with curiosity and openness, we allow ourselves to experience the richness of life's possibilities. Change can be daunting, but it also holds the potential for self-discovery, reinvention, and new beginnings. We are not defined by our past experiences or the identities we have built around them. We are constantly evolving, and each new chapter in our lives offers the opportunity to learn, grow, and transform.

To embrace uncertainty, we must first let go of the need for control. We cannot control every outcome or predict every twist and turn of life. However, we can control how we respond to the challenges and changes that come our way. By adopting a mindset of resilience and adaptability, we can navigate the unknown with confidence and grace. It's important to recognize that, even in moments of doubt or fear, we have the power to choose how we react to uncertainty. Instead of resisting change, we can lean into it, trusting that it will guide us to new experiences and opportunities.

Hemant's journey is a testament to the power of embracing uncertainty. He could have stayed in the safe, predictable world of industrial engineering, but instead, he chose to venture into the unknown, even when the future was uncertain. This decision allowed him to discover his true calling, build a successful career in teaching and coaching, and ultimately find greater fulfillment.

In our own lives, embracing uncertainty is a powerful tool for reinvention. It opens the door to new opportunities, new ways of thinking, and new ways of being. By letting go of the need for certainty and control, we make space for the unknown to reveal its potential. As we embrace the uncertainty of life, we not only grow as individuals, but we also create the conditions for new beginnings to unfold. The future may be unclear, but it is also full of endless possibilities—waiting for us to step into it with courage, curiosity, and an open heart.

Create Rituals of Release

Letting go can often feel like an overwhelming and emotional experience, but it doesn't always need to be a grand or dramatic gesture. Sometimes, small and simple actions can help us symbolize the process of release and make it more tangible. Rituals of release offer us a way to mark the act of letting go, making it feel more intentional and meaningful. These rituals can be especially helpful when we are releasing emotional baggage, old beliefs, or attachments to past identities that no longer serve our growth.

One of the most powerful ways to create a ritual of release is to physically symbolize the act of letting go. A simple yet effective practice could be to write down the things you wish to release—whether they are negative emotions, regrets, limiting beliefs, or attachments to old successes—and then physically discard the paper. This act of writing down your thoughts helps you externalize what you have been holding onto mentally or emotionally, making it easier to confront and release them. Once the paper is discarded—perhaps by burning it, tearing it up, or simply throwing it away—it serves as a symbolic gesture of shedding the old, allowing space for something new to emerge.

This ritual doesn't need to be elaborate; the power lies in the intention behind it. By actively performing this symbolic act, you create a sense of closure and give yourself permission to move on from what no longer serves you. It's like cleaning out a closet full of clothes that no longer fit or no longer reflect who you are today. Each item you let go of creates room for new possibilities. It's a way of saying goodbye to the past while embracing the potential of the future.

Another way to create a ritual of release could involve physical movements or gestures that represent letting go. For example, standing outside and allowing yourself to breathe deeply, envisioning the release of negative emotions with each exhale, can help you release the tension and stress associated with your attachments. You could also create a visual representation of your attachment—such as drawing or creating an object that represents what you wish to let go of—and then consciously destroy or alter it as an act of freeing yourself. This can be a therapeutic process that enables you to release your emotional grip on what no longer serves you.

For some, rituals of release may involve ritualized activities such as meditative practices, prayers, or affirmations. These acts can help center the mind, bringing focus to the intention of release and helping you let go of the attachment. For example, you might use visualization techniques in which you imagine the things you wish to release as clouds drifting away or as heavy weights being lifted from your shoulders. By using mindfulness and intention, you can make the process of letting go a conscious and deliberate action rather than something that feels forced or reactive.

Rituals of release can also be tied to significant milestones or life transitions, such as the ending of a relationship, a career change, or the closing of a chapter in your life. These moments can serve as natural opportunities for reflection, where you look back on what you've learned and identify what you want to release in order to move forward. Holding a small ceremony or ritual that marks the end of one phase and the beginning of another can provide a sense of closure, peace, and renewal.

In Hemant's journey, creating personal rituals of release played a crucial role in his ability to let go of past identities and find new beginnings. Every time he made a significant transition—whether in his career or his personal life—he took time to reflect, release old beliefs, and symbolically let go of attachments. This process wasn't always immediate or easy, but it was essential in helping him create space for new opportunities and personal growth.

Rituals of release are not just about the act of letting go but also about honoring the process of change. It's a way to acknowledge that certain things, people, or phases of our lives have served their purpose and that it's time to move forward. By creating a personal ritual, we actively take control of our journey, making the process of release feel intentional rather than passive. These rituals act as a way of clearing away what is no longer needed, so we can step into the future with a renewed sense of purpose, clarity, and readiness for what's next.

These small rituals can have a powerful impact on our emotional and mental well-being. By taking the time to consciously release what holds us back, we create space to grow, heal, and embrace new opportunities. Each ritual acts as a reminder that change is not something to fear, but something to be embraced. It is a symbol of your willingness to transform, adapt, and move forward with intention. Through these small yet meaningful actions, we can continuously shed the old, make room for the new, and stay open to the possibilities that lie ahead.

Focus on the Present

A powerful component of letting go is the ability to live in the present moment, fully embracing what is happening now, without being weighed down by the past or consumed by the uncertainty of the future. In today's fast-paced, hyper-connected world, we often find ourselves caught up in a constant cycle of thinking about what has already happened or worrying about what might happen next. These thoughts can create an emotional burden, preventing us from truly engaging with the present. Learning to focus on the present, however, is one of the most effective ways to release these attachments and find peace.

When we dwell on past mistakes, regrets, or unresolved issues, we carry that emotional weight into our current experiences, limiting our ability to move forward. Likewise, focusing too much on the future creates a sense of anxiety and fear of the unknown, leaving us paralyzed by what could happen. The key to letting go, then, lies in shifting our attention to the here and now—acknowledging that the present is the only time we truly have control over.

Focusing on the present moment doesn't mean ignoring the past or being oblivious to the future—it means making a conscious decision to not let them dominate our mental and emotional states. The past has already happened, and the future is full of uncertainties that cannot be predicted. By letting go of the need to control or regret either of these, we allow ourselves to experience the richness of the present, which is where real change and growth occur.

For Hemant, focusing on the present moment was a transformative practice that helped him release the emotional baggage of his past and stop worrying about future uncertainties. In his career transitions, he could have easily been overwhelmed by thoughts of his previous successes as an engineer or the fears of starting anew in teaching and coaching. However, Hemant found peace by dedicating his energy to the work he was doing right then. He embraced his current purpose, channeling his focus on what he could contribute in the present, rather than feeling weighed down by past accomplishments or anxious about what might come.

One way to cultivate present-moment awareness is through mindfulness practices. Mindfulness involves paying full attention to your thoughts, feelings, and sensations in the present moment without judgment. This practice helps you become more aware of how often your mind drifts to the past or future, and it empowers you to gently redirect your attention back to the here and now. Whether through meditation, mindful breathing, or simple moments of reflection, mindfulness allows you to create a sense of presence that calms the mind and alleviates stress.

Another way to focus on the present is by embracing the activities and people around you. When you're engaging in a task, whether it's working, spending time with loved ones, or even enjoying a hobby, immerse yourself fully in that activity. Instead of thinking about what's next on your to-do list or rehashing past experiences, give your full attention to the experience at hand. This approach helps you feel more grounded and connected to what you're doing in the moment, providing a sense of fulfillment and clarity.

Living in the present also involves recognizing that the moment you're in is all you truly have. When you focus on the here and now, you become more conscious of the opportunities that exist in each moment. Instead of wasting time wishing things were different or fearing what's to come, you become more open to embracing the experiences and lessons that are unfolding in front of you.

For Hemant, this meant releasing the desire to fix everything or control every outcome. He began to understand that progress isn't about worrying over every step or clinging to the past, but about showing up and doing your best in the present. This perspective helped him not only overcome setbacks but also find joy and meaning in the work he was doing. As he moved forward in his new career, Hemant recognized that each day was an opportunity to learn, grow, and contribute, and he found fulfillment by living in the present rather than allowing past fears or future uncertainties to dictate his actions.

Letting go and focusing on the present also allows you to build a more resilient mindset. When you're not caught up in past regrets or future anxieties, you free up mental and emotional energy that can be better used for growth, creativity, and problem-solving. In this way, you become more adaptable, able to respond to challenges as they arise, rather than being paralyzed by what has been or what might be.

In summary, focusing on the present is a powerful tool for letting go of what no longer serves you. By living in the now, you can release the weight of past burdens and stop worrying about the future. This allows you to create a space for new opportunities, deeper connections, and a more fulfilling life. Hemant's journey highlights how, by centering attention on his current purpose, he was able to release the hold that past identities and future fears had on him. He embraced each moment with clarity and intention, which empowered him to make the most of every opportunity that came his way. By focusing on the present, you, too, can begin to let go of what's holding you back and step into a life full of new possibilities.

Accept that Letting Go is a Continuous Process

Letting go is not a one-time act or a single decision; it is an ongoing process that evolves throughout your life. While certain moments may mark significant releases, such as leaving behind a career, a relationship, or an outdated belief system, the true nature of letting go is that it requires continuous awareness and willingness to release what no longer serves you. Each phase of life presents new challenges, attachments, and patterns that need to be addressed, and as you grow, the process of letting go deepens.

In the beginning, the idea of letting go may seem like a discrete action, something you do once and then move on. However, as you journey through life, you come to realize that attachments—whether they are to people, possessions, habits, or identities—are not static. They evolve, they change, and they shift based on your personal growth and the different stages of your life. What was once vital to your sense of self and purpose might no longer fit as your goals, values, and circumstances change.

Therefore, letting go must be seen as an ongoing process, a continual practice of self-awareness and reflection. Each time you reach a new level of personal growth, you will find that you need to let go of something in order to make room for the next chapter of your life. This can be challenging, as it often involves confronting parts of yourself or your life that you've deeply identified with. But it is through this continuous practice of letting go that you make space for transformation, renewal, and deeper fulfillment.

Hemant's journey is a powerful example of this continuous process of letting go. Over the course of his life, he has had to repeatedly shed old identities and attachments in order to grow. When he moved away from a stable and successful career in industrial engineering to pursue coaching and teaching, he didn't see that transition as a one-time act. It was a shift in perspective that required him to let go of the identity he had spent years building. He had to let go of the title, the reputation, and the lifestyle associated with his engineering career, but that wasn't the end of the story. As he grew in his new career, he had to continue letting go of the comfort of established success, the fear of failure, and the pressure of meeting others' expectations.

Hemant's ability to embrace change, step into new challenges, and let go of old identities again and again opened up space for him to grow in ways he never could have imagined. He let go of limiting beliefs that might have kept him stuck, as well as material possessions and relationships that no longer aligned with his evolving purpose. And with each release, he gained the freedom to pursue new opportunities and deepen his understanding of himself and his role in the world.

Letting go is not always easy. It often involves difficult emotions, a sense of loss, and a temporary feeling of uncertainty. But this process is necessary for your evolution. Just as the seasons change and nature sheds old leaves to make way for new growth, you, too, must release what no longer serves you to allow your personal growth to flourish.

To truly embrace the idea of letting go as a continuous process, it is essential to cultivate the habit of regularly checking in with yourself. Ask yourself: *What no longer aligns with my goals? What attachments am I holding onto that are holding me back? Are there any beliefs or fears that are no longer relevant to the person I am becoming?* This self-reflection allows you to be aware of when it's time to release something in order to make space for something new. It may be an attachment to a certain way of thinking, an outdated version of yourself, or a past success that no longer serves your current purpose.

This process of regularly letting go also involves being patient and compassionate with yourself. It's natural to resist change, especially when it comes to long-held beliefs or identities. But just as you wouldn't expect a tree to grow all at once or a butterfly to emerge without a process of transformation, you must understand that letting go takes time. You may need to release things in layers, allowing yourself the space to process and adjust with each phase of release. Some things may require more time than others, and that's okay. What matters is that you stay committed to the ongoing process of letting go.

Hemant's story teaches us that this process doesn't stop at any single moment; it continues to unfold as you evolve and reach new milestones in life. The more Hemant let go, the more freedom he found to explore new opportunities, to deepen his impact on others, and to continue growing personally and professionally. Each act of release was a step toward a more fulfilling and meaningful life.

Letting go also means accepting that nothing in life is permanent, and change is inevitable. Rather than fearing it, you learn to embrace it as an opportunity for growth. The more you practice letting go, the easier it becomes to navigate the inevitable transitions and challenges of life with grace and resilience.

Ultimately, letting go is not just about release, but about creating space. It's about making room for new experiences, new ways of thinking, and new opportunities that can enrich your life. It's about becoming more aligned with who you are becoming, not just who you have been. By accepting that letting go is a continuous process, you can allow yourself the freedom to evolve, the courage to embrace new possibilities, and the wisdom to recognize when it's time to release what no longer serves you.

In summary, letting go is not a single act but a lifelong journey of releasing attachments, beliefs, and identities that no longer align with your purpose and growth. Hemant's experience shows us that each release opens up space for new beginnings, growth, and opportunities. By committing to this ongoing process, you can live a more authentic, fulfilled, and evolving life, knowing that each step you take towards letting go brings you closer to becoming the person you are meant to be.

Conclusion

The wisdom of letting go is deeply intertwined with the philosophy of keeping your bags packed—being ever-ready to release what no longer serves your growth and stepping forward with openness, courage, and clarity. Life is an ongoing journey of transformation, and just as a traveler must occasionally discard old baggage to lighten their load, we too must be willing to shed the outdated, the limiting, and the unnecessary in order to move forward more freely. Hemant's journey illustrates this profound truth, showing us that letting go is not an act of defeat or loss, but a powerful, intentional choice that enables us to step into new possibilities.

When Hemant transitioned from industrial engineering to coaching and education, he demonstrated the strength of recognizing when an old identity no longer aligned with his evolving purpose. He didn't view his departure from the past as a failure; instead, he saw it as an opportunity to make room for a career that felt more authentic and meaningful. This willingness to release what he had outgrown allowed him to open the door to a fulfilling new chapter in his life. His story is a testament to the fact that sometimes, the best way forward is by letting go of the old, even when it feels comfortable or familiar.

Letting go is not about erasing the past or abandoning everything that once held meaning; rather, it is about making room for new growth, new ideas, and new relationships. Just as Hemant's decision to leave behind his former professional life was not about discarding his experiences but about creating space for something deeper, we too must recognize that releasing attachments—whether to a job, a relationship, a belief, or a past failure—is ultimately an act of empowerment. It is about freeing ourselves from the constraints of the past so that we can move toward a future that resonates more fully with our true selves.

As you reflect on your own life, consider how the wisdom of letting go can play a pivotal role in your own transformation. Letting go does not mean losing something important; it means gaining the freedom and clarity to pursue what truly matters. It allows you to move beyond fear, guilt, or resentment and to embrace new opportunities with a sense of purpose. When you let go, you make room for healing, growth, and new opportunities that are in alignment with your authentic self.

Letting go also offers you the chance to transform past wounds into valuable lessons. Hemant's ability to view failure not as an endpoint but as a learning experience allowed him to embrace setbacks and turn them into stepping stones toward greater success. Similarly, when we let go of the emotional baggage that weighs us down—be it regret, fear, or resentment—we create space for healing and growth. It is through this process of release that we can truly transform our past experiences and use them to fuel our future progress.

Furthermore, letting go empowers you to create a future that aligns with your true purpose. The act of releasing old identities, beliefs, and attachments is not just about clearing the past; it is about crafting a vision for the future that reflects who you are becoming. When you let go of limiting ideas and outdated expectations, you free yourself to dream bigger, think more creatively, and live more authentically. Letting go allows you to create a life that is truly aligned with your values, passions, and aspirations.

In summary, the wisdom of letting go is essential for personal growth and transformation. By adopting a mindset that views letting go as an empowering choice—one that creates space for new beginnings, fresh opportunities, and a future aligned with your true purpose—you can cultivate the courage and clarity needed to move forward. Hemant's story is a reminder that letting go is not a sign of weakness but a declaration of your readiness for the next phase of your journey. It is through releasing the old that you make room for the new, and it is by embracing this process with openness and strength that you can create a future that is truly fulfilling.

As you embrace the act of letting go, trust that the best is yet to come. Each release creates space for new possibilities to emerge, and each step forward brings you closer to the life you are meant to lead. With every act of release, you unlock the potential for growth, healing, and transformation that can lead you to a more meaningful, authentic, and purposeful life.

Chapter 15: Living with the Bags Packed

The journey we've explored in this book has been a profound one, from understanding the power of adaptability and readiness for change, to embracing uncertainty, non-attachment, and resilience. Now, we reach the culmination of this exploration—the philosophy of **Living with the Bags Packed**.

Living with your **bags packed** is not about constantly preparing for a specific future event or having one foot out the door. It's about embracing a mindset of **flexibility, readiness, and openness** in every moment. It's the art of being prepared for change, while simultaneously being deeply connected to the present. It's living with the understanding that life is always in motion, and your bags are packed not because you're leaving, but because you are **always ready** for whatever comes next.

In this chapter, we'll examine how **Hemant** has internalized the philosophy of living with the bags packed throughout his journey. We'll reflect on how this philosophy has shaped his experiences, decisions, and outlook on life. Moreover, we'll explore the **core principles** that define this lifestyle and provide actionable steps to help you incorporate them into your daily existence.

The Culmination of the Philosophy of "Keeping Bags Packed" as a Lifestyle

Throughout this book, we've explored the profound power of the "keeping bags packed" philosophy, not as a literal practice, but as a mental, emotional, and philosophical approach to life. The concept extends far beyond the idea of physical bags; it symbolizes the mental and emotional preparedness we cultivate in our daily lives as we navigate the inevitable changes, challenges, and transitions that life brings. It's about fostering a mindset that allows us to be flexible, open, and resilient in the face of the unknown, whether that involves a new job, a shift in personal circumstances, a change in relationships, or stepping into an entirely new chapter of our life.

At its core, the "bags packed" philosophy speaks to the importance of being ready for change—not in a state of panic or anxiety, but in a way that allows us to embrace new opportunities and challenges with grace, confidence, and ease. It's not about anticipating change with fear, but rather with a quiet readiness, understanding that change is a natural part of life. The philosophy encourages us to approach life with a mindset that is both grounded and adaptable. While we remain rooted in the present moment, we also hold a sense of readiness for what comes next, without becoming attached to past experiences or overly anxious about the future.

Living with "your bags packed" means being fully present in each moment, equipped to handle whatever life throws your way. It means not being weighed down by what has already passed, nor obsessing over the uncertainties of tomorrow. Instead, it's about recognizing that each day offers a new opportunity for growth and learning, and that we must remain mentally and emotionally agile to fully embrace these opportunities. By keeping our emotional and mental "bags packed," we create space for ourselves to move freely, make conscious decisions, and adapt to the ever-evolving circumstances of life.

Hemant's journey serves as a vivid illustration of how this philosophy can transform the way we approach life. From his career transitions to his personal challenges, Hemant consistently demonstrated the principles of living with his bags metaphorically packed. Each reinvention, each shift in direction, was approached not with fear or hesitation, but with an inner readiness to embrace whatever came next. His journey didn't involve a constant state of motion; rather, it involved an ongoing process of adapting to new circumstances and allowing his mindset to evolve in response to the changing landscape of his life.

For Hemant, living with his "bags packed" meant being prepared for change, not as an indication of instability or lack of direction, but as a sign of openness and resilience. When he made significant transitions—whether moving from industrial engineering to coaching or shifting careers after facing business setbacks—he did so with the understanding that each change was an opportunity for personal and professional growth. His ability to adapt, learn, and thrive in new environments stemmed from his ability to remain mentally and emotionally prepared for anything that came his way.

The "keeping bags packed" philosophy does not imply that we must be in a constant state of motion or that we should always be looking for the next big opportunity. It is not about being restless or constantly searching for change for the sake of change. Instead, it's about being ready to embrace the next step when the time is right, without being bogged down by past attachments or the fear of future uncertainty. It's about knowing that life is a series of transitions, and that each transition is an opportunity for growth and self-discovery.

By adopting this philosophy, we begin to see that life's twists and turns are not disruptions, but invitations to evolve. The key to thriving in these transitions lies not in resisting change, but in cultivating a mindset of openness and readiness. When our "bags are packed," we have the emotional space to let go of what no longer serves us, the mental clarity to make bold decisions, and the resilience to face the unknown without fear or hesitation.

Living with your bags packed means understanding that growth often requires leaving behind the comfort of the known, and being willing to step into the unfamiliar with confidence and grace. It doesn't mean running away from what's familiar, but rather having the wisdom to recognize when it's time to move on to something new. Hemant's journey is proof that this mindset doesn't just help us navigate life's inevitable changes—it enables us to thrive in the face of them. By staying grounded yet flexible, prepared yet open, we create the space to live a life that is in alignment with our evolving purpose.

In conclusion, the philosophy of "keeping bags packed" as a lifestyle is about more than just being ready for change—it's about adopting a mindset that embraces change as a natural, enriching part of life. It's about remaining rooted in the present while also being emotionally and mentally prepared to step into new possibilities. This philosophy empowers us to live life with intention, purpose, and an open heart, knowing that every transition is an opportunity to grow, evolve, and create a life that aligns with our truest selves.

Hemant's Reflections on How the Philosophy Shaped His Journey and Continues to Guide Him

As Hemant reflects on his life's journey, the philosophy of "keeping his bags packed" has been a cornerstone of his personal and professional transformation. He views it not just as a metaphor but as a living principle that has shaped how he approaches challenges, decisions, and growth. In his own words, "Life is an ongoing journey of reinvention. Every time I reached a crossroads, I realized that the real challenge was not in facing what lay ahead, but in the ability to release what was behind me."

This recognition of the importance of releasing attachments to the past has been the key to his success in navigating the many transitions he has experienced. Hemant's path is a testament to the power of reinvention—moving from a successful technical career in industrial engineering to becoming a mentor, coach, and educator. Each new role was not a detour but a natural progression, guided by his willingness to let go of old identities and embrace new ones. Whether stepping away from business ventures that no longer served him or redefining his version of success, Hemant has consistently demonstrated that the act of "keeping his bags packed" is not about being aimless or restless but about being prepared for the unknown.

One of the most profound lessons Hemant has learned over the years is that "keeping your bags packed" is not a sign of instability or indecision, but rather an expression of deep faith in the flow of life. It is about trusting that life's unpredictable twists and turns are not roadblocks but opportunities for growth and self-discovery. When you're mentally and emotionally ready to release what no longer serves you, it frees up the space to welcome the new. Hemant understands that this mental readiness does not come from a place of fear, but from an innate confidence that, no matter what challenges lie ahead, he has the tools, wisdom, and adaptability to navigate them.

His journey is one of continual adaptation and openness to change, which he believes is essential for both personal and professional growth. Hemant's commitment to "keeping his bags packed" means that he does not become overly attached to any one phase of his life. When opportunities arise, whether they are career shifts, new business ideas, or challenges in personal relationships, he is ready to engage with them fully, without the emotional weight of the past holding him back. This philosophy has helped him evolve not only as an individual but also as a mentor and guide to others.

As Hemant shares with his students, "The world is constantly changing, and you must be willing to unpack and repack your bags—shed your outdated beliefs, and be open to new knowledge and experiences. Only then can you truly grow." Through his own experiences, he teaches that transformation is a necessary part of life, but it requires the courage to step into the unknown and leave behind the comforts of the past. Each chapter of his life has been defined by the willingness to let go and embrace the next phase of his journey, even when it seemed uncertain or intimidating. His story is not just one of personal success but also of the power of embracing change with an open heart and mind.

Hemant's ability to adapt and thrive through multiple reinventions—first from engineer to educator, then from educator to coach—has shown him that change is inevitable and constant. What matters most, however, is how we approach change. It's about having the mental flexibility to navigate new challenges with curiosity and resilience. Through the years, he's cultivated an understanding that life is not a straight path but a series of opportunities for growth, and with each transition, he has learned to trust the process, knowing that he is always prepared for the next phase of his evolution.

His reflections also highlight the ongoing nature of growth. "Keeping your bags packed" is not just about preparing for the next big transition; it's about remaining present in the moment and cultivating an openness to the unknown that keeps the process of learning and evolving active. Hemant has found that every new experience—whether personal, professional, or educational—offers the opportunity to repack his metaphorical bags. He has learned to let go of beliefs, practices, and goals that no longer serve his current purpose, and in doing so, he makes space for new ideas, new people, and new opportunities that align with his evolving self.

Through this continuous process of unpacking and repacking, Hemant has discovered that the real key to growth is not just about letting go of the past, but also about being willing to change your mindset, beliefs, and actions when necessary. It is this willingness to shed the old and embrace the new that enables him to keep evolving in both his personal and professional life. By embracing change as a constant companion, Hemant teaches that we can live more intentionally, moving forward with clarity, adaptability, and confidence.

His journey continues to be shaped by this philosophy. Hemant remains committed to living with his "bags packed"—to continue learning, growing, and evolving. His story serves as a powerful reminder that no matter where we are on our path, the ability to adapt and embrace change is essential to moving forward. Whether facing uncertainty or stepping into new roles, we can all benefit from the mindset that our "bags are packed," and we are always ready for the next chapter in our journey.

In the end, Hemant's story is not just about his own reinvention but about the way he has used his experiences to inspire others. As a mentor, he encourages his students and those around him to adopt this philosophy, teaching them that success is not a static state but an ongoing process of growth and change. By embracing the idea of "keeping your bags packed," we can all learn to navigate life's transitions with resilience, openness, and a deep belief in our ability to adapt and thrive.

Core Principles and Actionable Steps to Live with Your "Bags Packed" Every Day

To live with your bags packed is a dynamic and ongoing practice. It's a lifestyle that keeps you **mentally agile**, emotionally resilient, and spiritually grounded. The following are core principles, along with practical steps, to help you adopt this philosophy in your own life:

Stay Open to Change:

The first and most fundamental step to truly living with your bags packed is accepting that change is not just inevitable, but necessary for growth. Life is in a constant state of flux, and it continuously presents us with opportunities to evolve—whether in our careers, relationships, or personal development. To make the most of these opportunities, we must be open to change and willing to embrace it with an open heart and mind. When we resist change, we limit our potential and remain stuck in old patterns that no longer serve us.

One of the core challenges in life is our attachment to the familiar. We often hold on to things—whether they are physical possessions, relationships, or even outdated beliefs—because they provide a sense of comfort, security, or control. However, the truth is that nothing in life remains static. Change is the only constant, and as much as we might try to hold on to what we know, life will continue to move forward, with or without our consent. Therefore, it becomes essential to develop the ability to let go of attachments that no longer align with who we are becoming or where we are going.

Living with your bags packed means recognizing that change isn't something to fear but rather something to anticipate and welcome. Just as a traveler prepares for a new journey by packing and adjusting their mindset to the unfamiliar terrain ahead, we, too, must prepare ourselves for the adventures that await us. Each transition, whether it's a new job, a shift in a relationship, or a change in our belief system, is an opportunity to reinvent ourselves and expand our horizons.

Start by identifying areas in your life where you may be holding on too tightly. These could be things that once served you but now feel limiting or stagnant. Perhaps it's a job that no longer excites you or a relationship that has outlived its purpose. Maybe it's a belief system that's no longer in alignment with who you are today. Acknowledging where you're holding on tightly is the first step to releasing those attachments. The more we resist change, the more we delay our potential for growth. But the moment we allow ourselves to open up to new possibilities, we begin to create space for new opportunities to flow into our lives.

Actionable Step: Practice Mindfulness Each Day

To cultivate an open mindset towards change, it's essential to practice mindfulness. This involves slowing down and reflecting on the present moment, without judgment or resistance. Spend a few minutes each day in quiet reflection, tuning into your thoughts, feelings, and experiences. Ask yourself: *What am I holding on to, and how can I embrace change instead of resisting it?*

In this reflective space, allow yourself to feel whatever emotions arise but do not get attached to them. See them as transient experiences rather than permanent fixtures. By developing a practice of mindfulness, you train yourself to become more aware of your attachments and patterns, allowing you to shift them when necessary. It's also a way to become aware of the opportunities for change that are already present in your life. Often, we miss these opportunities because we are too focused on what we've already done or what we think we should do.

By practicing mindfulness, you can begin to identify areas where you're resisting change and where you might be able to let go. Whether it's through letting go of outdated habits, shedding unnecessary material possessions, or releasing old ways of thinking, each small step in releasing what no longer serves you brings you closer to the freedom of living with your bags packed—ready for the next chapter of growth and transformation.

Remember that life is not a destination but a journey, and in this journey, change is your constant companion. Embracing it wholeheartedly allows you to experience life's fullness and empowers you to live in alignment with your truest self, always ready for the next phase.

Develop Mental Flexibility:

One of the most powerful tools we can develop in life is mental flexibility. This trait is essential for not only navigating the uncertainties of life but also for thriving in the face of change. Mental flexibility allows us to adapt to new circumstances, pivot when necessary, and open ourselves up to new possibilities. Without it, we can become stuck in rigid ways of thinking that limit our potential and close us off to opportunities that might otherwise enhance our lives.

When we approach life with rigidity, whether it's in our beliefs, career expectations, or even daily routines, we start to see the world in black-and-white terms, failing to appreciate the nuances and infinite possibilities that exist in the gray areas. Hemant's ability to move seamlessly from one career to another, constantly reinventing himself, is a testament to the power of mental flexibility. It wasn't simply his technical skills or expertise that allowed him to transition—it was his mindset. Hemant understood that challenges and setbacks were not barriers, but opportunities to learn, grow, and explore new horizons.

Having a flexible mind means being able to shift perspectives when things don't go according to plan, to challenge existing assumptions, and to see obstacles as stepping stones. This is a mindset that embraces change as a natural part of life rather than something to fear. When we are flexible, we give ourselves the space to explore alternatives and innovate, making room for growth and new experiences.

Actionable Step: Cultivate Curiosity and Seek to Understand Different Perspectives

To develop mental flexibility, we must consciously cultivate curiosity and a desire to understand different perspectives. This can start with small, everyday actions—such as asking yourself, *What if there's another way to view this situation?* or *What can I learn from someone with a completely different perspective than mine?* By fostering curiosity, we remain open to ideas and viewpoints that may challenge our existing beliefs, which is essential for developing a more adaptable, flexible mindset.

An excellent way to expand your mental flexibility is by actively seeking out new learning experiences. Dedicate time each day to exploring something new. This could be reading a book on a subject you're unfamiliar with, taking a course on a skill outside your usual interests, or engaging in conversations with people from diverse backgrounds. Each piece of new knowledge adds a layer of understanding and broadens the range of possibilities you see in the world.

For example, if you've always been in a particular field—say, finance—you might try learning about technology, art, or even philosophy. This new knowledge doesn't just expand your understanding of those areas; it also enables you to apply fresh perspectives to your own work or life. It creates cross-pollination of ideas that can lead to more creative problem-solving and innovative thinking.

Mental flexibility also involves being open to feedback, especially constructive criticism. Instead of viewing feedback as a personal attack, approach it as an opportunity to grow. Ask questions like, *How can I improve based on this?* or *What am I missing in my current approach that this feedback addresses?*

This ability to stay open to new information, different opinions, and novel ideas enables us to make smarter decisions, adapt quickly to changing circumstances, and open ourselves to possibilities that would otherwise remain closed off. The more we practice mental flexibility, the easier it becomes to embrace change, challenge assumptions, and reframe challenges as opportunities.

In essence, mental flexibility is the art of approaching life with an open mind and heart, free from the constraints of rigid thinking. It allows you to evolve and reinvent yourself as Hemant did—constantly ready to seize new opportunities, adapt to new situations, and grow beyond your current limitations. By cultivating mental flexibility, you become not just a passive recipient of life's changes, but an active participant in your own evolution.

Focus on the Process, Not the Outcome:

One of the central tenets of living with your bags packed is embracing the journey, rather than fixating solely on the destination. When we live with our bags packed, we cultivate a mindset of readiness for whatever comes next, which encourages us to focus on the process rather than the outcome. This approach allows us to be present in each moment, fully engaged with the experiences, challenges, and growth opportunities that unfold, rather than always being consumed by the desire to achieve a specific result. Hemant's story exemplifies this philosophy—his journey wasn't just about reaching a particular milestone, but about learning, evolving, and gaining wisdom at every stage along the way.

Often, in our fast-paced world, we become overly obsessed with achieving certain outcomes—whether that's landing a dream job, building a successful business, or reaching a particular life goal. While goals are important, they can become a source of stress and dissatisfaction if we treat them as the only measure of success. When we fixate too much on the end result, we risk missing out on the richness of the process and the lessons that life is offering us in each step of the journey. It's easy to overlook the value in small, seemingly insignificant actions if we're constantly chasing the next big thing.

In Hemant's case, his numerous career transitions and personal transformations were not defined by a singular outcome. Instead, he was focused on the experiences he gained and the lessons he learned during each phase. Each career change or new challenge became an opportunity for growth, a way for him to adapt and refine his approach to life. When you focus on the process, you allow yourself the freedom to grow organically, without the pressure of achieving perfection or meeting external expectations. You become more resilient, more adaptable, and more open to the changes that life inevitably brings.

Living with your bags packed means being ready to embrace change and to grow continuously, and that growth happens most powerfully when we focus on the small steps, actions, and lessons learned along the way. It's not about rushing to the finish line, but rather about savoring the journey—the little victories, the insights, the moments of learning, and the evolution of who we are becoming. By focusing on the process, you engage fully with life and allow the unfolding of your path to shape you in ways that rigid focus on an outcome never could.

Actionable Step: Focus on the Small Actions and Celebrate Progress

To adopt this mindset, it's important to shift your daily focus from outcomes to actions. Each day, dedicate time to reflecting on the small, incremental steps you are taking toward your personal or professional growth. Whether it's learning something new, making a small adjustment to your routine, or simply showing up with a positive attitude, these actions accumulate over time, leading to transformation.

Celebrating progress is essential in maintaining motivation and momentum. Too often, we overlook the small wins, thinking they don't matter. But each small step forward is a part of the bigger journey, and acknowledging them helps to reinforce positive behavior. For example, if you're learning a new skill, focus on your improvement rather than how far you still have to go. Celebrate each milestone along the way, whether it's successfully completing a task, mastering a new concept, or receiving positive feedback. These small celebrations act as reminders that you are progressing, even if it feels like you're not yet where you want to be.

Additionally, learning from every experience—both the successes and the setbacks—allows you to refine your approach and grow. If a particular action didn't bring the expected result, instead of seeing it as a failure, view it as a valuable lesson in how to improve. Life's challenges are often the most potent teachers, and when you approach them with an open mind and a focus on the process, they become opportunities for deeper growth.

By focusing on the process, you allow yourself to detach from the pressure of specific outcomes. You shift your energy into the present moment, where the work happens, and where transformation is taking place.

You free yourself from the anxiety that comes with chasing future outcomes and instead embrace the freedom that comes from being fully immersed in the now. Each step you take is a vital part of your evolving story, and living with your bags packed means being open to every part of that story, trusting that it will unfold exactly as it's meant to.

Embrace Uncertainty:

Uncertainty is a constant companion in life. No matter how much we plan or try to control our circumstances, the future remains inherently unpredictable. It's easy to be afraid of uncertainty because it challenges our sense of control and security. However, true growth and transformation happen when we are willing to lean into the unknown, rather than avoiding it. Embracing uncertainty allows us to explore new possibilities, take risks, and discover opportunities we may never have considered otherwise.

Hemant's life is a clear example of how embracing uncertainty can lead to incredible reinvention. He didn't shy away from the unknown when his career and personal life took unexpected turns. Instead, he saw each uncertain moment as an opportunity to learn, evolve, and grow. His willingness to embrace uncertainty enabled him to step away from the safety of his previous careers and move toward new ventures, each bringing its own set of challenges and rewards. Hemant's journey is a testament to the idea that life's most fulfilling opportunities often arise when we are open to the unpredictable and are willing to take risks.

When we resist uncertainty, we limit ourselves to the familiar, which might feel safe, but it also keeps us from experiencing the richness that life has to offer. The truth is, the familiar can become a trap. We can easily get stuck in routines, relationships, or careers that no longer serve our growth, simply because we fear what might happen if we step into the unknown. However, when we learn to embrace uncertainty, we break free from the constraints of what's known and step into the vast possibilities of what could be.

Embracing uncertainty requires a shift in mindset. Instead of viewing uncertainty as something to fear, we can begin to see it as a doorway to opportunity. The unknown is where innovation, creativity, and new experiences reside. It's where we get to test our limits, push ourselves beyond what we thought possible, and find new paths for growth. Whether it's a new job, a new relationship, or a new skill, uncertainty brings with it the potential for transformation.

One of the biggest challenges in embracing uncertainty is learning to let go of the need for control. We often feel that if we can't predict the outcome of a situation, we shouldn't engage in it. But by trying to control everything, we miss out on the excitement of discovery and the rewards of stepping outside of our comfort zones. The process of embracing uncertainty isn't about having all the answers, but about being willing to venture forward without knowing exactly what will happen next. This willingness to explore with an open heart and mind is what allows us to evolve into the best version of ourselves.

Actionable Step: Take Small Steps into the Unknown

The key to embracing uncertainty is to start small and gradually build your comfort with the unknown. It's not necessary to dive into major life changes immediately; rather, you can begin by incorporating small steps into your daily routine that push you out of your comfort zone. These could be as simple as trying a new hobby, taking on a new project at work, or engaging in a conversation with someone you don't know well. By taking small risks, you can begin to cultivate a mindset of adaptability and resilience, which will serve you well when larger uncertainties arise in life.

As you take these small steps, notice how you feel. It's normal to feel nervous or uneasy when facing uncertainty, but these feelings often diminish as we move through them. The more you expose yourself to uncertainty, the more comfortable you become in navigating it. With each small step, you build confidence in your ability to handle whatever comes your way.

The more you embrace the unknown, the more you'll realize that uncertainty isn't as threatening as it may initially seem. It's a space where you can grow, expand your horizons, and experience life in its fullest form. Over time, you'll find that uncertainty becomes less of a source of fear and more of an exciting adventure that sparks new ideas, perspectives, and opportunities for your personal growth.

By consistently stepping into the unknown, you start to see life as a series of exciting possibilities rather than something to control or predict. And just as Hemant demonstrated in his own life, it is through embracing uncertainty that you truly discover the extent of your own potential and the vast opportunities life has to offer.

Keep the Present in Focus:

While it's essential to be ready for what comes next in life, it's equally important to remain deeply connected to the present moment. This balance of staying open to future possibilities while appreciating the present moment is one of the cornerstones of the philosophy of "keeping your bags packed." Living with your bags packed doesn't mean being consumed with the idea of constantly moving or preparing for the next step at the cost of the now—it means embracing the present fully, while still holding a sense of readiness for change.

In Hemant's journey, his ability to be grounded in the present moment while simultaneously planning for future transitions has been pivotal to his peace of mind and success. He didn't lose sight of the blessings of today while he was focused on preparing for tomorrow. This balance allowed him to experience fulfillment and joy in the present, without being consumed by the anxiety of what might come next. Hemant's approach to life teaches us that true peace and clarity emerge when we live mindfully, anchoring ourselves in the present, even as we stay prepared for the future.

The act of staying present is often more challenging than it seems, particularly in our fast-paced, future-oriented world. Many people tend to live either in the past, ruminating on old mistakes or missed opportunities, or in the future, filled with worry and anxiety about what might happen. This constant focus on past regrets or future uncertainties can pull us away from experiencing the richness of the current moment, where true growth and contentment can be found. When we don't stay in the present, we miss out on the beauty and opportunities that life offers us right now.

Living in the present allows us to create a strong foundation for the future. It helps us recognize what is truly important, what opportunities we can seize today, and how we can improve ourselves in the now. By staying connected to the present, we not only experience more joy and satisfaction but also enhance our ability to make decisions and take actions that will positively shape our future. The present moment is where we have the most power; it is where we take the steps that will lead to future success, growth, and change.

Practicing mindfulness and gratitude are essential tools in keeping ourselves anchored in the present. When we express gratitude for what we have now, we shift our focus from what's lacking or uncertain to what's already abundant in our lives. This mindset shift not only makes us feel more connected and at peace, but it also fosters a positive outlook, which can pave the way for new opportunities and success in the future. Hemant's ability to practice gratitude helped him remain grounded and focused, which in turn created space for greater personal and professional growth.

Actionable Step: Practice Gratitude Daily

One simple yet powerful way to stay present is by practicing daily gratitude. Taking a few moments each day to reflect on what you are thankful for can dramatically shift your perspective and bring you back into the present. Whether it's gratitude for your health, your relationships, your work, or even just the simple fact that you are alive and breathing, acknowledging these blessings helps you stay connected to the now.

Start by setting aside a few minutes each morning or evening to reflect on the positive aspects of your life. You can do this by writing them down in a gratitude journal, mentally listing them, or even sharing them with a loved one. The goal is to focus your attention on the present and appreciate what you have in this moment, rather than getting lost in what's coming next or regretting what's been left behind.

In addition to gratitude, mindfulness practices can also enhance your ability to stay present. These practices help you become aware of your thoughts, emotions, and physical sensations in real-time, without judgment or distraction. By being mindful of your surroundings and your inner experience, you can improve your ability to remain calm and centered in any situation, whether it's a challenging moment or a joyous occasion.

When you anchor yourself in the present, you create a solid foundation from which to approach future challenges and opportunities. You will find that your mindset becomes more positive, your actions more intentional, and your ability to handle uncertainty and change stronger. Staying present doesn't mean you ignore the future; it simply means you acknowledge that the most important thing you can do right now is to make the most of today. And as you continue to grow and evolve, this focus on the present will help you live a life of greater fulfillment, purpose, and readiness for whatever comes next.

By practicing gratitude and mindfulness, you build a resilient mindset that not only enhances your current experience but also sets you up for future growth and success. Hemant's journey exemplifies how staying grounded in the present moment, while being prepared for change, is key to living a life that is both meaningful and full of potential.

Let Go of Attachments:

At the core of the philosophy of living with your bags packed is the powerful practice of letting go of attachments. Attachments—whether to material possessions, specific outcomes, people, or even the identities we create for ourselves—can weigh us down and keep us from fully experiencing the freedom and growth that life has to offer. When we become overly attached to something, it often leads to anxiety, stress, and a sense of limitation, preventing us from embracing new possibilities and opportunities.

The idea of letting go doesn't mean abandoning what is meaningful or neglecting responsibilities. Rather, it is about releasing the emotional or mental grip that we hold on to certain things, whether they are possessions, expectations, or past experiences. Just as a traveler would pack only the essentials in their bag and leave behind the rest, we too can learn to travel light emotionally and mentally, freeing ourselves from the burden of unnecessary attachments.

In Hemant's journey, he has consistently demonstrated the importance of letting go of attachments to outdated beliefs, past failures, and even rigid career paths. Each time he faced a new phase in life, whether it was shifting careers, letting go of old relationships, or redefining his values, he understood that holding on to the past would only limit his potential for the future. The act of letting go allowed him to step into new opportunities with a sense of clarity, freedom, and openness.

For Hemant, letting go wasn't a one-time act but an ongoing process. It was about regularly checking in with himself to identify what no longer served his growth or aligned with his evolving purpose. The more he practiced releasing attachments, the more space he had to cultivate new ideas, experiences, and connections. This act of release opened the door for personal transformation, enabling him to reinvent himself time and time again.

Letting go of attachments requires a deep level of self-awareness and courage. Often, attachments are tied to fear—the fear of losing something important, the fear of uncertainty, or the fear of change. But in reality, holding on to attachments often causes more pain and restriction than simply releasing them. Life is constantly evolving, and holding on too tightly to the past or to rigid outcomes only prevents us from moving forward.

To live with your bags packed means you are always ready for what life brings, but to do that, you need to be willing to release the things that no longer serve you. This is not a sign of weakness or loss; rather, it's an empowering act of growth and self-liberation. It's about accepting that life is a journey of constant change and that by letting go of what we no longer need, we create the space for new experiences, relationships, and opportunities to enter our lives.

Actionable Step: Identify One Attachment You Can Release Today

A simple but impactful way to begin practicing this concept is to identify one attachment that you can release today. This could be anything from a material possession that you've been holding onto out of sentimentality or a belief system that no longer aligns with your current values. It might also be a past failure, a painful experience, or even a person or relationship that no longer supports your growth.

Start by taking a moment to reflect on areas of your life where you feel restricted or burdened. Is there something that you're holding onto, believing it to be essential, but in reality, it's keeping you stuck? It could be an old goal you've been pursuing for years but no longer excites you, a job that no longer challenges you, or even a toxic relationship that you're afraid to let go of.

Once you've identified what you need to release, take concrete action to let go of it. This might mean donating or discarding an item that has emotional weight, writing a letter to release pent-up feelings or old grudges, or making a decision to step away from something or someone that is holding you back. It's important to approach this process with compassion and non-judgment. Release doesn't mean rejecting or devaluing the past—it simply means making room for something new and more aligned with who you are today.

To make the process of letting go more tangible, you can create a ritual of release. For example, write down your attachment on a piece of paper, read it aloud, and then physically let go by tearing it up, burning it, or burying it. This symbolic act can create a powerful sense of closure and help you truly release that attachment, giving you a fresh start.

By consistently letting go of attachments, you free yourself from unnecessary emotional baggage. You will start to feel lighter, more flexible, and better equipped to embrace change and opportunities. This practice of release doesn't only benefit you in the short term—it cultivates a deeper sense of inner peace and resilience, enabling you to live life with greater openness and a deeper connection to your true self.

As you continue to practice letting go of attachments, you will notice that you become more adaptable, more present, and more able to seize new opportunities without hesitation. The more you release, the more you create space for the new—and the more you make room for growth, learning, and transformation. Just like packing light for a journey, letting go of attachments allows you to move freely and confidently toward the next phase of your life.

Conclusion

Living with your bags packed is far more than just a philosophy—it's a mindset, a lifestyle, and a framework for navigating life with openness, readiness, and resilience. It's a mindset that encourages you to stay prepared for change, to be open to new opportunities, and to remain adaptable in the face of life's unpredictability. Hemant's journey illustrates that living with your bags packed doesn't mean constantly being in motion or running from one place to the next. Instead, it's about being mentally and emotionally ready to embrace the unknown, while staying grounded in the present.

In Hemant's experience, this mindset of readiness has not only been a tool for overcoming challenges but a guiding principle for creating and nurturing opportunities for personal and professional growth. Every change, transition, or challenge he faced was approached not with fear or resistance but with an open heart and a willingness to evolve. Living with your bags packed, for him, meant carrying the essential mindset that each step forward is an opportunity for reinvention and growth. It's not about clinging to the past, but about continuously evolving with an awareness that each phase of life brings something valuable to the journey.

As you begin to integrate these principles into your own life, it's important to remember that living with your bags packed is not about abandoning the concepts of stability or inner peace. Instead, it's about finding the balance between being rooted in the present while maintaining a flexible, ready-to-adapt stance for the future. It's about embracing evolution—not as an external force that disrupts you, but as a natural progression that invites growth, learning, and transformation.

By living with your bags packed, you cultivate the ability to embrace change without fear or resistance. You trust that whatever comes your way will serve as a stepping stone to the next level of personal and professional development. This philosophy invites you to step into each new chapter with confidence, knowing that your journey is an unfolding path that will guide you to where you need to be. Whether that means letting go of old attachments, reinventing yourself, or embracing uncertainty, you are equipped with the mental and emotional tools to face the future with courage.

In the end, the philosophy of living with your bags packed offers a roadmap to living a life of freedom, purpose, and constant growth. It is a call to let go of rigid expectations, embrace change with grace, and be open to the opportunities that come with every new phase of life. It reminds us that while we cannot control everything that happens, we can control how we respond to life's challenges. We can choose to remain flexible, open, and ready to take the next step on our journey, knowing that each change is an opportunity to grow, to learn, and to continue becoming the best version of ourselves.

So, as you reflect on your own journey and the path that lies ahead, ask yourself: Are your bags packed? Are you ready to embrace the changes that come with life's ever-changing landscape? The freedom and growth you seek are waiting for you, just around the corner, when you choose to live with openness, adaptability, and a readiness for what's next. The journey is yours to take—embrace it fully, with your bags packed, and step into the future with confidence and purpose.

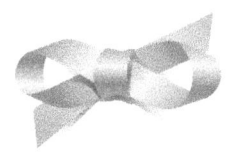

Conclusion: The Journey Continues

As we reach the end of this book, it's important to reflect on one fundamental truth: the philosophy of **"Keeping Bags Packed"** is not a destination, but a **continuous journey**.

Throughout these chapters, we've explored how living with our bags metaphorically packed—remaining adaptable, open to change, and detached from outcomes—helps us navigate life with greater ease, resilience, and purpose. Hemant's story has been an anchor for understanding this mindset, showing us that it is not about being prepared for one specific change, but about living with the understanding that life itself is fluid, unpredictable, and full of possibilities.

But the journey doesn't end here. The philosophy of **keeping your bags packed** is not something to adopt once and then forget about. It is a lifelong practice. **Life is constantly evolving**, and the mindset of staying ready for the next step is essential to living a fulfilling, meaningful existence. Whether it's embracing new opportunities, overcoming challenges, or simply being open to the unknown, this philosophy is about continuously evolving along with the changing tides of life.

A Call to Action

Now, it's your turn to carry the philosophy of "keeping your bags packed" forward into your own life. This mindset isn't just for Hemant or for a select few—it's a universal call to action that invites everyone to embrace change, growth, and opportunity. The essence of this philosophy is rooted in the understanding that life is fluid, dynamic, and full of constant transitions. Whether you realize it or not, the world around you is shifting. People evolve, careers change, and new challenges and opportunities emerge.

Embrace the Mindset of Readiness: By adopting the mindset of always being prepared, you open yourself to the vast potential that life offers. You become someone who is never too settled, too attached, or too comfortable in their current situation. This doesn't mean you should live in constant motion or anxiety, but rather that you approach life with the quiet confidence that you are ready for whatever comes your way. Being mentally and emotionally flexible doesn't mean you lack stability; in fact, it's the key to developing a more resilient, adaptable, and fulfilling life.

The world will continue to shift, and those who are ready to adapt will unlock countless opportunities for growth, fulfillment, and success. Change, when embraced, becomes a catalyst for transformation. When you stay ready, you gain the freedom to live with purpose, knowing that the unexpected can bring something wonderful.

Action Step 1: Let Go of What Holds You Back: Ask yourself this question: *What am I holding on to that's preventing me from moving forward?* Take a deep look at the attachments in your life—whether they're to past failures, outdated beliefs, unfulfilling relationships, or even material possessions. Ask yourself honestly whether these things are serving your growth or whether they're weighing you down. Letting go is not about abandonment; it's about freeing yourself from what no longer serves your purpose. This allows space for new opportunities, fresh perspectives, and growth.

To begin, choose one thing today—big or small—that you can release. It could be a belief that has limited your progress, a fear that has held you back, or a situation that no longer aligns with your goals. By letting go of these attachments, you clear the path for new experiences to come into your life. You are not losing anything; you are simply making room for more aligned, purposeful energy.

Action Step 2: Commit to Daily Readiness: Every day, commit to one small action that keeps you mentally and emotionally prepared for whatever the future holds. This is where the true power of living with your bags packed lies—it's about consistency and small, incremental actions. Whether it's learning something new, trying a different approach, or simply practicing mindfulness in the present moment, you are making a conscious effort to stay open and adaptable.

Start small. Perhaps it's dedicating a few minutes each morning to reflect on the changes you'd like to embrace or taking on a new skill that aligns with your goals. These small actions will compound over time, ensuring that you are always moving forward, regardless of the challenges or changes you face.

By making it a habit to stay ready for what's next, you strengthen your ability to handle anything life presents. Life's unpredictability becomes an exciting adventure, rather than a daunting obstacle, because you know you are always prepared.

Action Step 3: Embrace the Freedom of Change: Remember that true happiness and fulfillment are not found in static certainty, but in the freedom of living a life where you are ready to evolve, adapt, and face new challenges with courage. The path to success is not linear or predefined. It's not about where you end up but about how you show up for each chapter of the journey. When you embrace uncertainty with readiness, you unlock your potential to create a life that's rich with meaning, growth, and satisfaction.

The adventure of life is not in knowing exactly what will happen, but in your ability to embrace the unknown. Success is found in the willingness to change, to evolve, and to continuously prepare for new beginnings. Life is a fluid journey—your readiness to evolve with it is what will allow you to thrive, regardless of the circumstances.

As you begin this journey of keeping your bags packed, remember that it's not about being in a constant state of movement or instability. It's about preparing yourself for the beautiful unknown, staying rooted in the present moment, and allowing the future to unfold naturally. By living with this mindset, you'll not only become more adaptable to change but also more connected to the flow of life.

The world is constantly changing, and by staying ready for whatever comes your way, you'll not only unlock opportunities for growth, but you'll also discover a deeper sense of purpose, fulfillment, and success in the process. Keep your bags packed—and embark on the adventure of life with courage, openness, and the knowledge that the best is yet to come.

The Continuous Journey

In closing, it's essential to understand that life is not a destination but a continuous journey. The philosophy of "keeping your bags packed" is not merely a tactic for navigating through transitions; it's a profound approach to embracing life itself. The act of keeping your bags packed represents an openness to life's unfolding narrative—a mindset that allows you to embrace each new chapter, regardless of the unknowns it may bring. This philosophy teaches us that life is ever-evolving, and our ability to stay prepared, adaptable, and open to change determines how we navigate this ever-shifting landscape.

We often think of transitions as disruptions, but in reality, they are invitations for growth and reinvention. By remaining ready for change, we don't just survive life's twists and turns—we thrive within them. When we view life as a journey rather than a series of destinations, every step becomes an opportunity to evolve. The key is not to fear the unknown but to embrace it, trusting that with each step, we are learning, growing, and becoming more of who we are meant to be.

This mindset opens up a world of possibilities. Each day, we can approach life with the understanding that we are not locked into one path, one identity, or one version of ourselves. Instead, we are free to evolve, adapt, and explore new directions. The philosophy of keeping your bags packed encourages you to remain fluid, to shed outdated beliefs and attachments, and to stay open to the lessons each new phase of life brings.

So, as you continue on your own journey, remember that your bags are always packed. Not because you are running away from what you have, but because you are ready to receive whatever comes next. Whether it's an unexpected challenge, an exciting opportunity, or a new phase of personal growth, you approach it with a mindset of readiness. You aren't attached to the past or fixated on any particular outcome—you are simply open to what life has to offer, trusting that it will bring exactly what you need for your next step.

Every new experience is a doorway to greater understanding, and every challenge you face is an invitation to stretch beyond your current limitations. Even in moments of uncertainty, there is the potential for profound transformation. When you adopt the mindset of "keeping your bags packed," you are saying yes to the adventure of life. You are telling yourself that you are not bound by the past or by fear of the future—you are fully present and prepared for whatever the journey brings.

Living this way frees you from the weight of overthinking and overplanning. It allows you to trust the natural flow of your journey, knowing that with each step, you are exactly where you need to be. This mindset cultivates an inner peace, because you no longer feel the need to control every outcome. Instead, you focus on staying grounded in the present and trusting that you are ready for what comes next.

True happiness, fulfillment, and success are not about reaching a final destination. They are found in the ongoing journey—the ongoing process of growth, learning, and becoming. When you live with your bags packed, you align with the freedom to evolve and adapt. You realize that life is not a race or a series of fixed points, but a fluid, ever-changing experience.

So, take a moment to embrace the freedom that comes with knowing you are prepared for anything. Let go of the need to have all the answers or to control every outcome. Trust that you are always ready, and in that readiness, you will find the true essence of happiness. Life's most fulfilling moments often emerge from the willingness to embrace uncertainty, from the courage to step into the unknown, and from the openness to receive life's blessings in all their forms.

In the end, the journey is not about where you're headed but how you move through each moment along the way. Live with the knowledge that your bags are packed, your heart is open, and you are ready to embrace everything life has in store for you. In that readiness, you will find the richness of life, the depth of purpose, and the fulfillment that comes from knowing you are prepared to evolve at every stage of the journey.

"Life is not about waiting for the perfect moment, but about being ready to embrace the unexpected with open arms, knowing that each new step is an opportunity to grow, evolve, and become who we are meant to be."

Acknowledgments

Writing this book has been a journey of introspection, exploration, and countless discoveries along the way. I am profoundly grateful to all those who have contributed, directly and indirectly, to bringing this work to life.

First and foremost, I thank my family for their unwavering support, patience, and encouragement. To my wife, whose understanding and wisdom have been my guiding light, and my children, who inspire me daily to be a better person—I could not have done this without you.

I extend my heartfelt appreciation to my friends and mentors, who have shared their own journeys, insights, and experiences, reminding me of the resilience and adaptability that this book seeks to celebrate. Your stories and perspectives have enriched my own understanding of life's challenges and possibilities, and I am thankful to each of you for being part of my journey.

To my students and colleagues, past and present: you have been my teachers as much as I have been yours. Your curiosity, questions, and drive have continually inspired me to reflect on what it means to keep learning, adapting, and growing. Thank you for challenging me to be the best version of myself and for reminding me of the importance of lifelong learning.

I would also like to thank my editorial and publishing team, whose guidance and expertise helped shape this book into what it is today. Your keen insights, meticulous attention to detail, and belief in this project have been invaluable. I am grateful for your commitment and dedication in helping bring my words to readers.

Finally, to the readers who have opened this book, thank you for allowing me to share these ideas and philosophies with you. My hope is that this book encourages you to embrace life's uncertainties with open arms and a packed bag, ready for whatever lies ahead.

With deep gratitude,

ALWAYS KEEP YOUR BAGS PACKED

Sandeep Chavan

Don't miss out!

Visit the website below and you can sign up to receive emails whenever SANDEEP CHAVAN publishes a new book. There's no charge and no obligation.

https://books2read.com/r/B-A-EPGPC-QHDHF

BOOKS 2 READ

Connecting independent readers to independent writers.

Did you love *Always Keep Your Bags Packed*? Then you should read *You are just a Version of Your Original*[1] by SANDEEP CHAVAN!

[2]

In *You Are Just a Version of Your Original*, author Sandeep Chavan embarks on a journey to illuminate the intricate relationship between our evolving selves and the essence we carry within. This book seeks to address a timeless question: who are we beneath the layers of versions we adopt throughout our lives? With a background in engineering and teaching, Chavan brings a unique perspective that fuses philosophy, psychology, and human nature to explore what it means to "version" ourselves as we grow.

The book presents the idea that each of us, like evolving technology, embodies numerous versions that form over time in response to experiences, relationships, and the changing world. Yet, while technology often upgrades to reach an ideal functionality, humans are on a different path—a cyclical journey of transformation, adaptation, and rediscovery, guided by an original self that lies within our subconscious.

---

1. https://books2read.com/u/4NqZKY

2. https://books2read.com/u/4NqZKY

As humanity advances, author makes the intriguing parallel between our own development and technological growth, particularly with artificial intelligence. Technology, he suggests, is a reflection of our ingenuity and adaptability but remains a tool in our hands, never a replacement for the human experience. This book reminds readers that true growth lies not in "perfecting" oneself but in moving fluidly between change and reconnection with our core essence.

At the heart of the book, author encourages readers to adopt practices like self-reflection, mindfulness, and introspection as tools to "reset." Through these resets, we can temporarily strip away the accumulated layers, discover aspects of ourselves that may be dormant, and come closer to understanding our purpose. By doing so, we do not regress; instead, we access a state of genuine presence that illuminates our path forward.

Sandeep Chavan wrote *You Are Just a Version of Your Original* to offer a perspective that embraces the balance between transformation and constancy. The author's intention is to guide readers toward a deeper awareness of their own cyclical journey, helping them recognize that each version is a step in a larger, meaningful rhythm of life. The book encourages readers to accept the shifts and versions they encounter as expressions of both resilience and purpose, underscoring that the ultimate goal is not to settle on an "ideal" self but to keep evolving while remaining rooted in the unchanging essence that defines who we are.

In a world advancing rapidly, Chavan's work reminds us that our versions, when viewed through this lens, are opportunities for rediscovery and growth. By reconnecting with our original selves, we can navigate the journey of life with intention, understanding that true fulfillment comes from honoring both the journey forward and the return to our core essence.

Read more at www.gyrusvision.com.

Also by SANDEEP CHAVAN

It's Not AI, It's AHI - Amplified Human Intelligence
The Decision Paradox
The Four Sapiens
Malicious Script of Indian Polity
The IIT Legacy & Global Impact
The IIT Legacy & Global Impact
You are just a Version of Your Original
Win the Game You Didn't Choose
Always Keep Your Bags Packed

Watch for more at www.gyrusvision.com.

About the Author

Sandeep Chavan is a seasoned educator, industrial engineer, and lifelong learner with a career that spans over two decades in both the corporate and educational sectors. Starting his journey as a mechanical engineer, Sandeep built a successful career in industrial engineering and planning, working with renowned multinational companies. However, his passion for meaningful contribution and helping others navigate their own journeys led him to transition into teaching and mentoring.

Today, Sandeep is not only a dedicated teacher but also a trusted guide for countless students aspiring to excel in engineering, science, and beyond. His approach to education is rooted in real-world experience, bridging the gap between theoretical knowledge and practical application. Known for his thoughtful perspective on adaptability and resilience, he has inspired many to face life's challenges with a "keep your bags packed" philosophy, viewing each transition as an opportunity for growth.

Sandeep's own journey of transformation—from corporate professional to educator, from technical expert to a mentor in life's broader lessons—shapes his writing and resonates through every chapter of this book. Living by the values of lifelong learning, adaptability, and purpose-driven growth, Sandeep continues to empower others to find fulfillment beyond traditional success, encouraging them to embrace change as a constant and inspiring force.

Read more at gyrusvision.com.

Milton Keynes UK
Ingram Content Group UK Ltd.
UKHW030905151124
451262UK00006B/1000

9 798227 168399